M000237863

America's Great-Power Opportunity

August 31, 2022

Dear Ben:

You render the following judgment in your essay "Them and Us": "Defining the United States' purpose in the world and American identity through a new 'us versus them' construct risks repeating some of the worst mistakes of the war on terror." I issue precisely that warning in *America's Great-Power Opportunity*: even as Washington will increasingly have to contend with and manage the challenges posed by a resurgent Beijing and a revanchist Moscow, it must resist the temptation to pursue a foreign policy that is centered upon contesting them reflexively and ubiquitously.

I would be grateful for any reactions that you might have, and I hope to continue our conversation soon.

Sincerely,

Ali

America's Great-Power Opportunity

Revitalizing US Foreign Policy to Meet the Challenges of Strategic Competition

Ali Wyne

polity

Copyright © Ali Wyne 2022

The right of Ali Wyne to be identified as Author of this Work has been asserted in accordance with the UK Copyright, Designs and Patents Act 1988.

First published in 2022 by Polity Press

Polity Press
65 Bridge Street
Cambridge CB2 1UR, UK

Polity Press
101 Station Landing
Suite 300
Medford, MA 02155, USA

All rights reserved. Except for the quotation of short passages for the purpose of criticism and review, no part of this publication may be reproduced, stored in a retrieval system or transmitted, in any form or by any means, electronic, mechanical, photocopying, recording or otherwise, without the prior permission of the publisher.

ISBN-13: 978-1-5095-4553-7
ISBN-13: 978-1-5095-4554-4 (pb)

A catalogue record for this book is available from the British Library.

Library of Congress Control Number: 2021947326

Typeset in 10.75 on 14pt Adobe Janson
by Cheshire Typesetting Ltd, Cuddington, Cheshire
Printed and bound in the UK by TJ Books Limited

The publisher has used its best endeavours to ensure that the URLs for external websites referred to in this book are correct and active at the time of going to press. However, the publisher has no responsibility for the websites and can make no guarantee that a site will remain live or that the content is or will remain appropriate.

Every effort has been made to trace all copyright holders, but if any have been overlooked the publisher will be pleased to include any necessary credits in any subsequent reprint or edition.

For further information on Polity, visit our website:
politybooks.com

Contents

Acknowledgments

This book would not exist without Colin Clarke, a former colleague at the RAND Corporation who generously shared my interest in great-power competition with Louise Knight at Polity. I hope I can repay his quiet kindness one day, and I promise to pay it forward. My next debt, of course, is to Louise. Patient, discerning, and encouraging, she is the editor every writer dreams of having. She commissioned three superb reviewers to critique my initial proposal and another three to critique my first draft. Their combined feedback was instrumental in helping me determine the book's structure, crystallize its arguments, and define its tone. Inès Boxman kept me on schedule and offered detailed guidance at every step of the publication process. And Manuela Tecusan copy-edited my final draft with extraordinary rigor and care, strengthening both the clarity of my prose and the logic of my arguments.

Elmira Bayrasli played an invaluable role in the completion of this book. I realized soon after I began formulating my proposal that I would need an extended period of uninterrupted time to grapple with great-power competition in a considered manner. The only way I would secure such a window would be to step down from a rewarding job I had at the time, not knowing when I would next find a position. Elmira gave me the courage I needed to take that leap of faith, impressing upon me that some of life's most compelling opportunities arise when we take a detour and trust that we will be able to navigate the attendant uncertainty.

Joseph Nye took time out of a frantic schedule to read my first draft and to offer detailed feedback, which proved indispensable as I refined my arguments and produced the final version. Graham Allison urged me to follow my intuition that great-power competition was underspecified, stressing that policy can be only as thoughtful as the constructs underpinning it are rigorous. Joe and Graham have been my foremost mentors and champions for the better part of the past two decades, and I hope they will see in this book the intellectual seeds they have planted in me.

Two seminars were essential in helping me stress-test and refine my initial arguments. First, Bruce Jones of the Brookings Institution arranged and hosted a discussion with William Burke-White, Tarun Chhabra, Alexandre Marc, William Moreland, and Thomas Wright on June 29, 2020. In addition, Tom took time to participate in a written exchange with me from February to June 2020, on Pairagraph, a vibrant platform that convenes debates on the pressing issues of the day. Second, Sarah Donahue and Grace Headinger of the Belfer Center for Science and International Affairs arranged and Aditi Kumar hosted a discussion held on July 27, 2020 with some two dozen individuals from across the Belfer network. William d'Ambruoso, Steven Miller, Mina Mitreva, and Jane Perlez all sent detailed written feedback after the session.

I also benefited enormously from conversations with scholars, journalists, editors, and past and present public servants: Emma Ashford, Alyssa Ayres, Caroline Baxter, Robert Blackwill, Brian Blankenship, Nicholas Burns, William Burns, Jessica Chen Weiss, Elbridge Colby, Bernard Cole, Ivo Daalder, Richard Danzig, Benjamin Denison, Abraham Denmark, Rhys Dubin, Naz El-Khatib, Alexandra Evans, Richard Fontaine, Daniel Franklin, Lawrence Freedman, Uri Friedman, Michael Fullilove, John Gans, Francis Gavin, Andrew Goodhart, Jorge Guajardo, Richard Haass, Ryan Hass, Kathleen Hicks, Fiona Hill, Frank Hoffman, Timothy Hoyt, John Ikenberry, Van Jackson, Elsa Kania, Mara Karlin, Michael Kofman, Daniel Kurtz-Phelan, Mark Leonard, Jessica Libertini, Rebecca Lissner, Kelly Magsamen, Hunter Marston, Michael Mazarr, Michael McFaul, Shivshankar Menon, Jim Mitre, Daniel Nexon, Meghan O'Sullivan, Yashar Parsie, Robert

Person, Sara Plana, Ionut Popescu, Patrick Porter, Christopher Preble, Mira Rapp-Hooper, Gregory Sanders, Nadia Schadlow, Anne-Marie Slaughter, Constanze Stelzenmüller, Stephen Walt, Odd Arne Westad, and Gavin Wilde.

Many individuals gave me writing opportunities that allowed me to articulate initial versions of the various arguments I have attempted to weave together: David Barboza, Samuel Bresnick, Daniel Byman, Sarah Canna, Evan Corcoran, Daniel Flitton, Stéphanie Giry, Judah Grunstein, Jacob Heilbrunn, Susan Jakes, Sahar Khan, Alex Lennon, Kathleen Miles, James Palmer, Sam Roggeveen, and Shannon Tiezzi.

Many others, in addition, gave me speaking opportunities: Bunmi Akinnusotu, John Amble, Wardah Amir, Christopher Ankersen, George Beebe, Colonel Jason ("JP") Clark, Mick Cook, Meaghan Fulco, Eric Gomez, Nikolas Gvosdev, Paul Haenle, Mark Hannah, Grant Haver, Laicie Heeley, Liam Kraft, Kaiser Kuo, Thomas Lynch, Katherine Mansted, Jennifer Mustapha, Captain Antony Palocaren, Ankit Panda, Johannes Perterer, Asad Rafi, Derek Reveron, Stephen Saideman, Kori Schake, Patricia Schouker, and Ben Watson.

Cliff Kupchan supported this project from the moment I began working at Eurasia Group, and he generously permitted me to take a sabbatical to complete a first draft. Ian Bremmer has nurtured about as stimulating and enriching an environment as one can imagine for those who are trying to process tectonic shifts in geopolitics.

Meg Guliford introduced me to Katerina (Kat) Kakkis in mid-2019, when Kat was an undergraduate student at Tufts University. Although I brought Kat on board as a research assistant, she soon became a colleague, critiquing every chapter thoroughly and supplying a steady stream of trenchant insights that helped me develop my perspectives on great-power competition. I am excited to see what the future has in store for her.

I submitted my final proposal on February 11, 2020 and received a contract from Polity on February 28, not knowing how profoundly a new virus—still quite contained at the time—would go on to shape our world. My sister and I decamped from Washington, DC to Fredericksburg, VA on March 13, to ride out the pandemic with our parents, and I returned shortly after submitting the final draft. My mother, father, and sister watched as our study room transformed from a tidy den into something of a hazard zone, as my research materials steadily occupied more and more space. They gave me the room (literally and figuratively) that I needed for thinking and the support that I needed for finishing. It is to my beloved family—Ammi, Abbu, and Zaahira—that I owe my greatest debt and I dedicate this book.

Preface

With the publication of its national security strategy (NSS) in December 2017 and its national defense strategy (NDS) the following month, the Trump administration helped propel the phrase "great-power competition" to the heart of US foreign policy discourse. While this term had been growing more prominent, particularly after Russia's annexation of Crimea in March 2014, it had not diffused broadly; it did not figure significantly in government conversations outside of the Pentagon and, although some esteemed scholars urged greater focus on it, great-power competition had yet to become a bedrock of mainstream analysis.[1]

With the release of the aforementioned documents, though, the term quickly became a backdrop of conversations in Washington.[2] As impressively, if not more, it achieved that status within a fraught political environment, not only transcending sharp disagreements between and within the two main parties over the foreign policy that the United States should pursue but also deepening ideological acrimony more generally, in Congress and among the public. Donald Trump's election, after all, did not just challenge the core precepts that had undergirded America's strategic outlook for the better part of the past seven decades; it also surfaced the extent to which the political center on Capitol Hill had narrowed and the degree to which Americans of different ideological persuasions had come to regard one another less as fellow travelers than as threatening strangers.

The frequency with which policymakers and analysts now discuss great-power competition would suggest that they have converged upon a common interpretation. And yet, while increasingly encountering the term in articles, reports, interviews, speeches, and testimonies, I consistently found myself unable to define it succinctly. I initially conceived of this book, then, as an attempt to redress my own ignorance. The more research I conducted and the more conversations I had while drafting it, though, the more I came to conclude that the shared understanding whose existence I had assumed is overstated. The late Colin Gray, one of the foremost strategic thinkers of the past half-century, observed that this discrepancy between invocation and elucidation plagues many a construct: "A problem with popular formulas can be that their familiarity breeds an unwarranted confidence in interpretation."[3]

There are, of course, certain basic propositions with which most observers agree. First, the phenomenon of interstate competition is longstanding. Second, the emergence of great-power competition as a (if not as *the*) principal analytical basis for formulating US foreign policy nods to the reality that the United States is no longer as influential as it was at the end of the Cold War. Third, acting upon their longstanding dissatisfaction with the settlement that emerged in the aftermath of the Soviet Union's collapse, China and Russia are challenging US national interests and the postwar order; and they are doing so individually and, increasingly, in concert.

But disagreements surface soon after one moves beyond these assertions. What is the essence of contemporary strategic competition? Over what is the United States competing? For what is it competing? What policies should it adopt to be more competitive? How should it assess whether it is succeeding? What would durable strategic arrangements with China and Russia entail? Even a simple list of foundational questions would be far more exhaustive.

It is plain enough to see that the United States confronts a more competitive external landscape. It is more vexing to decide how Washington should adapt. There is a gap, in brief, between description and prescription: while great-power competition captures an important element of geopolitics, articulations of that construct generally do not do enough to illuminate the challenges the United States should prioritize in competing with China and Russia—or the trade-offs it should accept to that end. Many envision instead an all-encompassing contest that will occur in perpetuity, broaching virtually every geographic theater and functional domain.

The management of strategic tensions with China and Russia will be essential to shaping America's role in the world. But a foreign policy that is predicated upon contesting their actions risks being reactive. Rather than relying upon Beijing and Moscow to furnish its strategic objectives, Washington should identify the contours of the order it would like to help bring into existence alongside its allies and partners—and only then, having formulated an affirmative vision, consider where selective competition with those two countries might contribute to its execution. Selective, because the United States should not and need not compete with them everywhere. Selective, because it will be unable to advance its own vital national interests if it concludes that cooperation with China and Russia on transnational challenges is impossible and that the pursuit of collaborative possibilities signifies competitive weakness. And selective, because neither the American public nor America's friends will be inclined to participate in an unrestricted competition with Beijing and Moscow.

Whether the United States will be able to formulate a more forward-looking conception of foreign policy remains to be seen. There is little doubt, though, that discussion of great-power competition will continue to grow. There was already a prodigious volume of commentary about it in October 2019, when I submitted the first draft of my book proposal. That volume has increased steadily over the past two and a half years and, as observers assess the Biden administration's unfolding approach to strategic competition, it will surely continue to grow.

Since I have already mentioned both the Trump administration and the Biden administration, I hasten to note that I have tried to avoid writing a partisan text. There are, of course, likely to be important differences between a Republican-led and a Democrat-led foreign policy. Considering, though, that concerns over China and Russia are growing on a bipartisan basis, the concept of great-power competition is likely to influence America's approach to world affairs for at least the next few decades. It accordingly demands rigorous nonpartisan examination.

While I have attempted to offer several reasons why I believe that it would be mistaken to adopt great-power competition as the guiding framework for US foreign policy, I am not looking to convince readers of any one critique. I hope, more modestly, that, if they consider those

critiques in their totality, they will appreciate the importance of inter-
rogating that framework more rigorously and will consider different
ways of conceptualizing how the United States understands its role in
the world. One senses in the embrace of great-power competition a
relief of sorts that Washington can once more define itself on the basis
of its challengers, as it did most notably during the Cold War. There
are, however, more compelling and sustainable ways for it to cultivate
its identity, two of which readily come to mind: first, reaffirming the
promise of its democratic example; and second, contributing to an
order that can better withstand the stresses of globalization. The United
States is unlikely to recover the degree of preeminence it inherited after
the Soviet Union's dissolution. If it focuses on those two undertakings,
though, there is every reason to believe that it will be able to reinvent
itself: America's great-power opportunity is to play a role in the world
that will enhance its strategic position no matter what decisions China,
Russia, or any other competitor makes.

Fredericksburg, VA
December 15, 2021

Notes to Preface

1   One example is Thomas J. Wright's *All Measures Short of War: The
    Contest for the 21st Century and the Future of American Power* (New
    Haven, CT: Yale University Press, 2017).
2   Uri Friedman, "The New Concept Everyone in Washington Is Talking
    About," *Atlantic* (August 6, 2019).
3   Colin S. Gray, *Modern Strategy* (New York: Oxford University Press,
    1999), p. 21.

1

Searching for a Post-Cold War Ballast

The final draft of this book was completed in fall 2021, shortly after the Taliban stormed back to power in Afghanistan. Though most observers had anticipated that the drawdown of US forces would encourage the organization to reassert itself, the speed with which it advanced—and with which the Afghan army collapsed—stunned even the most pessimistic of them: on August 15, just nine days after it had captured its first provincial capital, the Taliban entered the presidential palace in Kabul.

The outcome elicited a heated debate in Washington. Some observers argued that the United States should have maintained a small military presence in Afghanistan to hold the Taliban at bay. Others concluded that it should have accepted defeat and cut its losses far sooner. Some feared that the Taliban's resurgence would undermine US credibility in world affairs. Others believed that it was the decision to stay in Afghanistan for so long that called America's judgment into question. Some warned that America's departure would only exacerbate instability in the Middle East and make it harder for Washington to rebalance to the Asia-Pacific.[1] Others assessed that it was precisely this kind of argument that had kept the United States preoccupied while China's resurgence was transforming world affairs. Although America's intervention in Afghanistan has concluded, the reckoning over what lessons Washington should learn is likely just beginning.[2]

The Rise of a Unifying Construct

That reckoning, in turn, both shapes and reinforces a much broader debate US observers have been having about the foreign policy that Washington should pursue in a world of growing disorder. While the debate itself is longstanding, it has acquired growing urgency as America's relative decline has become more apparent and as domestic political currents have called into question some of the assumptions that had long guided the country's engagement abroad. Jessica Mathews observes that "the shock of failure in America's longest war may provide an open moment to reexamine the lengthy list of earlier interventions and to reconsider US foreign policy in the post-Cold War era more broadly."[3] Consider three questions.

First, how should it respond to particular challenges, geographic and functional? Turning to the former, China has emerged as an increasingly formidable competitor, especially within the Asia-Pacific, but increasingly beyond. Russia has hived off territory in its near abroad; has promulgated disinformation campaigns aimed at undercutting the internal cohesion of western democracies; and has supported Bashar al-Assad's brutal rule in Syria. The Middle East is plagued by civil wars in Yemen, Libya, and Syria; by fragile security environments in Afghanistan and Iraq; and by a resurgent Islamic State. The European Union is contending with disintegrationist forces from within and strategic pressures from without. North Korea's nuclear and missile capabilities are advancing. The scope and complexity of this problem set raise other questions. How should the United States apportion its strategic equities across different regional theaters, and how can it achieve more balanced burden-sharing security arrangements with its longstanding European and Asian allies and partners?

On the functional front, how should the United States incorporate transnational challenges such as climate change, pandemic disease, and cyberattacks into its assessment of today's geopolitical landscape? Because it is harder to put a nation-state "face" on them, they do not fit as readily into traditional international relations frameworks, even as it grows clearer by the day that such challenges undercut global security and—especially in the case of climate change—amplify a wide range of extant threats.

Second, what role should the United States attempt to play in the world? While this question has preoccupied the country for at least eight decades—and, arguably, for many more, if one assesses that the United States became a global, or at least a transpacific power in the late nineteenth century—it provoked an unexpected conversation with the arrival of the Trump administration, which, unlike its postwar predecessors, challenged the judgment that the United States advances its national interests by undergirding a global order. With a deep skepticism of international institutions and multilateral arrangements, the administration embraced an "America First" posture that sometimes appeared to make little distinction between longstanding allies and avowed competitors. It did not so much cause the debates that are occurring in the US foreign policy community as it affirmed their endurance and intractability. In early 2020, *Foreign Affairs* published an issue with a "Come Home, America?" theme, featuring six responses that weighed the strategic virtues of a more restrained US foreign policy.[4] The postwar era has abounded with such conversations, perhaps most notably in the aftermath of the Vietnam War. Still, considerations of America's role in the world have not, until recently, had to contend with the possibility that potent challenges to the resilience of the postwar order would come from its principal architect.

Third, how much effort should the United States put into developing a grand strategy?[5] The frequency with which this question is posed has not dulled the vigor with which it is debated. Daniel Drezner, Ronald Krebs, and Randall Schweller argued in a widely discussed article that the absence of "a clear understanding of the distribution of power, a solid domestic consensus about national goals and identity, and stable political and national security institutions" has "rendered any exercise in crafting or pursuing a grand strategy costly and potentially counterproductive."[6] Some critics rejoined that the uncertainty this confluence of phenomena has created has rendered efforts to formulate a grand strategy even more important.[7] Complicating this debate, explains Rebecca Lissner, is that, while "most scholars who research and write about grand strategy agree on its basic definition, they employ the concept in markedly different ways."[8]

Debates over these three questions occur not only between, but also within, ideological tents that are growing increasingly capacious. Van Jackson observes that "progressives have failed to articulate . . . *how* their preferred pattern of foreign policy decisions defines and realizes US interests."[9] Colin Dueck contends, meanwhile, that "[c]onservative nationalists have tended to stress US sovereignty, while conservative internationalists have tended to stress the need for US strategic engagement overseas."[10]

But, amid these debates over the contours of US foreign policy, there is at least one high-level judgment that has significant and growing traction in policymaking and analytical circles: namely, that the world has reentered a period of great-power competition. A little over a year before the 2020 presidential election, a member of the National Security Council (NSC) under the Obama administration observed that "there seems to be only one bipartisan consensus in Washington: We are living in a new era of great-power competition. For the United States to win (whatever that means), it must compete—economically, militarily, technologically, and politically."[11]

The emergence of a construct that could orient US foreign policy is notable for several reasons: the number and scope of the aforementioned disagreements; the increasing extent to which partisan polarization is undermining America's ability to pursue a patient, sustained diplomacy that endures from one administration to the next; and the sheer number of crises that compete for policymakers' attention.

Although observers define the term "great-power competition" in different ways, most interpretations begin with some version of the following judgment: the world's two foremost authoritarian powers, China and Russia, are increasingly challenging US national interests and undermining the postwar order, individually and in partnership. That conclusion has steadily gained prominence; Russia's incursion into Ukraine in early 2014, China's steady militarization of the South China Sea, and the Trump administration's 2017 national security strategy and 2018 national defense strategy all served as important reinforcements. The judgment grew especially entrenched, though, in the early months of 2020, as a virus that had originated in China's Hubei Province in December 2019 swiftly morphed into a health-cum-economic emergency of global proportions.

While the COVID-19 pandemic should have occasioned a modicum of great-power cooperation, even if haltingly and begrudgingly, the gravest crisis of the twenty-first century thus far has only intensified mutual distrust, especially between Washington and Beijing but also between Washington and Moscow, as nationalistic impulses in all three capitals increasingly frame cooperative overtures as strategic concessions. Further destabilizing this fraught environment, the United States, China, and Russia are all rapidly modernizing their nuclear arsenals—without, it would appear, having given sufficient thought to the impact of those pursuits on "the delicate calculus of nuclear deterrence."[12]

Before considering the analytical underpinnings and prescriptive implications of great-power competition, it is helpful to trace, even if briefly, how this construct came to assume its present centrality in US foreign policy conversations. The end of the Cold War is a good place to start.

A Pyrrhic Victory?

In a September 11, 1990 address before a joint session of Congress, President George H. W. Bush famously proclaimed that "a new world order" was within reach: "A world where the rule of law supplants the rule of the jungle. A world in which nations recognize the shared responsibility for freedom and justice. A world where the strong respect the rights of the weak."[13] The August 1991 NSS sustained that prospect, declaring that Americans had "an extraordinary possibility . . . to build a new international system in accordance with our own values and ideals, as old patterns and certainties crumble around us."[14] A few months later, delivering his first State of the Union address since the formal dissolution of the Soviet Union, President Bush spoke in language befitting the profundity of the moment: "[I]n the past 12 months, the world has known changes of almost biblical proportions." He went on: "A world once divided into two armed camps now recognizes one sole and preeminent power, the United States of America."[15]

Not all US observers greeted the end of the Cold War with comparable exuberance. In June 1990 a professor at Hofstra University asserted that West Germany and Japan, not the United States, were the true victors, because they had avoided "the treadmills of the arms race and occasional 'small' wars."[16] In August, as the disintegration of the Soviet Union was gaining momentum, John Mearsheimer warned that the world would rue the Cold War's conclusion; that outcome would eliminate the three factors that, in his judgment, had accounted for the absence of a third world war, among them Washington's and Moscow's comparable military capabilities and their possession of a vast nuclear stockpile each.[17] Testifying before the Senate Select Committee on Intelligence in February 1993, James Woolsey cautioned that, while the United States had "slain a large dragon," it now lived "in a jungle filled with a bewildering variety of poisonous snakes." He assessed that those lower-grade threats were more difficult to monitor and counter than the ones posed by a clear antagonist.[18] A year later, Robert Kaplan hazarded that the Cold War's conclusion would unshackle a range of destructive forces that had been overshadowed by, or at least framed within, an overarching struggle between nuclear-armed adversaries. He specifically envisioned "worldwide demographic, environmental, and societal stress, in which criminal anarchy emerges as the real 'strategic' danger."[19]

One concern loomed especially large: had the United States won a Pyrrhic victory? While the implosion of the Soviet Union had eliminated the principal threat to US vital national interests, the central basis for defining America's role in the world had now disappeared. The editor of *Foreign Policy* warned in early 1990, for example, that observers "could disagree about the importance for victory in the Cold War of the Western position in Laos or Zaire, but at least all knew they were discussing the same problem. As the Cold War ends, therefore, American foreign policy will lose more than its enemy. It will lose the sextant by which the ship of state has been guided since 1945."[20]

An especially compelling—and perhaps unexpected—formulation to this effect came from George Kennan. On February 15, 1994 the Council on Foreign Relations held a party in New York City to celebrate the 90th birthday of the celebrated diplomat and author. Kennan would have been well within his rights to offer a triumphant address at the Council. He was, after all, the foremost avatar of containment—a doctrine that, although interpreted and implemented differently by eight presidents, had endured throughout the Cold War. But he struck a measured, cautionary tone. Kennan acknowledged that the world had entered into a period "marked by one major blessing: for the first time in centuries, there are no great-power rivalries that threaten immediately the peace of the world." He feared, though—presciently, in retrospect—that, having spent more than six decades dealing with frontal challengers such as Japan, Germany, and the Soviet Union, the

United States would struggle to adapt to "a world situation that offers no such great and all-absorbing focal points for American policy."[21]

Some observers expressed even greater anxiety, warning that the absence of an external antagonist might not only deprive US foreign policy of its anchor but also, more fundamentally, deprive Americans of their identity. In early 1992, commenting on a slew of recently published books that had urged the United States to mobilize against Japan's seeming economic ascendance, Robert Reich posited that "[t]he central question for America in the post-Soviet world . . . is whether it is possible to rediscover our identity, and our mutual responsibility, without creating a new enemy."[22] Samuel Huntington articulated that question starkly in late 1997: "If being an American means being committed to the principles of liberty, democracy, individualism, and private property, and if there is no evil empire out there threatening those principles, what indeed does it mean to be an American, and what becomes of American national interests?"[23]

But concerns over the prospect of strategic disorientation—and attendant calls for strategic discipline—did not command as much attention as they deserved, perhaps because they seemed incongruous with the realities of America's post-Cold War inheritance. Josef Joffe observed in mid-1997 that "the United States isn't just the 'last remaining superpower.' It is a continent-size 'demonstration effect.'" While predicting that the twenty-first century would witness Russia's convalescence and China's military modernization, he concluded that, for the time being, Washington resembled "a gambler who can play simultaneously at each and every table that matters—and with more chips than anybody else."[24]

It would be an exaggeration to say that the United States exercised hegemony after the Cold War; indeed, a number of searing episodes challenged its seeming omnipotence. In October 1993 the Battle of Mogadishu left eighteen Americans dead and seventy-three wounded, raising doubts about the country's ability to intervene militarily without sustaining fatalities. Shaken by that outcome, the Clinton administration was determined not to repeat it when, less than a year later, the Hutu government and its allies began slaughtering Rwanda's Tutsi minority, even moderate Hutus, and up to a million Rwandans died in just under 100 days. The United States was criticized once more for inaction in July 1995, when Bosnian Serbs massacred some 8,000

Muslims in Srebrenica, marking the worst atrocity in Europe since World War II.

The Search for a New Anchor

Even as these horrors raised questions about America's willingness to deploy military force where it did not have vital national interests at stake, they did not change the prevailing perception that it was far and away the world's foremost power. Indeed, as Richard Haass summarized shortly before the turn of the century, during the 1990s Washington had accumulated sufficient military and economic strength as to be not quite sure how to apply it: "What to do with American primacy?" was the question.[25]

An answer appeared to come with the terrorist attacks of September 11, 2001, which made it seem self-evident that counterterrorism should be—or perhaps had to be—the new ballast for US foreign policy. In his 2002 State of the Union address, President George W. Bush declared that the United States would commit itself to "the pursuit of two great objectives. First, we will shut down terrorist camps, disrupt terrorist plans, and bring terrorists to justice. And, second, we must prevent the terrorists and regimes who seek chemical, biological, or nuclear weapons from threatening the United States and the world." The president warned that America's counterterrorism efforts had only begun.[26] Vice President Dick Cheney supported that judgment in early 2004, venturing that fighting al-Qa'ida and other terrorist organizations would burden the United States indefinitely.[27]

While counterterrorism proved to be the Bush administration's central focus, it did not ultimately gain enough traction to serve as an enduring basis for US foreign policy. The prospect of a terrorist organization's acquiring a nuclear weapon was—and remains—sobering, but it did not represent the kind of existential threat to the United States that the Soviet Union did. Elite and public opinion increasingly questioned the strategic rationale for open-ended interventions in Afghanistan and Iraq, and the notion of a "global war on terrorism" lumped together the distinct threats posed by state actors such as Iran, Iraq, and North Korea and by non-state actors such as al-Qa'ida.

America's emphasis on counterterrorism also seemed increasingly disconnected from the challenges of accelerating globalization and thickening interdependence. In his 2006 book *The Audacity of Hope*, Senator Barack Obama observed that, in the past, "America's greatest threats came from expansionist states like Nazi Germany or Soviet Russia, which could deploy large armies and powerful arsenals to invade key territories, restrict our access to critical resources, and dictate the terms of world trade." But he argued that the landscape was now different; citing terrorism, pandemic disease, and climate change, he concluded that "the fastest-growing threats are transnational."[28] Richard Haass offered a comparable assessment in mid-2008, noting that the primacy of those threats marked

> a fundamental change from much of modern history, which . . . was shaped by great-power competition and often great-power conflict. This is now a different world . . . because the fact that great-power competition and conflict is no longer the driving force of international relations means that the world has opened up the possibility of meaningful cooperation between . . . the major powers of this era, including the United States and China.[29]

Shortly before the 2008 presidential election, Robert Kagan concluded that "very few nations other than the United States consider terrorism to be their primary challenge." Indeed, he continued, to most of the United States' allies and partners, "it has been at best an unwelcome distraction from the issues they care about more."[30] If counterterrorism was too narrow a basis for US foreign policy, no self-evident successor appeared to be in the offing—though a brief episode in the fall would hint at one that would emerge as a linchpin of US foreign policy a decade later.

Russia and Georgia went to war in August 2008: it was the culmination of tensions that had emerged in the waning days of the Cold War and escalated sharply in 2003, with the Rose Revolution in Tbilisi that brought to power a pro-western president, Mikheil Saakashvili. The fight itself lasted only five days, concluding on August 12, 2008. President Saakashvili signed a French-brokered ceasefire agreement on August 15, and Dmitry Medvedev, the Russian president, followed suit the next day, marking the official end of the conflict. Ten days later, though, President Medvedev signed an order that declared the Georgian territories of Abkhazia and South Ossetia to be independent.

Mercifully the conflict did not result in a third world war, despite some anxious speculations at the time. Still, Michael Kofman assesses that it "presaged the return of great-power politics and the end of the post-Cold War period. In 2008, Moscow demonstrated the will and ability to ... challenge Washington's design for a normative international order where small states can determine their own affairs independent [*sic*] of the interests of great powers."[31]

Despite its symbolic significance, the war was overshadowed by the summer Olympics, which took place in Beijing from August 8 through 24. It was a spectacle that spotlighted China's growing stature. And the war faded further into the recesses of global consciousness with the collapse of Lehman Brothers on September 15, which precipitated the world's severest macroeconomic crisis since the Great Depression. Given how sharply relations between the United States and China have deteriorated in the intervening years, it is hard to believe that these two countries coordinated as vigorously as they did in late 2008 and early 2009, spurring the G20 into action and helping to arrest a fast-moving recession. Their cooperation offered preliminary evidence that strategic distrust between the world's lone superpower and a rapidly emerging power need not preclude partnership during global crises or marginalize existing international institutions. Reflecting on that result, Daniel Drezner notes that, "[d]espite initial shocks that were more severe than those of the 1929 financial crisis, global economic governance responded in a nimble and robust fashion in 2008."[32]

The Obama administration's initial experience of dealing with China imbued it, understandably, with confidence about the potential for US–China cooperation. For some time Washington and Beijing even expressed a shared interest in developing a "new model" of great-power relations—a nebulous but attractive call to elevate cooperative imperatives over structural tensions.[33] The logic was compelling: the world would be unable to address pressing challenges without robust collaboration between its only superpower, which possessed the largest economy, and its principal driver of growth, which commanded the second-largest. Even so, the construct did not gain enduring support; the United States was reluctant to suggest that it regarded China as a peer, and China, though agitating for greater sway in prominent international fora, did not want to imply that it bore as much responsibility for maintaining the postwar order as the United States did. Still, the two countries undertook several joint efforts, launching the US–China Clean Energy Research Center in November 2009, signing a landmark climate change agreement in November 2014, and inking a deal to promote greater trust in cyberspace in September 2015. So, even as strategic frictions between them intensified, the two countries seemed able—and, as importantly, willing—to prevent competitive dynamics from crowding out the cooperative ones.

The Obama administration notched a number of cooperative successes with Russia as well. Washington and Moscow partnered to shore up the Northern Distribution Network, which played a key role in routing supplies to US troops when they were deployed in Afghanistan. On February 5, 2011, the two countries signed New START, a major nonproliferation agreement that was effective for ten years and restricted each signatory to 1,550 deployed strategic warheads. Russia joined the World Trade Organization (WTO) at the end of the year, becoming the last G20 member to do so. In late 2013 and early 2014, Washington and Moscow worked together to secure and transport out of Syria 1,300 tons of its chemical weapons. Finally, they collaborated on the negotiations that would ultimately result in a breakthrough deal to constrain Iran's atomic activities: the Joint Comprehensive Plan of Action (JCPOA).

Aggression in Europe and Tension in Asia

Despite these glimmers of hope, US observers began to express growing concerns over renewed strategic competition during the second term of the Obama administration. Russia's annexation of Crimea proved to be a pivotal inflection point: the Congressional Research Service characterizes it as "[t]he sharpest single marker of the shift in the international security environment to a situation of renewed great-power competition."[34] In March 2014, in a referendum that the Obama administration pronounced illegitimate, Crimea voted to secede from Ukraine. Five days afterward the secretary general of the North Atlantic Treaty Organization (NATO) declared that "Russia's military aggression in Ukraine is the most serious crisis in Europe since the fall of the Berlin Wall." He went on: "We had hoped this kind of revisionist behavior was confined to the nineteenth century. But we see it is back in the twenty-first century."[35] His language spoke to a

deepening anxiety among western—and especially US—observers that
the post-Cold War configuration was more tenuous than it had seemed
in the 1990s. Shortly after Moscow's wresting of Crimea, Walter
Russell Mead warned that Russia, China, and Iran were all contesting
that arrangement. Although downplaying the suggestion that the three
countries formed an alliance or would eventually emerge into one (he
cited critical differences between their material capacities and their
strategic objectives), Mead stressed their shared belief that "US power
is the chief obstacle to achieving their revisionist goals."[36]

While Russia tended to capture attention as a result of its discrete
provocations, China came into focus because of its overall trajectory.
Contrary to longstanding US hopes that Beijing would take steps in
the direction of political liberalization as its economy grew, the country
became more authoritarian under its new leader, President Xi Jinping,
and more explicit in its rejection of liberal norms. In April 2013 the
Chinese Communist Party (CCP) issued a document warning that
China had to guard against "Western forces hostile to China" that "are
still constantly infiltrating the ideological sphere."[37] Beijing also grew
more assertive in its neighborhood. That November, without consulting
its neighbors, it declared an air defense identification zone in the East
China Sea that overlapped with Japan's, South Korea's, and Taiwan's
existing zones. Discussions of a "new model" of great-power relations
began to fade during the second half of the Obama administration, as
more observers started to question whether deep interdependence and
extant cooperation could forestall a fundamentally antagonistic turn in
US–China relations.[38]

By February 2015, when President Xi announced that he would
make his first state visit to the United States in September of that year,
Washington and Beijing were at loggerheads over a rapidly expanding
set of issues.[39] The following month, the Council on Foreign Relations
published a report by two distinguished scholars-cum-practitioners,
Robert Blackwill and Ashley Tellis, which concluded that "Washington
needs a new grand strategy toward China, one that centers on balancing
the rise of Chinese power rather than continuing to assist its ascend-
ancy." They warned that "[t]he long-term US effort to protect its vital
national interests by integrating China into the international system
is at serious risk," stipulated that "China seeks to replace the United
States as the leading power in Asia," and urged the United States to

discard its "self-defeating preoccupation . . . based on a long-term goal of US–China strategic partnership that cannot be accomplished in the foreseeable future."[40]

US observers expressed growing concern not only about China and Russia individually but also about the strengthening of their relationship. Isolated and sanctioned by much of the West after its annexation of Crimea, Moscow moved to deepen its ties with Beijing. In April 2014 Russia approved in principle the sale of four to six S-400 missile defense system battalions to China (the deal was finalized the following April, and it made China the first foreign buyer of the S-400 system). In May the two countries signed a $400 billion deal whereby Moscow agreed to supply Beijing with natural gas for thirty years, beginning in 2018 (the Power of Siberia gas pipeline did not actually open until December 2019). The pact had been under discussion for more than a decade, but the immediate precipitant for the completion of negotiations proved to be the crisis over Ukraine, for Russia needed to secure an alternative to its main energy market, Europe. A year later, when marking the 70th anniversary of Nazi Germany's defeat, China and Russia signed thirty-two bilateral agreements that included a framework for avoiding frictions between their economic initiatives in Central Asia; more than $6 billion in Chinese funding for a railway between Moscow and Kazan; and, perhaps most notably, a mutual pledge to avoid conducting cyberattacks on each other. Shortly after concluding that roster of deals, the two countries conducted joint naval exercises in the Mediterranean Sea for the first time.

China's resurgence and Russia's revanchism were hardly America's only foreign policy concerns during the second term of the Obama administration. The Islamic State was wreaking havoc across the Middle East and North Africa and, by late 2014, controlled roughly 100,000 square kilometers of territory, primarily in Iraq and Syria.[41] North Korea continued to make progress toward mating a nuclear warhead to an intercontinental ballistic missile and conducted two nuclear tests in 2016. Finally, on June 23, 2016, with 52 percent of voters in favor, the United Kingdom moved to leave the European Union, casting doubts on America's "special relationship" and on the resilience of the European project.

Still, China and Russia began to occupy increasingly central roles in US foreign policy thinking, especially within the defense community. In

December 2015, Deputy Secretary of Defense Robert Work stated that the revival of great-power competition would be "the most stressing" challenge over the coming quarter-century. Tasked with implementing the "third offset" strategy that Chuck Hagel, the former secretary of defense, had announced in November 2014, Work argued that "Russia and China present the United States, our allies, and our partners with unique and increasingly stressing military capabilities and operational challenges."[42]

Many of Work's colleagues shared his concerns. In January 2016 the navy released a maritime strategy in which it warned: "For the first time in 25 years, the United States is facing a return to great-power competition. Russia and China both have advanced their military capabilities to act as global powers."[43] The following month, Hagel's successor, Ash Carter, observed: "Russia and China are our most stressing competitors. They have developed and are continuing to advance military systems that seek to threaten our advantages in specific areas. And in some cases, they are developing weapons and ways of wars that seek to achieve their objectives rapidly, before, they hope, we can respond."[44]

Despite the Pentagon's advocacy, the construct of great-power competition did not diffuse across the government.[45] In fact, the *Navy Times* reported in September 2016 that "a recent directive from the National Security Council ordered Pentagon leaders to strike out that phrase and find something less inflammatory."[46] The authors of that guidance argued that the term mischaracterized a relationship with China that, albeit increasingly competitive, nevertheless retained important cooperative dynamics.

Under a new administration, though, the notion of great-power competition would soon assume center stage. Although Donald Trump and his top advisors did not forswear the possibility of multilateral cooperation, they stressed that countries would pursue their sovereign prerogatives and that competitive dynamics would predominate in world affairs. The president stated in his inaugural address that, while the United States would "seek friendship and goodwill with the nations of the world," it would "do so with the understanding that it is the right of all nations to put their own interests first."[47] National Security Advisor H. R. McMaster and National Economic Council Director Gary Cohn argued in an influential article that "the world is not a 'global community' but an arena where nations, nongovernmental actors, and businesses engage and compete for advantage."[48] In a September address to the UN General Assembly, President Trump focused on the theme of sovereignty, avowing that "we are renewing our commitment to the first duty of every government: the duty of our citizens."[49] These various statements paved the way for the White House's December 2017 NSS, which observed that the United States had pursued a misguided foreign policy after the Cold War:

> Since the 1990s, the United States displayed a great degree of strategic complacency. We assumed that our military superiority was guaranteed and that a democratic peace was inevitable. We believed that liberal–democratic enlargement and inclusion would fundamentally alter the nature of international relations and that competition would give way to peaceful cooperation.

In truth, the document concluded, "after being dismissed as a phenomenon of an earlier century, great-power competition returned. China and Russia began to reassert their influence regionally and globally." And, it added, "they are contesting our geopolitical advantages and trying to change the international order in their favor." While the NSS did not focus exclusively on Beijing and Moscow—it regarded "the rogue states of Iran and North Korea" and "transnational threat organizations" as two additional sets of challengers—its primary concerns were a resurgent China and a revanchist Russia.[50] The January 2018 NDS echoed the NSS's core messages: warning that the United States was "emerging from a period of strategic atrophy," it described "[l]ong-term strategic competitions with China and Russia" as the Pentagon's chief priorities "because of the magnitude of the threats they pose to US security and prosperity today, and the potential for those threats to increase in the future."[51]

The Follies of Triumphalism

The Trump administration rightly argued that the landscape it confronted was a far cry from the soaring prophecies that had pervaded much US commentary in the aftermath of the Cold War, and key trends that it spotlighted have endured. Democracy, for example, is under growing stress. Freedom House reported in 2021 that "[c]ountries with aggregate [freedom] score declines . . . have outnumbered those with gains every year for the past 15 years," warning that 2020 contributed to "a new global status quo in which acts of repression went unpunished and democracy's advocates were increasingly isolated."[52] While technological advances have aided those who seek to hold power to account, they have also proven far more conducive to the consolidation of authoritarian rule than most observers would have predicted at the turn of the century—or even in the early 2010s, when a series of revolutions across the Arab world spurred renewed optimism over the political power of social media platforms. "Between 2000 and 2017," according to a recent study, "37 of the 91 dictatorships that had lasted more than a year collapsed; those regimes that avoided collapse had significantly higher levels of digital repression, on average, than those that fell."[53] Chief among them is China, which, harnessing artificial intelligence-powered surveillance, has built a sophisticated apparatus for ensuring that it can censor information as it sees fit, prevent mass mobilizations that might challenge the CCP's authority, and still give Chinese "netizens" a release valve for airing their grievances. Having defied many prognostications of collapse, the CCP is now one of the longest surviving authoritarian parties in history.

Forecasts of deglobalization are overwrought, but resistance to integration—geographic, technological, and geopolitical—is growing. According to Elisabeth Vallet, there were fifteen border walls in 1989; today there are at least seventy.[54] Deteriorating relations between the United States and China, meanwhile, have led many observers to conclude that some degree of decoupling between the two countries' economies is inevitable and has the potential to fracture global supply chains and even to produce technological blocs that may operate on the basis of different norms, standards, and arrangements. And countries as diverse as Austria, Brazil, Hungary, India, Poland, and Turkey are witnessing a revival of what Jan-Werner Müller calls "nationalist populism," which threatens to yield "more closed societies and less global cooperation to address common problems."[55]

Finally, it seems highly misguided, in retrospect, to have hoped that either China or Russia would accept the post-Cold War settlement. Beijing was unnerved by the Soviet Union's dissolution and continues to study it. The speed with which the United States defeated Iraq during the Persian Gulf War and the ease with which it conducted maritime operations in the vicinity of mainland China in the 1990s—perhaps most vividly during the 1995–6 Taiwan Strait Crisis—impressed upon the CCP that it had to accelerate the modernization of China's armed forces in order to preempt challenges to its rule. Moscow, of course, viewed the disintegration of its erstwhile imperium as a colossal indignity, taking umbrage at Washington's assertion that America's conception of exceptionalism illuminated the path to a more just future. Russia felt further aggrieved by the discrepancy between its own experiences during the 1990s, marked as they were by economic hardship and societal convulsion, and those of the United States, characterized by growing prosperity and geopolitical ascendance.

At the beginning of 2000, amid discussions of purported US unipolarity, Condoleezza Rice argued that one of the country's five central tasks was to develop "comprehensive relationships with the big powers, particularly Russia and China, that can and will mold the character of the international political system."[56] Their grievances did not register as loudly in the first two decades after the Cold War, in part because America's margin of preeminence was much more significant. Today, though, Beijing and Moscow are considerably more capable of channeling long-lived dissatisfaction into meaningful resistance, individually and collectively. China possesses the world's second-largest economy and is both the largest exporting and the largest trading country. It occupies a commanding position within the vast mesh of global supply chains, and its Belt and Road Initiative has deepened its commercial heft across vast stretches of the developing world. Investing heavily in the development and application of frontier technologies, China is emerging as a center of global innovation. It is rapidly modernizing its armed forces and continues to militarize the South China Sea on the basis of a "nine-dash line" that the Hague unanimously ruled illegal in July 2016. It is also using economic coercion and aggressive diplomacy to make the world more conducive to authoritarianism.

As for Russia, it continues to threaten provocations along its own periphery, to inflame social divisions in western democracies, and to prop up Assad in war-ravaged Syria. And, while the entente between Beijing and Moscow may not be a natural one—their historical interactions give them reasons to be suspicious of each other and their national interests sometimes diverge—it is nonetheless gaining momentum.

The Need for an Affirmative Vision

Great-power competition would appear, then, to have clear virtues as an organizing principle of US foreign policy. It distills, in broad brushstrokes, a core element of contemporary geopolitics, intensifying strategic tensions between the world's most powerful democracy and two significant authoritarian competitors. Because it occupies a central role in high-level government documents such as the NSS and the NDS, it lends coherence to interagency priorities and efforts. And, in keeping with Kennan's Council on Foreign Relations address, it puts policymakers in a familiar frame of mind: that of dealing with a menacing other (or others, in this case).

Certain realities, though, bely that familiarity. The United States has won three decisive victories over overt challengers: Nazi Germany surrendered on May 7, 1945, imperial Japan surrendered just under four months later, and the Soviet Union formally dissolved on December 26, 1991. But the United States is less accustomed to achieving and sustaining stable cohabitations with complex competitors; the putative "long peace" that prevailed during the Cold War discounts not only the number of times Washington and Moscow came to the brink of nuclear conflict but also the maelstrom of proxy wars, civil wars, and genocides that sowed instability across the world during that period. It is not clear what "victory" over China or Russia would look like, nor how either one's collapse would advance US national interests. During its sole experience of long-term multifaceted competition that was the Cold War, the United States was a relatively ascendant power that contested just one other. Today it is a relatively declining power that contests two others.

The United States will face considerably different circumstances as it competes today. Amy Zegart accordingly cautions against policy by analogy, warning that "in a genuinely new moment, the old playbook won't win."[57] There is a more fundamental problem, though, with elevating great-power competition to the position of defining America's role in the world: it is descriptive, not prescriptive. That is to say, interstate competition is a characteristic of world affairs—much like the balance of power—not a blueprint for foreign policy. Competitive dynamics vary in nature, scope, and intensity over time, but they are always present. As Matthew Kroenig explains, "recognizing that competition exists is not a strategy"—and neither is treating competition as an imperative unto itself.[58] A foreign policy that is centered upon repelling Chinese and Russian assertions of influence would be risky on at least three grounds:

- It could lull the United States into an increasingly expansive, yet poorly specified struggle against two formidable powers, undermining America's sense of strategic balance and unnerving its allies and partners: these countries have little desire to be instrumentalized in the service of a reactive US foreign policy, however potent their apprehensions about China and Russia may be.
- It could elicit defensive, even alarmist US responses to Beijing and Moscow, accelerating Sino-Russian rapprochement in the process.
- Given that transnational challenges increasingly shape geopolitics, such a policy could undercut the United States' vital national interests if it sets the United States on a path of permanent antagonism with China and Russia.

While Washington will increasingly have to contend with and manage the challenges posed by a resurgent Beijing and a revanchist Moscow, it should not pursue a foreign policy that is driven by or beholden to their actions. It should instead articulate a forward-looking conception of its role in the world, identifying cases where circumscribed competition with China and Russia might further that vision. Near the end of his famed "long telegram," Kennan exhorted the United States to "formulate and put forward for other nations a much more positive and constructive picture of [the] sort of world we would like to see than we have put forward in [the] past . . . And unless we do, [the] Russians certainly will."[59]

The second part of his judgment may not obtain to the same extent as it did during the Cold War. Russia's vision—to be recognized as a great power within a system it hopes will continue to grow more multipolar—does not rouse individuals across the developing world in the way the Soviet Union's appeals to the proletariat did. China's vision, meanwhile, traffics in underspecified abstractions—"a community of common destiny for mankind," for example—that have acquired a more ominous dimension as the country's aggregate power has grown and its abandonment of foreign policy restraint has become more apparent. What both Beijing and Moscow can do, though, even if they lack compelling alternative visions of their own, is to highlight the weaknesses of the present order, which COVID-19 has amply displayed. They can also, disingenuously yet potently, adduce the convulsions now roiling US domestic politics as evidence that the United States is unfit to govern itself, let alone lead others. The more traction such critiques gain globally, the harder it will be for the United States to marshal either the internal or the external support it will require to pursue a sustainable foreign policy.

It remains critical, then, according to the first part of Kennan's judgment, for the United States to offer an affirmative vision that can elicit enduring support from the American public as well as from its longstanding allies and partners. A starting point for constructing that vision is the recognition that, despite renewed concern over the prospect of deglobalization, transnational challenges are increasingly likely to define our future, be they climate change, pandemic disease, or macroeconomic instability. With tragic irony, COVID-19 may leave the world less prepared to manage such challenges, for it has reduced the agency of core international institutions, amplified nationalistic sentiments, and, perhaps most concerningly, undercut the willingness of great powers to cooperate with one another: transnational challenges are increasingly exacerbating a competition that renders their mitigation less likely.

The more the demand for collective action outstrips the supply of it, the greater the strategic return on investment will be for actors that transcend parochial impulses and undertake to narrow that gap. Henry Farrell and Abraham Newman argue that "a retreat from globalization would make generosity an even more powerful tool of influence for states that can afford it."[60] Two kinds of mobilization must occur in parallel among governments, corporations, philanthropies, advocacy organizations, and other stakeholders in today's geopolitics: short-term, emergency mobilizations to contain crises when they arise; and long-term, patient mobilizations to boost collective resilience against transnational challenges.

The United States is one of the countries that are best positioned to play the role of chief galvanizer. It has the world's largest economy, accounting for roughly a quarter of gross world product (GWP). The US dollar remains the sole reserve currency, and its position has endured despite concerns that the global financial crisis and America's initial mismanagement of the pandemic would prompt widespread de-dollarization. Washington has a network of alliances and partnerships that, while under considerable strain, remains unrivaled. And, whether one considers the fight against Ebola in 2014 or the Marshall Plan that facilitated postwar Europe's resuscitation, the United States has a longstanding record of forging coalitions to contain emergencies and build capacity.

It cannot assume, however, that it will automatically be entrusted to serve as the world's principal mobilizer. The Trump administration's foreign policy strained well-established US alliances and partnerships and, if "America First" proclivities manage to have an enduring impact on the United States' strategic outlook, Washington's friends may be reluctant to make commitments to it, or maybe even to join it in common undertakings. The United States will have to work hard over multiple administrations to demonstrate that it has resumed a more traditional approach to international institutions and multilateral agreements. It will also have to inspire greater confidence in its ability to stay economically competitive and technologically innovative over the long haul, especially vis-à-vis China. The challenge Beijing poses to Washington's diplomatic network—a network that is essential to the latter's ability to mobilize collective action—lies less in ideological allure than in commercial pull: if, through actual performance and the accompanying rhetoric, China can persuade the United States' allies and partners that it is inexorably resurgent, they may decide to rebalance eastward over time.

Now, if the United States is to reemerge as the focal point for collective action, external repositioning will not suffice; it will have to come alongside domestic revitalization. Samuel Huntington once observed that "[t]he ultimate test of a great power is its ability to renew its power."[61] Although the United States has marshaled that regenerative capacity time and again, Michèle Flournoy cautions that one of its "biggest risks is assuming that our advantages are inherent as opposed to something we have to work for to sustain."[62] In addition, while Washington remains the lone superpower, it would be remiss to presume that the rest of the world will wait for, or proceed from, its directives as to how to construct a more resilient post-pandemic order. On the contrary, the initial phase of America's response to COVID-19 heightened the urgency other countries felt to coordinate among themselves:

> Countries in Europe and Asia are forging new bonds on issues like public health and trade, planning for a future built on what they see as the pandemic's biggest lessons: that the risks of China's authoritarian government can no longer be denied, and that the United States cannot be relied on to lead when it's struggling to keep people alive and working, and its foreign policy is increasingly "America first."[63]

Despite having just over 4 percent of the world's population, the United States accounts for roughly 18 percent of global COVID-19 infections and 14 percent of fatalities.[64]

The good news is that significant progress has been made: by the time this book was completed, 60 percent of the US population was fully vaccinated and 72 percent of Americans had received at least one dose.[65] There still are, of course, many causes for concern. A Delta variant that could be twice as transmissible as the original strain is surging among unvaccinated Americans, many of whom are likely to continue resisting vaccination. There have been a few breakthrough infections in which fully vaccinated individuals have nonetheless managed to contract the virus. And, as epidemiologists are unsure how long fully vaccinated Americans will remain protected, the Biden administration initiated a booster shot program in September 2021. On balance, though, the United States is in a substantially better place than it was just a year before. At the same time, a growing body of evidence suggests that Chinese vaccines are substantially less efficacious than Pfizer, Moderna, and AstraZeneca. Given that just 7 percent of individuals in low-income countries have been partially inoculated, the United States has an extraordinary opportunity—and obligation—to help the rest of the world recover (it has purchased 1.41 billion vaccine doses).[66] It also has a profound interest in doing so; the longer COVID-19 persists, the more likely it is that new variants will emerge against which current vaccines offer less protection, or even none.[67]

As the United States works to sustain its recovery from the pandemic, it must also grapple with a range of other domestic challenges that the crisis has placed in sharp relief, including the frailty of the country's middle class, the scourge of racial injustice, and the corrosiveness of political polarization. Internal renewal is not only a moral imperative unto itself; it may also be the most powerful antidote there is to Chinese and Russian suppositions of—and narratives around—terminal US decline. External repositioning and domestic revitalization, moreover, are inextricably intertwined. The United States cannot hope to sustain a constructive role in world affairs if it is unable to restore the appeal of its domestic example. Nor can it protect its public from climate change, pandemic disease, and the like if it is diplomatically isolated.

A Critique and an Alternative

When we are sailing through uncharted waters, we instinctively draw upon our accumulated experiences, looking to see if any of them might offer guidance. It is unsurprising that observers often invoke the interwar period and the Cold War when assessing contemporary great-power competition. With its combination of economic stagnation, authoritarian momentum, and aggrieved nationalisms, the 1930s feel uncomfortably relevant. And the decades-long, globe-spanning competition that pitted Washington's assertion of exceptionalism against Moscow's would seem to be the natural prequel to the increasingly expansive contest that unfolds now between the United States and China. While each period holds insights important for the present, I will suggest in chapter 2 that these insights may obscure the characteristics of contemporary geopolitics more than they clarify.

If one accepts that those historical comparisons are limited, one has to work harder to diagnose America's competitive predicament and generate fresh prescriptive guidance. The prevailing starting point for those conversations is that the United States must adapt to an environment of increasingly acute great-power competition. Chapter 3 expounds more fully the concern around this construct: the notion needs to undergo significant analytical refinement before it can evolve from a partial descriptor of contemporary geopolitics into a prudent basis for US foreign policy. For the United States to have the confidence to compete with China and Russia on a considered, selective basis rather than on a reflexive, reciprocal one, it must take their respective measures with temperance, making sure that it neither discounts nor aggrandizes them.

The 2017 NSS and the 2018 NDS often juxtaposed those two countries, and many discussions in Washington continue to lump Beijing and Moscow together when aiming to articulate the great-power challenge as a whole. But, given the differences between the two countries' material capacities, strategic objectives, and foreign policies, it is important to consider them separately. Chapter 4 begins that deconstruction, exploring how the United States should assess China's competitive strengths and weaknesses. That it is the longest chapter in the book testifies to the central place that Beijing's resurgence now occupies in US foreign policy discussions. While China is undeniably a formidable and multifaceted competitor, it is actively undercutting its own strategic potential by doubling down on both authoritarian rule and coercive foreign policy—and, in the process, alienating major powers within and outside the Asia-Pacific. Indeed, COVID-19 has illuminated a paradox of its trajectory that had been growing more apparent for some time: while increasingly embedded economically and technologically, Beijing is also increasingly isolated militarily and diplomatically, at least among the advanced industrial democracies that still anchor the postwar order.

Chapter 5 continues the disaggregation. It considers how the United States should weigh both Russia's competitive challenge and a deepening relationship between Beijing and Moscow. While Russia possesses a range of assets that make dismissals of its relevance unwise, the problem it poses is more of a disruptive than systemic nature. Similarly, while its relationship with China continues to grow in scope and intensity, the ideological allure and geopolitical potential of their entente will be constrained so long as it defines itself more on the basis of what it opposes—US influence—than on the basis of what it espouses. Rather than considering misguided efforts to drive a wedge between Beijing and Moscow, Washington should concentrate on renewing the power of its democratic example and demonstrating that it can mobilize allies and partners around the urgent task of constructing a more resilient post-pandemic order.

I had originally intended to make this fifth chapter the last one in the book. Soon after I began putting pen to paper, however, I concluded that it would be irresponsible to do so. After all, the more strenuously one objects to a prevailing construct, the more conscientiously one must strive to offer an alternative—or, less satisfactorily, admit that one cannot think of an alternative. With that perspective in mind, the sixth and final chapter outlines eight principles designed to inform a more affirmative vision of US foreign policy, one in which a circumscribed competition with China and Russia influences but does not determine America's role in the world.

* * *

I should note upfront that, for two reasons, I do not attempt to propose US responses to each specific competitive challenge raised by a resurgent Beijing, a disruptive Moscow, and a deepening entente between them. First, it would be impossible to do justice to that task in a book of this length. Second, my goal is not so much to offer a comprehensive playbook for dealing with those challenges as it is to articulate a broader framework in which to examine them. That framework is grounded in the judgment that China and Russia, while significant competitors, are not overwhelming ones, either individually or in concert. If the United States accepts that judgment, it will have the confidence to believe that it will be able to address whatever challenges they end up presenting. It will also have the composure to conduct a foreign policy in which the management of great-power tensions does not overwhelm the pursuit of other imperatives.

While Washington can play a significant role in shaping the external environment Beijing and Moscow confront, particularly if it exercises greater discipline in making common cause with allies and partners, it can fully control only its own choices. That judgment is no cause for despair. On the contrary, if the United States focuses on investing anew in its unique competitive advantages, it will be well positioned to endure as a pillar of geopolitics, even with a reduced margin of preeminence. Hence it has a great-power opportunity to renew itself without having to invoke China or Russia, let alone base its course upon their calculations. If it can formulate a foreign policy that is largely justified on its own merits, one whose prudence endures no matter what steps its competitors may take, it will have gone a long way toward seizing that opportunity.

2

Drawing Historical Analogies

As the United States' relations with China and Russia continue deteriorating, it is becoming increasingly common to hear variants of two propositions: one, that history is returning; the other, that history never disappeared in the first place. The latter is a more forceful critique of those who had hoped that the Soviet Union's dissolution might inaugurate a less competitive era in geopolitics. A representative articulation of the former comes from the *Economist*, which observed, after Donald Trump's election as president, that the fall of the Berlin Wall "was when history was said to have ended ... After a titanic ideological struggle ... open markets and Western liberal democracy reigned supreme." With Trump's victory, though, "that illusion was shattered. History is back—with a vengeance."[1] Stephen Kotkin memorably captured the latter judgment in mid-2018, when great-power competition was rapidly becoming a pillar of US foreign policy discourse: "Geopolitics didn't return; it never went away. The arc of history bends toward delusion."[2]

Which historical periods might help illuminate the contours of contemporary geopolitics? There are numerous comparisons one might consider. The centenary of the outbreak of World War I compelled many observers to wonder whether the United States and China might be heading down a path similar to the one that the United Kingdom and Germany traversed in the late nineteenth and early twentieth centuries.

Some go further back, citing the kind of geopolitical dynamics that emerged with the Treaty of Westphalia in 1648. Thomas Lynch characterizes great-power competition as "a framework for understanding global interstate relations that dominated global political affairs for centuries prior to World War II."[3] And some date the phenomenon to antiquity, often beginning their inquiries with the war between Athens and Sparta, which destroyed the city-state system in the classical Greek world.

Perhaps most common in current discussions of great-power competition, though, are suggestions that the United States is poised to confront an external landscape comparable to the one it faced in the 1930s or in the Cold War. Hence it is essential to revisit those turbulent stretches, both to spotlight important differences and to identify potential lessons.

1930s Redux?

Comparisons with the 1930s generally center around three concerns: democratic recession, deglobalization, and the disintegration of order.

At the beginning of 2021, Freedom House reported that 2020 marked the "15th consecutive year of decline in global freedom." It warned that prominent Chinese and Russian observers are both celebrating and hastening that decline, at a time when COVID-19 has "exposed weaknesses across all the pillars of democracy, from elections and the rule of law to egregiously disproportionate restrictions on freedoms of assembly and movement." It observed, perhaps most concerningly, that erstwhile stalwarts of democracy such as the United States and India are themselves proving susceptible to illiberal currents.[4]

In short, democracy is under duress from without as well as from within. To make matters worse, authoritarian countries are increasingly entrenching their rule by coopting the very digital platforms one might have expected would undercut any grip they had on power, if not end it. Drawing on data from 154 countries, a January 2020 report by the Center for the Future of Democracy at the University of Cambridge found that 2019 marked "the highest level of democratic discontent" since 1995, feelings of dissatisfaction having grown especially pronounced after 2005.[5]

While this picture is concerning, the situation was more dire in the second half of the interwar period, which saw the ascension of hyper-nationalism and fascism in major European powers. Those forces had made sufficient progress during the 1930s that only 11 electoral democracies remained by 1941; in 2020 there were 115.[6] Daniel Treisman observes that, while the democratic stalling that has occurred since 2005 is worrisome, it is not as alarming as it might seem at first blush—and perhaps could even be expected, if one considers the democratic surge that occurred in the three decades before.[7] Steven Levitsky and Lucan Way, meanwhile, caution against conflating democratic stagnation with democratic backsliding: "The failure of authoritarian regimes in China, the Middle East, or Central Asia to democratize should not be taken as evidence of democratic retreat (doing so would be akin to taking a glass that is half full and declaring it not to be half empty but to be emptying out)."[8]

That democracy has lost some of its luster does not mean that authoritarianism is necessarily stealing a march. For starters, that binary is overly reductionist; there are varieties of democracy and varieties of authoritarianism. Nor is any one mode of governance self-evidently better equipped than the rest to manage the challenges of modernity. Martin Wolf concludes that "[l]iberal democracy is corroded, even at its core. But the authoritarian politics that challenge it are vastly worse."[9]

Indeed, the range of responses to the pandemic challenges the narrative that authoritarianism is clearly and confidently in the ascendant. While China's success in containing COVID-19 has been impressive, its punishment of whistleblower doctors such as Li Wenliang (who died of the virus in February 2020), its promulgation of conspiracy theories concerning the origins of the outbreak, and its unwillingness to cooperate with independent inquiries have all undercut its soft power. Other authoritarian countries, including Russia and Iran, have struggled to rein in their outbreaks, while some democracies, such as Taiwan and New Zealand, have won nearly universal plaudits.

Jonathan Freedland reminds us that "when we contemplate our forebears from eight decades ago, we should recall one crucial advantage we have over them . . . We have the memory of the 1930s. We can learn the period's lessons and avoid its mistakes."[10] We should take heart that, even as it is newly stressed, democracy is far more pervasive today than it was in that perilous decade.

The contemporary wave of concern over economic fragmentation probably dates to the global financial crisis. In early 2009 the *Economist* observed that the downward economic spiral that followed the collapse of Lehman Brothers had made the term "deglobalization" fashionable.[11] The intensification of trade and technological tensions between the United States and China in the late 2010s renewed those concerns. Shortly after the Trump administration announced its first tranche of tariffs on China, Harold James speculated that "the world [may have] reached 'peak finance' and 'peak trade,' and possibly 'peak globalization.'"[12]

Understandably, the pandemic occasioned another wave of obituaries for globalization, as it precipitated the worst global downturn since the Great Depression. Referencing the number of individuals who at one time were sheltering in place, Gita Gopinath, research director at the International Monetary Fund (IMF), called it "the great lockdown."[13] International air travel plunged, as many countries imposed strict restrictions on the foreign nationals who were allowed to enter, and the International Air Transport Association estimates that travel may not resume its pre-pandemic level until 2024.[14] Countries are considering how to onshore a greater proportion of their manufacturing, lest they rely too heavily upon others for vital commodities in times of crisis. And the recovery from the pandemic will be highly variegated within and across countries. Near the end of 2020 the UN forecast that an additional 44 million people could enter into extreme poverty by 2030 under a "baseline COVID" scenario and warned that that figure could rise to 207 million under a "high damage" scenario.[15]

But the world appears to have averted the kind of protracted depression it experienced in the 1930s; the IMF forecasts that gross world product will expand by 5.9 percent in 2021 and by 4.9 percent in 2022.[16] It is also notable that, despite concerns over decoupling, many trade and investment deals have recently been concluded. The Regional Comprehensive Economic Partnership (RCEP), which covers fifteen countries—Australia, China, Japan, New Zealand, South Korea, and the ten member countries of the Association of Southeast Asian Nations (ASEAN)—went into effect near the end of 2020, accounting for roughly 30 percent each of the world's population and GWP. Marking the first time China, Japan, and South Korea have belonged to a free trade agreement (FTA) together, the RCEP has imparted momentum to conversations the three countries have had about signing their own FTA. China and the European Union inked an investment agreement soon after the conclusion of the RCEP, thus bringing seven years of negotiation to a close (though Beijing's coercive diplomacy has jeopardized its ratification). The United Kingdom and the European Union signed a FTA that went into effect on January 1, 2021. Trade within the African Continental Free Trade Agreement began that same day, with thirty-four of Africa's fifty-five countries as ratifiers. And, looking ahead, India and the European Union are resuming talks over a possible FTA.

Because the pandemic forced so many businesses and schools to shift their operations online, an explosion in digital connectivity followed: platforms such as Zoom, WebEx, and Microsoft Teams became lifelines for employees and students. Survey evidence suggests, in addition, that there is a significant, pent-up desire to resume travel once the pandemic has abated. The 2020 edition of the DHL Global Connectedness Index summarized the situation: "Trade and capital flows . . . have already started to recover. And digital information flows have surged as people and companies have rushed to stay connected online."[17]

The world is unlikely to resume the kind of freewheeling globalization that gained momentum in the 1990s. Selective disentanglement between the United States and China is poised to continue, as the former has announced its commitment to "a twenty-first-century American industrial strategy" and the latter is intensifying its push for greater technological self-reliance.[18] Clashes over digital norms—not only between democracies and autocracies but also among democracies themselves—mean that global information flows are likely to grow more fragmented. And the ongoing devastation inflicted by COVID-19 compels many countries to consider how they can develop more secure supply chains for active pharmaceutical ingredients, rare earth minerals, semiconductors, and a whole host of other commodities that are increasingly seen as essential for both economic and security reasons.

Globalization is a multifaceted phenomenon and, if certain manifestations stall while others accelerate, there is no self-evident methodology for gauging the net impact of those trends on its trajectory. But we should be skeptical of eulogies, considering how often observers have expressed concern over its prospects. On balance, this phenomenon has grown more entrenched across eight decades of upheavals such as World War II, the Cold War, September 11, 2001, the global financial crisis, and the pandemic. Globalization is more likely to continue evolving than to collapse.[19]

Finally, the erosion of the postwar order prompts many observers to revisit the 1930s. Under the Trump administration, the principal underwriter of that order became one of its sharpest critics—pursuing a foreign policy that, like an autoimmune condition that unleashes the body's own defenses against itself, undercut many of the enduring pillars of US influence. China and Russia have grown increasingly vocal in touting their partnership and pressing for an architecture that centers less on US-led institutions and liberal norms. And COVID-19 has illuminated the order's frailties about as starkly as one can imagine: far from inducing a level of great-power cooperation commensurate with the gravity of the crisis, it has set in motion a precipitous deterioration of Washington's relations with Beijing and Moscow, introduced into the world's consciousness the disturbing phenomenon of "vaccine nationalism," and hollowed out the very health and humanitarian institutions that will be essential to managing future pandemics.

Observers debate both how the pandemic will shape the postwar order and how enduring any effects are likely to prove. Some believe that they will be transformational. Henry Kissinger, for example, assesses that, when the crisis is deemed to have passed, "many countries' institutions will be perceived as having failed . . . the world will never be the same after the coronavirus."[20] Others speculate that the crisis will not usher in a dramatic reconfiguration of geopolitics so much as intensify trends that predated the pandemic. Stephen Walt argues that it "will not transform the essential nature of world politics."[21] Still others opine that this crisis is likely to prove less consequential than one might expect. Joseph Nye predicts that there is less than a 50 percent chance that COVID-19 "will profoundly reshape geopolitics by 2030."[22] Finally, there are those who adopt a more contingent perspective. Thus, Richard Fontaine ventures that "[a]t a minimum . . . the pandemic will accelerate geopolitical changes already in progress. At a maximum, it will usher in a new global era, with as-yet-undefined characteristics."[23]

But now, unlike in the 1930s, there is at least a structure that can theoretically be updated, even if the window for doing so is shrinking. The United States still remains the world's foremost power, and the arrival of the Biden administration has generated hope among longstanding US allies and partners that the postwar order can be reinvigorated, if not restored to the perch it occupied at the turn of the twenty-first century. While it is unlikely that we will witness the emergence of a global coalition of democracies that aim to counter China and Russia, the combined power of democracies far outstrips that of autocracies. One tends to discount this reality if one focuses exclusively on the capabilities that Washington can unilaterally bring to bear against those two countries.

China and Russia, meanwhile, are of a different ilk from the frontal challengers that asserted themselves in the 1930s. Having depended inordinately upon its integration into the postwar order to spur its contemporary resurgence, Beijing attaches high priority to strengthening its influence within that system—as opposed to agitating for dissolution. And, while the descriptor "revisionist" seems to imply a dichotomy between countries that are content with the status quo and countries that are not, China's approach to the postwar order is complex and issue-specific. Stipulating "a world of multiple orders in different domains . . . rather than a single, US-dominated liberal order," Iain Johnston concludes that "China interacts differently with different orders, supportive of some, unsupportive of others, and partially supportive of still others."[24] It is therefore a challenge to distill an overarching Chinese disposition. A recent study by Michael Mazarr, Timothy Heath, and Astrid Cevallos of the RAND Corporation questions the materialization of scenarios in which Beijing "simply accedes to a US-led order and meekly follows its rules" or "becomes so aggressively revisionist that it aims to tear down most of the institutions, rules, and norms that have arisen since 1945." The authors conclude that "China will be neither a friend nor an enemy of the global order."[25]

Russia is less embedded in the postwar order than China, and its pronouncements betray a greater sense of disillusionment with that system than Beijing's. Moscow contends that, in its post-Cold War triumphalism, the United States spurned overtures by Russia to reintegrate itself into the West and failed to make core international institutions more inclusive. Russia is more skeptical than China that it can advance its national interests from within; indeed, it seems to have assessed that it can more readily demonstrate its weight by fomenting disruption. But Moscow does not have the capacity to overturn an entrenched order like the current one on its own, and it probably would not benefit from such a pursuit in any case. Even as it makes extra-system efforts to assert its influence, it appreciates that its status as a permanent member of the UN Security Council and its participation in institutions such as the World Bank, the IMF, and the WTO help burnish its great-power credentials. Indeed, Andrew Radin and Clint Reach conclude that "Russia continues to see the possibility of adapting several components of the international order to reflect its interests rather than US domination."[26]

The geopolitical landscape was considerably more alarming in the 1930s. While the United States had become the largest economic power by the late nineteenth century, several decades would elapse before it would project its military power and assert its national interests in a manner befitting a superpower. World War I culminated with the collapse of the Austro-Hungarian, Ottoman, and Russian empires, destroying an erstwhile Eurocentric balance of power and giving way to new players such as Japan. The protracted stagnation borne of the Great Depression, meanwhile, had helped incubate a confluence of reactionary ideologies: Stanley Hoffmann observed that the 1930s pitted "cosmopolitan liberal nationalism" against communism, against the "squabbling particularistic nationalisms" that found expression in newly formed European countries, and against "the messianic and imperialistic nationalisms of fascist Italy, Nazi Germany, and [a militarized] Japan."[27] That decade, in brief, witnessed a set of aggressive revisionists that confronted far less resistance than they would face today.

A New Cold War?

And what of the Cold War? When observers use the phrase "a new cold war" or variants thereof, especially with reference to US–China relations, it is important to consider whether they are suggesting that strategic tensions between Washington and Beijing indeed exhibit crucial similarities with those that unfolded between Washington and Moscow or they are using the term "cold war" loosely, simply to reinforce the reality that the United States and China have systemic frictions that are likely to endure and intensify. The way one employs this term matters, because the analogy with the Cold War may well obscure more than illuminate—and, accordingly, yield misguided policy recommendations.[28] Observers have suggested a number of alternative terms to capture the downward trajectory of US–China relations, among them "diplomatic ossification," "uneasy peace," and "cooperative rivalry."[29]

Policymakers and observers invoke the Cold War as often as they do in part because of its singularity: it furnishes America's only experience with protracted strategic competition. Kathleen Hicks, now deputy secretary of defense, explains the risks of drawing too heavily upon that one case, referencing an episode of *The Office* in which the lead character, Michael Scott, drives his car into a lake after misinterpreting the instructions from its GPS system: "We have this road map, kind of the Cold War. It doesn't exactly work, but we don't know what else to follow, and we don't really know where it's going. There isn't a plan, but . . . it's following some kind of vague sentiment about what's been wrong in the past. And where do we end up? You know, we end up with the car in a lake."[30]

Of the many differences between Cold War-era strategic tensions and those that exist today, nine come to mind. First, the danger to US security was much more immediate during the Cold War. While a growing number of US observers contend that China poses an "existential threat" to the United States, that term once had a much more literal meaning. Washington and Moscow were nuclear-armed antagonists that contemplated seriously the possibility of a confrontation in which tens of millions might perish. On June 22, 1981, speaking at a hearing on his nomination to be director of the Arms Control and Disarmament Agency, Eugene Rostow was asked if either the United States or the Soviet Union would survive a nuclear war. He assured his questioner, Senator Claiborne Pell, that "[t]he human race is very resilient." When pressed, Rostow admitted that "some estimates predict that there would be 10 million casualties on one side and 100 million on another. But that is not the whole of the population."[31] Washington and Moscow came close to having a nuclear war during the Cuban Missile Crisis of 1962, and a growing body of declassified literature documents that they also came close to having one—perhaps even closer—in 1983.[32] In addition, proxy warfare contributed to a military confrontation between the United States and the Soviet Union that spanned the globe. On balance, contemporary contrasts between today's disorder and the apparent stability of the Cold War reflect a misplaced nostalgia.[33]

Tragically, atomic dangers do endure, and observers cite a number of pathways through which a US–China or a US–Russia conflict could escalate to the nuclear level. But arms races figure less prominently in contemporary competition. In addition, the military component of America's strategic tensions with China is largely confined to the Asia-Pacific; with Russia, it is mainly restricted to Moscow's immediate western periphery, even though security frictions between Washington and Moscow exist around the Black Sea and in some Middle Eastern countries that are mired in civil war. While China and Russia are both pursuing robust campaigns of military modernization, neither has demonstrated a capability to project force globally. Beijing has prioritized the augmentation of its regional deterrence capacity and, while Moscow's activities in Syria demonstrate an upgrade in its expeditionary capabilities, Russia is primarily focused on raising the costs of western military intervention in its near abroad.

Second, the United States did not have the benefit of a highly developed postwar order when its relationship with the Soviet Union began to deteriorate; the Cold War started shortly after the most ruinous conflict in human history. Margaret MacMillan notes that, as gruesome a toll as World War I had exacted, "it had been possible to contemplate going back to business as usual" after its conclusion.[34] Indeed, the first half of the interwar period was largely "a time of cooperation, not confrontation, in international relations. For the most part, the leaders of the major powers, the Soviet Union excepted, supported a peaceful international order."[35] Although they proved short-lived and may appear ingenuous in retrospect, accomplishments such as the establishment of the League of Nations (1920), the conclusion of the Locarno Pact (1925), and the signing of the Kellogg-Briand Pact (1928) were among numerous demonstrations that seemed to suggest that the major powers of the time had seen the errors of their ways. At the outset of World War I they may have plausibly claimed that they could not have foreseen the grisly consequences of their brinkmanship; they could no longer feign such ignorance after its conclusion. One wonders whether the achievements of the 1920s would have had a greater opportunity to take root, entrenching more enlightened norms of international relations, had the Great Depression not intruded.

Alas, a decade of depression climaxed with the beginning of another world war, one that would inflict such staggering military and economic devastation that leaders could not credibly argue afterward that they had learned the lessons of World War I or contend that they simply needed an opportunity to pursue the peacemaking experiments of the 1920s with greater vigor. They deemed it necessary to construct a new order. The resulting "postwar order," now such a commonplace in mainstream discourse, was in its nascent stages when the Cold War began. John Ikenberry explains that it "did not begin as a global order. It was built 'inside' half of a bipolar system as part of a larger geopolitical project of waging a global Cold War. Its original bargains, institutions, and social purposes were tied to the West, American leadership, and the global struggle against Soviet communism."[36] Today, however, that system is far more deeply ingrained and diffuse, giving the United States a major source of "sticky" leverage. Constructing a coherent alternative to an entrenched system is a daunting undertaking, even for a resurgent China that has substantial power.

Third, the Soviet Union initiated its challenge to the United States after a period of upheaval. It was able to make strategic inroads into Europe and Asia in part because both had incurred such great devastation in so brief a period (historically speaking, anyway). World War I claimed some 20 million lives; the Great Depression wreaked havoc on the global economy and empowered authoritarian regimes during the 1930s; and World War II began at the end of that turbulent decade, ultimately taking some 65 million lives. Over the past three quarters of a century, however, both continents have experienced remarkable resuscitations, and several countries on each now serve as important components of the global strategic balance. In addition, where the three-decade prelude to the Cold War (1914–45) saw two global conflagrations and a decade-long downturn, the three-decade precursor to COVID-19 (1989–2019)—the crisis that set in motion an especially sharp deterioration of US relations with China—was largely a period of great-power peace and robust growth.

As a consequence, China challenges the United States from a significantly constrained regional position. It is hemmed in by highly capable democracies—Australia, India, Japan, and South Korea—as well as by the United States' naval power, a predicament that is likely to grow more vexing as Beijing's neighbors bolster their defenses and Washington rebalances in earnest toward the Asia-Pacific. In addition, the longstanding linchpin of America's postwar presence in the region, the US–Japan alliance, is far stronger today than it was after the Soviet Union's collapse. While China's relationship with Russia continues to deepen, its ties with most other major powers are deteriorating, principally on account of a belligerent course of diplomacy Beijing seems intent on continuing.

Russia, meanwhile, must contend with redoubtable, increasingly sophisticated NATO capabilities on its western border. While the alliance faces no shortage of stresses, increasingly from within, Moscow's incursion into Ukraine has proven to be an enduring catalyst for modernization. NATO conducted its largest military exercise since the end of the Cold War in 2018, and even European countries that do not belong to the alliance, such as Sweden and Finland, are upgrading their armed forces and strengthening security ties with one another.[37] In detaching Abkhazia and South Ossetia from Georgia and hiving off Crimea from Ukraine, Russia has demonstrated that it can undercut the norm of territorial integrity in its near abroad and make piecemeal gains. On balance, though, the Russia of today is a far cry from the one that presided over the Warsaw Pact: a significant Eurasian power, to be sure, and one that can rely upon a range of instruments to foment disruption well beyond its borders, but not a frontal revisionist with a global military presence and pretensions to a universal ideology.

Fourth, the Soviet Union had a more propitious set of circumstances in which to promulgate its ideology. A wave of decolonization gave birth to some three dozen African and Asian countries between 1945 and 1960. Happily from Moscow's perspective, a number of them contained receptive audiences. John Darwin explains that, "[i]n many new states, the Soviet model of industrial growth, the strength and efficiency (so it seemed) of the Soviet party state, and the dazzling alchemy of authoritarian rule and egalitarian values that Marxism–Leninism proclaimed were deeply attractive."[38] China, by contrast, has little intrinsic ideological appeal today, and it is not exporting revolution—though it now pushes back more forcefully, and often counterproductively, against perceived challenges to its sovereignty (or even affronts to its sensibilities). It also believes that, while the more enlightened of its onlookers may try to learn from its successes, it is fundamentally inimitable. It is true, of course, that China need not adopt a missionary orientation to make the world more receptive to its normative preferences; the example of its economic development and the growth of its trade and investment linkages with other countries will contribute to that goal. But its ideological challenge is not as pronounced as the one that the Soviet Union marshaled. Russia's ideological limits are even more apparent. Alina Polyakova ventures that its "low-tech model of digital authoritarianism could prove to be more readily adaptable and enduring" than China's.[39] On balance, though, Moscow has far less capacity than Beijing to inspire through economic performance or to transmit its ideological precepts in an ambitious Belt and Road Initiative style.

China and Russia undoubtedly benefit from the dysfunctions that are afflicting the United States, and the final year of the Trump presidency gave them ample grounds for schadenfreude. America's early misman-agement of the pandemic, the lengths to which Donald Trump, then president, went to deny that Joe Biden had won the November 2020 pres-idential election, and the insurrection that occurred while Congress was certifying the president-elect's victory all contributed to the impression of a superpower in distress. But the challenges confronting democracies do not obviate those that confront autocracies; nor does dissatisfaction with democratic governance imply enthusiasm for authoritarian rule. Thomas Pepinsky and Jessica Chen Weiss explain that

> the more proximate roots of democratic backsliding in most countries are domestic: popular resentment over the perceived loss of power and resources to immigrants, minorities, and robots; "out of touch" political and intellectual elites; economic dislocation resulting from globalization and deindustrialization; and polarization and disinforma-tion fed by a loosely regulated digital sphere.[40]

Fifth, the Cold War placed US-led and Soviet-led ideological blocs in competition with each other. Such blocs are less salient today. Thus, for example, the European Union is increasing its economic ties with America's principal strategic competitor, China, and India is strength-ening its military ties with America's other main strategic competitor, Russia. The United States should fully expect that longstanding allies and partners will maintain significant, multifaceted relationships with those two autocracies. Accepting that conclusion will be especially important in dealing with China. While major powers across Europe and Asia have long avowed their desire to maintain independent foreign policies toward Beijing, even smaller powers increasingly question why they should have to make a strategic "choice" between Washington and Beijing or favor one over the other. Bilahari Kausikan argues that the interdependence between the two countries gives Southeast Asia greater agency than it had during the Cold War: "During the Cold War, fundamental choices may have been very difficult, but they were essentially binary. The complex supply chains within which the US and China compete make their competition far from binary."[41]

Sixth, because of deliberate choices by the United States and the Soviet Union, there was little commercial entanglement between them. Avery Goldstein explains that "security concerns about the mutual vulnerabilities inherent in economic interdependence led both the Soviets and the US to preclude broad and deep economic exchanges with each other."[42] Roughly the converse characterizes the post-normalization phase of the relationship between the United States and China: they consciously and proactively built up their economic linkages, seeking to impart a baseline of stability to a relationship that had little organic basis for development. While the two countries are increasingly attempting to recalibrate their present configuration of interdependence, they remain highly intertwined; bilateral flows of foreign direct investment have fallen sharply in recent years, but two-way goods trade has held reasonably steady—and is substantial, at roughly $560 billion in 2020.[43] In addition, as Yen Nee Lee notes, Fitch Ratings observed in August 2020 that the two countries' supply chain linkages with each other had grown in the preceding decade.[44] Evidence from mid-2021 suggests that Washington and Beijing are not only adjusting to existing tariffs they have imposed on each other but also trading at a much higher level than most observers would have predicted.[45]

Seventh, because the Soviet Union was not a significant economic competitor—at its peak, in 1980, its gross domestic product (GDP) was roughly two fifths of that of the United States—Washington assessed containment to be viable.[46] China, by contrast, is already a potent economic competitor: it is the world's largest trading country and a key driver of technological innovation, and its GDP continues to close in on that of the United States. While the pandemic may, over time, undercut China's dominant position in manufacturing, as other countries gradually find ways of reducing their dependence upon its exports, the crisis has boosted Beijing's linchpin status for now.[47] The upshot is that the United States cannot credibly undertake to contain China; nor should it expect fellow democracies to attempt to decouple from China as much as it may wish. Europe now trades more with China than with the United States, and European companies are not planning to exit China in a significant way. The same holds for their Japanese counterparts.[48] Even forging a coherent US position will prove challenging; while the American government takes a harder line toward Beijing, Wall Street deepens its footprint there.[49]

Eighth, the United States and the Soviet Union were largely bound together by the sole imperative of avoiding mutually assured destruction. Today, however, there are many other challenges besides nuclear proliferation that Washington, Beijing, and Moscow must cooperate on if they are to safeguard their shared vital national interests; they must work to slow climate change, manage pandemic disease, and limit macroeconomic instability (to name but a few priorities).

Ninth, the Cold War ended with the implosion of one of the contenders. China and Russia each have numerous competitive vulnerabilities, of course, both at home and abroad, and it is unclear how a post-Xi Beijing and a post-Putin Moscow will evolve. It seems improbable, though, that either country will collapse in spectacular fashion. China's sheer demographic and economic proportions mean that it will likely endure as a central actor in world affairs. Many consultancies estimate that its GDP will overtake the United States' in absolute size well before the middle of the century. But one need not accept that this scenario will come to pass to appreciate that China will remain a pillar of the global economy. That judgment seems even more certain when one considers both the extent of its trading and investment relationships and the position it occupies within global supply chains. And, while there are questions about the willingness of younger Chinese citizens to accept authoritarian rule, the Chinese Communist Party enjoys broad domestic legitimacy for now.[50]

Russia may not be as formidable a competitor as China, and its long-term strategic outlook may not be as promising as it seemed in the early 2010s, when it avowed its ambition to serve as a thriving economic intermediary between Western Europe and the Asia-Pacific. Today it is laboring under sanctions, grappling with both the fallout of the pandemic and the volatility of oil prices, and achieving mixed results as it tries to "pivot" eastward. Still, whether one considers the vastness of its territory, the size of its gas reserves, or the number of its nuclear weapons, Russia cannot be dismissed. And President Vladimir Putin continues to command strong public support. Like China, then, Russia seems poised to continue muddling through domestic upheavals and external disturbances. Regarding both Beijing and Moscow, Washington will be tasked with maintaining a strained, dynamic balance; its objective is not—and cannot plausibly be—to prevail over a supreme antagonist but to cohabitate with a vexing competitor.

The Lessons and Limits of Analogies

The preceding section is not intended to strike a Panglossian tone. The differences between the present and the 1930s do not silence the echoes. Authoritarian countries continue to learn and adapt, and democratic decay now tends to occur more subtly and gradually than it once did.[51] Certain methodologies suggest that democracy is more imperiled than one might expect; the Democracy Report Team at the V-Dem Institute found that in 2019 the number of autocracies (92) surpassed the number of democracies (87) for the first time since 2001: "Almost 35% of the world's population live in autocratizing nations—2.6 billion people."[52] In addition, there is no law that requires an inexorable continuation of economic integration; World War I broke out after a period that observers sometimes call "the first globalization." Systemic shocks such as COVID-19 threaten not only to hobble institutional pillars of the postwar order but also to disillusion publics in democracies and to empower authoritarian leaders, who cite the chaos of a world in flux to justify and reinforce their grip on power. Finally, while chapter 5 will discuss some of the limits of Sino-Russian relations, the interwar period cautions against underestimating the ability of competitors to act in concert; Ian Ona Johnson explains that, even though "the Soviet Union and Germany had vastly different visions of their preferred order, they collaborated because their opposition to the status quo was greater than their concerns about each other."[53]

Nor do all the differences between the present and the Cold War period offer grounds for reassurance, particularly in dealing with China. While Beijing is a less menacing competitor than the analogy implies—Moscow was a nuclear-armed antagonist that used territorial

aggression and proxy warfare to export its ideology—it is a more formidable one in some ways. As the center of global growth and as a key
driver of technological innovation, one that is highly integrated into
the postwar order, China cannot be readily isolated.

There are in fact vital lessons one can learn from analogies with the
1930s and the Cold War, three of which come immediately to mind.
First, US observers should not minimize the potential appeal of ideologies they regard as self-evidently noxious, especially if democracies
themselves are underperforming. An initially prevalent narrative—that
the world's response to COVID-19 elevated the appeal of authoritarianism over that of democracy—looks premature in retrospect.[54] If,
however, China continues to sustain robust growth while the United
States is unable to renew itself domestically, the former may find a
more receptive audience for its ideological precepts, especially in the
developing world. In a July 2021 speech to representatives of some 500
political parties from 160 countries, President Xi posited that there
are "multiple ways and means to realize democracy" and rejected the
conclusion that there is a "fixed model for the path to modernization."
He also offered to "contribute more Chinese solutions and Chinese
strength to the poverty reduction process worldwide."[55]

Second, protracted competitions can be most dangerous at the
outset, after both countries appreciate that their relationship has taken
an adverse turn and its fundamental nature has changed, but before
they appreciate the urgency of circumscribing its further deterioration. Although the Cold War abounded in precarious moments, the
US–Soviet competition was, on balance, far more fraught before
the initiation of détente than after. Observers demarcate the inter-
val of greatest peril differently—1949 to 1962 versus 1953 to 1969,
for example—but the point is that Washington and Moscow were
more inclined to probe each other's red lines and to confront each
other militarily when they did not grasp the potential consequences
of their brinkmanship. The Cuban Missile Crisis impressed upon
them the imperatives of sustained communication—they concluded
a hotline agreement on June 20, 1963—and arms control—witness
the Limited Test Ban Treaty (1963), the Nuclear Nonproliferation
Treaty (1968), the Anti-Ballistic Missile Treaty (1972), and the pair of
treaties they signed to limit strategic arms, one in 1972 and another in
1979.

Historians are likely to mark 2020 as an inflection point in the US–China relationship, when Washington and Beijing both concluded that cooperative dynamics could no longer constrain competitive ones. The sooner they appreciate the sources of each other's resilience and the consequent unavoidability of competitive cohabitation, the sooner they will be able to stabilize their interactions. In the interim, they must fashion their own set of guardrails to ensure that they neither engage in an armed confrontation nor drift into a new cold war, especially since both countries increasingly view economic interdependence—the erstwhile stabilizer of their relationship—as a competitive liability.

Third, policymakers should neither overstate their enlightenment nor understate their agency. It surely seemed unthinkable after World War I that leaders would allow themselves to sleepwalk into another catastrophe of comparable proportions—yet a vastly more destructive one began just two decades later. Today the nexus of nuclear multipolarity and military artificial intelligence is cause for grave concern. Former Secretary of Defense William Perry, a doyen of the US national security establishment, fears that atomic dangers are far greater today than they were during the Cold War.[56] Whether they agree or disagree, policymakers cannot be overly sanguine. Nor, however, should they assume that disasters are preordained. President John F. Kennedy's leadership during the Cuban Missile Crisis offers enduring insights into the ability of creative diplomacy and patient deliberations to defuse tensions. The United States and the Soviet Union again came close to having nuclear exchange in 1983, twice; but, thankfully, historians never had to write about the aftermath of such an event. Soviet Lieutenant Colonel Stanislav Petrov played a decisive role in heading off a confrontation in September, and US Lieutenant General Leonard Perroots did the same in November.[57] That we have managed to avoid a third world war undoubtedly owes in part to luck. But this outcome also demonstrates the capacity of human intervention to triumph over the often invoked immutability of human nature.

As they heed history's warnings, policymakers must also guard against becoming its prisoners. Perhaps the greatest gift the past bequeaths to the present is its affirmation of human agency. The unavoidability of strategic tensions does not preordain great-power war any more than it precludes great-power cooperation. To compete effectively, the United

States must distill as accurately as possible the core characteristics and drivers of contemporary geopolitics, bearing in mind the lessons of the 1930s and of the Cold War, but appreciating the need—and embracing the opportunity—to develop a substantially new playbook.

3

Probing Great-Power Competition

The further one analyzes the construct of great-power competition, the more of a paradox it proves to be: it is, arguably, as ubiquitous as it is underspecified—at least beyond the baseline assessment that China and Russia are increasingly contesting US national interests and the postwar order. Despite the "remarkable extent to which the concept is linked to virtually every aspect of defense, strategy, and security," notes one observer, there is little agreement upon its definition: "Even a cursory search yields a multitude of answers across a variety of sources. This inevitably leads to differing views on how to carry out the broad directives in the keystone defense policy documents."[1] Another judgment in that vein notes that "numerous government stakeholders hav[e] differing assessments."[2] Mike Gallagher, a Republican representative for Wisconsin, notes that "we still don't really know what great-power competition means."[3]

The Competition Snowball

One reason why it has proven difficult to converge on a shared understanding is that no such understanding exists for either of the constituent terms, "great power" and "competition," taken separately. Observers continue to debate the criteria that a given country must fulfill to earn the designation of "great"—an intrinsically subjective descriptor. John

Mearsheimer contends that a great power has "sufficient military assets to put up a serious fight in an all-out conventional war against the most powerful state in the world."[4] John Copper defines a great power as one that "can exert global influence and is able to cause other nations to concur with its views and/or do what it asks or demands." He notes, though, that "[m]ore commonly today ... a great power is simply a nation that is perceived as that."[5] As chapter 5 will explain, these perceptions have generated an enduring debate over how to classify Russia. It is generally characterized as a great power, but many other nuclear-armed countries are not. There are also eight countries whose economies are smaller than China's but larger than Russia's, none of which is commonly classified as a great power.

A perfunctory review similarly reveals that, while there is a prodigious literature on terms such as "competition" and "strategic competition," neither the volume of scholarship nor the passage of time has brought observers closer to formulating common interpretations of what it means to be competitive or how to become more competitive. A Royal United Services Institute report laments that,

> despite the broad political consensus on the need to reorient national security strategies to secure "competitive advantage," there exists an absence of clarity about what this term means and how it might be secured. Existing definitions of the term tend towards either being tautological or conflat[ing] process with strategy. In many policy documents, the term is used loosely to refer to capabilities and the ability to secure desirable outcomes at different junctures.[6]

Considering how much uncertainty there is over how to understand the terms "great power" and "competition," it is not surprising that their concatenation produces further ambiguities. It would be unreasonable to call for the kind of precise definition one expects to find when looking up a word in a dictionary. It is nonetheless striking that a concept can be as doctrinally dominant as it is strategically inchoate. Stephen Biddle presciently envisioned the potential emergence of this discrepancy. In early 2005, when most US observers were understandably focused on terrorism and great-power competition was more of a scholarly consideration than of a policymaking one, he predicted that policies in support of countering the former would increasingly come into tension with policies in support of waging the latter. Biddle argued that high-level US foreign policy documents were "ambiguous on the nature of the problem itself" and concluded that they contained "no explicit discussion of long-term goals with respect to great-power competition."[7]

The conceptual challenges he identified have proven enduring. The summary of a November 2018 workshop at the Lawrence Livermore National Laboratory, for example, observes that a "fundamental uncertainty in the US approach to strategic competition is about the long-term goals. It remains unclear to what end the US is competing."[8] *Defense News* reported in May 2019 that the Pentagon "hasn't even settled on a definition for the 'competition' in 'great-power competition.'"[9] Mara Karlin, now acting deputy undersecretary of defense for policy, notes that "everyone is using the term great-power competition, kind of ad infinitum, and occasionally in contradictory manners."[10] The more frequently observers use it without having—or attempting to develop—a shared interpretation, the more its strategic utility diminishes. A gap between usage and understanding is especially problematic for a term such as "great-power competition," which, far from designating an esoteric concept that dwells at the margins of policy conversations, points to a core construct that lies at their heart. Socialization should occur in parallel with interrogation, clarification, and refinement.

One would not advise a team of doctors to perform a surgery if they disagreed over where to make incisions. Nor should one advise US officials to pursue a foreign policy that is oriented around great-power competition if they disagree over how to compete, where to compete, and what they seek to achieve by competing. A framework that is at once widely accepted and highly elastic is vulnerable to misappropriation. A report by the Finnish Institute of International Affairs cautions that "great-power competition and its manifold terminological siblings . . . risk becoming mere empty signifiers that obscure from view more than they illuminate . . . great-power competition may be evoked by political leaders to defend any number of disparate policies regardless of their strategic merit."[11]

Indeed, once an ambiguous construct has diffused so broadly across the policymaking apparatus, without any clear "owner" within the bureaucracy, retroactive attempts to circumscribe it are unlikely to succeed. Instead, when weighing differing conceptions, officials run the risk of attempting reconciliation through accumulation: when given an inherently permissive mandate, policymakers can more easily justify including additional missions than downsizing or eliminating existing ones. A mandate of that nature is akin to the proverbial snowball, which gains volume and momentum as it barrels down the side of a mountain.

Thus, even though the renewed focus on great-power competition was explicitly predicated upon reducing America's relative focus on counterterrorism, a growing number of analysts argue that the implicit trade-off is a misguided one. In mid-2018, for example, one observer expressed concern that prioritizing China and Russia would "once again give terrorism room to flourish, just as the premature drawdowns in Iraq and Afghanistan did."[12] In early 2020, another warned that "some in Washington have become myopic, using the focus on this grand game" to ignore the reality that terrorism remains a potent threat in South Asia and is a growing threat in both East and West Africa.[13] Around the same time, conveying anxiety over a prospective drawdown of US forces from Africa, a bipartisan group of lawmakers warned that "the narrow focus on great-power competition may create an environment in which the successes of our stability operations are lost."[14]

In addition, observers have begun warning that, while it is important to invest in higher-end military capabilities to deter formidable state competitors, sustaining preparations for low-end, unconventional conflict is essential to that undertaking. One analysis accordingly cautions against the presumption that "conventional military dominance will trump any need to specifically address irregular activities."[15] The former chief of irregular warfare policy in the office of the undersecretary of defense for policy goes further, concluding that present conceptualizations of great-power competition focus too narrowly on deterring conventional threats: "While America prepares for a traditional war neither Russia nor China seems eager to fight, these competitors are busy shaping conditions to their advantage through proxies, denying the United States military access to key terrain through coercion, and eroding American influence through disinformation—all without firing a shot."[16] Running in parallel with such assessments are growing calls to repurpose special operations forces so that Washington can deter Beijing and Moscow along a more expansive conflict spectrum.[17]

Finally, while the present prioritization of great-power competition initially stressed that the United States had overinvested in the Middle East, more observers now contend that it cannot maintain its strategic position in relation to China and Russia if it rebalances away from the region.[18] The United States' sheer preponderance of power ensures its ability to be omnipresent. But the accretion of capabilities does not diminish the need for priorities; it simply gives one more time to postpone an inevitable reckoning with trade-offs—trade-offs that even the world's lone superpower must make to pursue a sustainable foreign policy.[19] Competitive equipoise—and therefore strategic solvency—will require the United States to accept two propositions. First, even if it were to conduct a flawless foreign policy, it would be unable to lock in a certain level of relative influence in every region unless it could prevent competitors from growing their own capabilities. Second, the unavoidable consequence of rebalancing one's strategic equities away from one region and toward another is that one's competitors will have greater freedom of maneuver to extend their reach into the former. Accepting the limits of one's agency is not an expression of fatalism; it is a requirement of strategy.

Weaving together the three concerns mentioned so far—that prevailing conceptions of great-power competition mistakenly downgrade counterterrorism, unconventional conflict, and the Middle East—some observers conclude that those conceptions, while necessary, are insufficient. Perhaps it is the case that "today's turbulent world does not allow a single strategic focus."[20] In that case, argues Raphael Cohen, "the challenge becomes not how to compete with this or that great power, or engage in counterterrorism operations, but how to do all of the above."[21]

The Elusiveness of Victory

One reason why it is becoming harder for countries to formulate sustainable foreign policies is that they are experiencing greater difficulties in articulating clear strategic objectives. For much of human history, by contrast, the expansion of territory was an articulable supreme goal. Klaus Knorr observed in 1966 that, "until recently, European history involved an unending series of territorial conquests in Europe; and after European nations had begun to industrialize, it was easy for them to conquer vast areas outside of Europe." He noted that European countries had "colonized the entire Western hemisphere and Oceania" and "acquired colonial control over most of Africa and Asia" by the end of the nineteenth century.[22] It was not until the early twentieth century that territorial conquest began to encounter significant legal and normative challenges. Oona Hathaway and Scott Shapiro found that there was roughly one conquest every ten months between 1816 and the signing of the Kellogg–Briand Pact in 1928, and that almost 300,000 square kilometers of territory on average were conquered annually during that time. After 1948, by contrast, those figures changed from ten months to roughly every four years and from almost 300,000 to under 15,000 square kilometers.[23] Richard Lebow concludes that territorial conquest is increasingly rare because it has become less profitable for aggressors and because it has elicited growing opposition from those who are attacked.[24]

Russia's annexation of Crimea sent shockwaves around the world, in part because that kind of outcome is now such a rarity and in part because it is distressing to contemplate the possibility that such scenarios could one day push Washington to clash with Moscow or Beijing (if not with both). One cannot, of course, rule out the possibility of a great-power war. The hope, though by no means the presumption, of most observers is that the great powers will find ways of competing short of armed confrontation. Peter Layton observes that contemporary strategic competition is "seen as remaining below the level of great-power armed conflict, instead ranging across diverse areas including economic, diplomatic, cyber, information campaigns, and proxy wars."[25]

Most assessments corroborate Layton's, explaining that great-power competition involves an extensive set of levers and occurs in a wide range of domains. One formulation states that it entails "Chinese and Russian malign activities occurring below the threshold of armed conflict."[26] Another posits that it involves "nuclear-armed states and regional powers engaged in high-stakes standoffs mixing military threats, diplomatic warnings, and economic coercion."[27] The *New York Times* suggests that another variable to consider is the pace at which Beijing and Moscow can act as compared to Washington, framing great-power competition as America's "attempts to leverage its weight as a military and economic superpower, albeit one that sometimes operates with bureaucratic sluggishness, against the ability of China and Russia to send money, troops, and matériel, with speed—and little, if any oversight."[28] An especially telling interpretation stipulates that "a comprehensive great-power competitive space would comprise all military domains, multiple sectors, and every instrument of national power."[29]

Defining victory in so vast a competitive space is no trivial matter— let alone pursuing it. General Joseph Votel, former commander of US Central Command and US Special Operations Command, explains:

> Winning will not necessarily look the same as it did in the past; a parade, a very clear and distinct signing of surrender or some clear indication that hostilities are over, and that one side has prevailed over the other ... The definition of what winning in this very complex environment means has changed; winning matters, but winning looks quite different than what we might have thought about it in the past.[30]

It looks different in part because attempts to achieve something resembling a decisive victory today could be ruinous: in the nuclear era, an armed confrontation could not only have unfathomable consequences for the societies and economies of the warring countries but also deliver an irreversible blow to the legitimacy of the postwar order, whose central objective has been to avert another world war. How, then, should countries define, achieve, and sustain competitive advantage vis-à-vis one another? Lawrence Freedman distills the challenge:

> The fear of escalation—a function not only of nuclear weapons but also the dangers and uncertainties associated with conventional war—explains why the great powers work hard to prevent their forces clashing at any level, and therefore why so much conflict is conducted through means short of war, such as economic sanctions, information campaigns, or cyber war. The reluctance to escalate gives these conflicts their indecisive and indefinite quality.[31]

That ambiguous quality accounts for the increasing manifestations of strategic competition—witness the proliferation of commentary about "hybrid warfare" and competitive strategies within "the gray zone" (two terms that, like great-power competition, are defined in myriad ways and whose analytical utility is often questioned).[32]

Compounding the challenge that Freedman sets out are the characteristics of America's chief competitors. The opening chapter noted that the Soviet Union's implosion—however monumental a military, economic, and ideological victory for the United States it may have seemed at first glance—contributed to a sense of strategic disorientation in Washington. When the superstructure that had governed US foreign policy for nearly half a century disappeared, there was an immediate, overwhelming desire to find a comparable framework that could replace it. The United States would have appeared to identify such a successor, for the geopolitical reverberations of a resurgent China, a revanchist Russia, and a deepening alignment between these two authoritarian powers are becoming more apparent.

But neither country constitutes an existential threat in the way the Soviet Union did. Both are, of course, nuclear-armed powers that are bolstering their atomic programs. But Washington and Moscow actively prepared for a nuclear war, bound together by what amounted to a mutual suicide pact. Nuclear modernization does not figure as centrally in China's and Russia's respective competitive approaches vis-à-vis the United States. That conclusion is not intended to diminish the reality of nuclear dangers, which, tragically, endure and, in the eyes of some observers, grow more pronounced even as they recede from global consciousness.[33] It is simply intended to affirm that Beijing and Moscow will strive to compete with Washington differently, not only in the hope of avoiding an armed confrontation but also in the hope of reducing the competitive returns to military overmatch. Odd Arne Westad concludes that they "will attempt to nibble away at American interests and dominate their regions. But neither China nor Russia is willing or able to mount a global ideological challenge backed by military power."[34]

There are two other reasons why it is difficult to articulate what a victory over China or Russia would look like. First, they seem more likely to endure as central forces in world affairs than to implode in spectacular fashion. While their competitive liabilities are myriad and are manifest, both have defied many prognostications of collapse. Analyses that purport to explain how Washington can "beat" Beijing or Moscow discount the imperative of cohabitation, seemingly suggesting that it can wear them down over time.

Second, the inexorability of strategic tensions does not obviate the endurance of shared interests—interests that, in turn, will require the United States, China, and Russia to preserve a cooperative space. Cooperation is not, of course, a goal in and of itself; it is a means. Indeed, if Washington seems overly keen, even desperate when making overtures to Beijing and Moscow around possibilities for collective management of transnational challenges, it could validate their narratives about terminal US decline and embolden them to spurn US outreach. The more the United States demonstrates an ability to renew its unique competitive advantages, the better positioned it will be to pursue cooperative possibilities in its interactions with China and Russia—from a position of quiet confidence.

But the seeming banality of the proposition in question—that great-power cooperation is indispensable—does not nullify its basic truth, as the coronavirus pandemic has made all too clear. If, whether through shortsighted calculation or through equally misguided pride, great powers come to devalue high-level diplomacy, the world will find itself increasingly incapable of addressing the very phenomena that threaten its long-term prospects. As unpalatable as Washington might find the idea of collaborating with Beijing and Moscow, challenges such as climate change and pandemic disease will lend themselves less and less to the imposition of unilateral will over time. Indeed, in late 2020, as the coronavirus was tearing across the United States, Simon Reich and Peter Dombrowski observed that, in confronting naturogenic threats, "not only is the United States heavily dependent on the cooperation of other states for its own national security, that security is now contingent on the goodwill of others, because it has lacked (and currently lacks) the planning awareness, economic infrastructure, and integrated institutional apparatus needed to autonomously respond effectively."[35]

Competitive dynamics inhere in interstate relations. But codifying great-power competition as the organizing framework of US foreign policy signals more explicitly, even if unintentionally, that the United States is thinking in predominantly zero-sum terms, regarding cooperative possibilities as an afterthought more than as an imperative: "By making competition a ubiquitous descriptor, the US risks the inverse of what some see as a mistaken understanding of the post-Cold War period as one of great-power cooperation. In other words, we risk ignoring other aspects of great-power relations."[36] Here, then, is one of the paradoxes that characterize prevailing conceptualizations of great-power competition: they are at once too reductionist and too expansive—reductionist, because they orient the United States narrowly around competitive dynamics; expansive, because they invite an all-encompassing competition.

The Possibility of Boundless Competition

One way of probing the scope of great-power competition is to ask what its geographical delimitations are. Some observers believe that it occurs mainly in the Asia-Pacific, home to America's foremost strategic competitor. The Pentagon calls it "the single most consequential region for America's future."[37] Elbridge Colby, the principal author of the 2018 national defense strategy, and Wess Mitchell, assistant secretary of state for European and Eurasian affairs from 2017 to 2019, assert that great-power competition "applies both to the Asian nations that find themselves under growing economic and military pressure from Beijing and to the federating heart of the European continent and the more loosely affiliated states on its fringes." They urge the United States to "scale back its efforts in secondary and peripheral regions"—especially, in their judgment, in the Middle East.[38]

Some observers caution that retrenchment from the Middle East would have a spillover effect, calling into question the credibility of US security commitments in the Asia-Pacific and Europe.[39] A variant of this argument holds that maintaining a sufficient military presence in the region would reduce the possibility that a crisis there prevents the United States from maintaining a first-order prioritization of China and Russia.[40] Thus, for example, if there were to be another terrorist attack on the homeland and it originated in the Middle East, Washington would face overwhelming pressure to prioritize that region once more.

The record thus far suggests that the United States will find it difficult to reduce its focus even without such a shock. Two consecutive administrations, albeit with markedly different attitudes toward supporting multilateral institutions and upholding the postwar order, came into office with a strong desire to reduce America's military footprint in the Middle East, and both struggled. The devolution of Syria into civil war and the damage wrought by the Islamic State put pressure on the Obama administration almost immediately after it had announced that the US military intended to rebalance to the Asia-Pacific. In 2019, meanwhile, as tensions escalated between Iran and Saudi Arabia, the

Trump administration deployed an additional 14,000 troops to the Middle East. It sent another 3,500 or so in early 2020, amid concerns that the assassination of Major General Qassim Suleimani could invite Iranian retaliation against US military personnel and assets. And given how quickly the Taliban stormed back to power in Afghanistan after the drawdown of US troops in 2021, the Biden administration has faced significant pressure to reassert Washington's influence in the Middle East even as it prioritizes the Asia-Pacific. Given that the United States is looking to scale back, while China and Russia are looking to make inroads, some observers contend that the region "is at the epicenter of great-power competition."[41]

Other assessments expand the number of theaters under consideration. According to Nadia Schadlow, the principal author of the 2017 national security strategy, great-power competition is actively occurring in "Europe, the Indo-Pacific, the Middle East, and the Western Hemisphere."[42] One analysis ventures that, while the United States is "actively shifting its resources—military and otherwise—toward Europe and East Asia," where contestation is likely to be most pronounced, "as the frontiers nearest our competitors harden, interstate competition will displace to those geographies that offer space and provide broader economic opportunities." In these circumstances, it predicts that the Middle East, Central Asia, Latin America, and Africa, too, will become "pivotal spaces for great-power competition between the United States, China, and Russia."[43] And some inquiries conclude that the phenomenon has no geographic limits; one notes that "every country is a battleground."[44]

In addition to scrutinizing the geographic parameters of great-power competition, one might ask what its strategic objectives are. Here, too, one can construct a continuum of increasingly ambitious goals. Some observers argue the United States should pursue with renewed vigor the goal that has animated its foreign policy since at least the end of World War II—and, according to some historians, since Germany's invasion of Poland in the fall of 1939: forestalling the emergence of a belligerent power or coalition that dominates the Eurasian landmass.[45]

While ambitious, this prescription seems quite limited when one surveys an ascendant class of articulations, envisioning a far broader struggle with China and Russia to determine the evolution of geopolitics. A representative assessment explains that great-power competition, occurring in a range of domains and spanning a number of regions, is poised to endure indefinitely:

> Today, the United States and China, often with Russia at its side, are competing to shape security architectures, as well as norms and practices worldwide, including trade and investment regimes and the development and regulation of new technological infrastructures. These frictions will play out over decades, not only in Beijing, Washington, and Moscow, but in Africa and Europe, the Arctic, outer space, and cyberspace.[46]

Comparable distillations hold that the United States is "vying for a place on the world's economic stage, on the world's political stage, and even on the national security stage"; waging a "global struggle for military, economic, and ideological supremacy"; contesting "control of the modern levers of power"; and aiming to determine "nothing short of the world order's future contours."[47] Such formulations suggest a series of interlocking, system-level competitions. In March 2019 the assistant secretary of state for international security and nonproliferation concluded that great-power competition is "not just about *who* will dominate the twenty-first-century world, but also about what the *operating system* of that world will be, and the predominant mode of governance within it."[48] One observer concludes that the term "great-power competition" actually "obfuscates the gravity of the situation," which entails not merely contestation among the United States, China, and Russia, but "a competition between the systems of liberal democracy and authoritarianism."[49] Reviewing a wide swath of scholarship on the construct, one report observes that great-power competition would appear to involve "*wrangling over advantage on a grand, global scale*" and "*great,* that is all-encompassing, competition over the trappings of power. The dimensions of the competition are thus system-wide, and the potential implications pervasive."[50] Indeed, when surveying most interpretations of the phenomenon, the challenge is not so much to identify what mandates they prescribe as to determine which ones they exclude.

The more challenging it becomes to specify the objectives of competition, the harder it is to define progress. Nonetheless, if it is increasingly deemed essential for the United States to compete, then competition risks becoming an imperative unto itself, in perpetuity. Indeed, a circular logic is liable to take hold: the United States must compete more aggressively to achieve certain objectives that are self-evidently meritorious, even if highly unspecified; and, in turn, the existence of those objectives explains why Washington must engage in vigorous competition.

Boundless competition neither yields durable strategies nor points to steady states. Perhaps the United States can hope to secure only ephemeral advances. In a widely discussed June 2019 note, the Joint Chiefs of Staff promulgated the notion of a "competition continuum" comprising "cooperation, competition below armed conflict, and armed conflict." The document advanced the tripartite conception not only on the grounds that China and Russia can and do compete with the United States in many ways that do not involve military confrontation, but also on the grounds that competitive gains are at best fleeting. "In enduring competition," it observed, "the joint force does not *win* or *lose* but is in the process of *winning* or *losing*." It further posited that "[t]he enduring nature of competition below armed conflict poses unique challenges for consolidation of strategic objectives. Local successes rarely mean the end of the larger competition and few gains are reliably permanent."[51]

Such characterizations are growing more prevalent, both within and beyond military contexts. The army's chief of staff explains that the United States must adapt to "endless or infinite competition."[52] The head of Air Force Global Strike Command concludes that it is in "a long-term, strategic competition with two realist, autocratic nations with existential arsenals at their disposal"—a competition he compares to "an infinite game." In such a game, he observes, "there's no winning," only "the ability to continue to compete."[53] Another assessment stipulates that great-power competition "entails the distribution of relative gains with no finite terminal objectives."[54] Here is an especially vivid encapsulation of the purported challenge: "If the defining characteristic of post-primacy is that strategic advantage is in constant dispute, the persistent struggle to gain, exploit, and regain transient advantage must be the new object of American strategy . . . There is only the persistent contest to compete more effectively."[55]

Assessing whether one is competing more effectively is difficult, if not impossible, if strategic advantage is inherently and increasingly fleeting. Complicating matters, the perception of steadily shrinking

windows of opportunity in which to stitch together piecemeal competitive gains imposes greater pressure to act. That pressure, in turn,
heightens the temptation to proceed from a "do something" mentality
and, accordingly, places a higher premium on discipline.[56]

A Superpower's Anxiety

One might sympathize with expansive, if not maximalist, renderings
of contemporary geopolitics and conclude that the United States is
indeed competing with China and Russia across the world to determine
the parameters of world order. But we should not conflate description
with prescription. In and of itself, characterizing geopolitics as increasingly competitive does not yield priorities besides a nearly tautological
injunction: to compete more forcefully. And, when the description is
as capacious as to border on all-encompassing, it is more liable to sow
alarm than to provide clarity; it implies, after all, that the United States
will risk an erosion of its competitive position if it fails to match every
Chinese and Russian demonstration of influence, real or perceived.

Stanley Hoffmann warned near the end of the 1970s that "playing the
role of a superpower also means permanent insecurity."[57] The logic is
that, as the world's foremost power expands the reach of its influence, it
also increases the scope of its anxiety: there are now more points where
it could assess that a setback, actual or seeming, presages a systemic
reversal of its strategic position. The risk is that a sustained relative
decline will exacerbate this underlying unease, compelling a harried
US effort to slow that trajectory; such an effort could well accelerate it.

China and Russia will consider not only how to inflame the United
States' internal fissures but also how to convince it that they are
outflanking it with greater frequency and growing consequences. If
Washington prioritizes instinctive countermeasures over strategic discipline, Beijing and Moscow will be able to keep it off balance; it is less
costly to maneuver around a reactive superpower than it is to contest
a proactive one. In 1978, at a time of growing US concern over Soviet
inroads into Africa, Arthur Schlesinger, Jr. observed:

> A recurrent experience of the American people is to discover that
> some exotic locality of which they had not previously heard is vital to
> the national security of the United States. An unknown place that had

never before disturbed our dreams suddenly becomes a dagger pointed at the heart of something or other, a capstone to a hitherto undiscerned arch, the key to some momentous global conflict.[58]

While US anxieties have not proven debilitating to date, Beijing will seek to impress upon Washington—and upon the United States' allies and partners—that today's declinism is grounded in irreversible trends. Beijing's conduct in recent years, especially since the onset of the pandemic, suggests that it will try to gain traction for three major propositions. First, China can reduce its dependence on globalization while nonetheless playing a steadily greater role in shaping how that phenomenon evolves. Second, China need not pay undue heed to external criticisms of its internal politics or regional behavior so long as its economic centrality and technological capacity continue to grow apace. Third, China is an inexorably resurgent power, confidently moving to resume its rightful place in world affairs, while the United States is a terminally declining one, anxiously seeking to uphold a fraying order of global politics and an unsound model of domestic governance. In the run-up to 2049, the centenary of the founding of the People's Republic of China (PRC), the United States should expect China to announce a wide array of military, economic, and technological objectives it aims to achieve by that date. Beijing will seek to undermine Washington's self-confidence with each successive declaration.

While Russia cannot credibly offer a comparable narrative about the likelihood of its continued renaissance, it can find other ways of distracting the United States. For starters, it will continue touting its deepening partnership with China, which is a central pillar of its efforts to depict itself—and be perceived—as a great power. In addition, if and as Washington tries to sustain its rebalance toward the Asia-Pacific, Moscow will likely spotlight its own presence in other regions, even if tactical and improvised, to make the United States second-guess the prudence of an eastward reorientation. As it stands, many US observers are already concerned that Russia is emerging as a kingmaker in the Middle East, exerting worrisome influence across Latin America and sub-Saharan Africa, positioning itself to reap the military and economic dividends that will result from a warming Arctic, and otherwise playing an unfavorable hand with great dexterity. Overstatements of Russia's strategic acumen advance its great-power ambitions.

Insofar as the framework of great-power competition compels the United States to compete ubiquitously—by implying that it will compromise its credibility if it rebalances away from theaters of diminishing strategic importance (such as the Middle East) and moves toward ones of increasing strategic importance (such as the Asia-Pacific), or accords greater focus to certain functional domains than others—it undercuts Washington's ability to prioritize and projects a posture of anxiety. A more self-assured disposition would appreciate the limits to US influence. Stanley Hoffmann offers sage counsel again: "A great power cannot consider itself threatened by every tremor anywhere. It must establish a hierarchy of concerns and have a sense of proportion and perspective."[59]

Quiet Confidence

A timeless axiom holds that great power confers great responsibility—to wield that power justly. One might stipulate a corollary: great power also yields great temptation—to wield that power indiscriminately. The United States must resist this temptation if it is to husband its resources and maintain its composure. First, not all of the measures that China and Russia take will undermine US national interests. In some cases, in fact, as when Beijing invests more in politically unstable countries or Moscow involves itself further in civil wars, they may ultimately undercut themselves. Frank Hoffman accordingly explains that "the United States needs clear criteria for when to respond to Chinese or Russian influence efforts in Africa, the Middle East, and the Arctic. Not every Chinese infrastructure project is a threat to the free world, and not many of Putin's pronouncements constitute an attack on the West that warrants response."[60]

Second, neither country is immune to nearsightedness and hubris. China's deepening authoritarianism and heavy-handed diplomacy have undermined its reputation in the Asia-Pacific and across Western Europe, stimulated greater security cooperation among the members of "the Quad"—the United States, Australia, India, and Japan—and blunted the momentum of telecommunications giant Huawei among advanced industrial democracies. The pandemic is also testing the viability of China's Belt and Road Initiative, as many participating countries have applied to the Chinese government for debt relief.

Meanwhile Russia's incursion into Ukraine, as well as its footholds in Syria and Libya, are increasingly straining its economy, and its room for strategic maneuver is constrained by deteriorating relations with the West and growing economic dependence upon China.

Third, there will invariably be instances—on certain issues, in certain countries, and at certain gatherings—in which China or Russia exercises greater influence than the United States, so the latter will have to decide on a case-by-case basis whether attempting to redress that imbalance is a worthwhile use of its strategic bandwidth. In appraising the setbacks that will occur to its national interests, the United States must distinguish as clearly as possible between those it might have averted or mitigated had it acted differently and those that would likely have occurred regardless of what course it had pursued. Counterfactual analysis should not seek to absolve Washington of responsibility, but it should not overstate Washington's capacity to dictate the course of events either.

The Middle East offers an instructive example. In January 2020, as tensions between the United States and Iran were escalating and relations between Washington and Baghdad were deteriorating in tandem, some observers ventured that the United States would "hand" the region to China and Russia if it were to try to lessen its footprint. Now that the United States has concluded its combat missions in Afghanistan and Iraq, that concern is even more pronounced. It is true, of course, that both Beijing and Moscow are making military and economic inroads into the Middle East. To argue, though, that this outcome is solely the consequence of US retrenchment is to suggest that Washington can unilaterally control the decision-making processes of governments in the region. In truth, most, if not all of them see strategic value in maintaining different kinds of ties with the United States, China, and Russia all at once.[61] In addition, Beijing and Moscow will confront formidable challenges as they look to deepen their influence in the Middle East.

China's dependence on oil imports from the region is increasing and, no matter how strenuously it avows its commitment to noninterference in other countries' domestic affairs, it will invariably find it more difficult to navigate the Middle East's fractious geopolitics. It is simultaneously attempting to strengthen its ties with Iran and with other key oil suppliers in the region whose relations with Tehran are strained, if not downright antagonistic. At the same time, terrorist attacks and sectarian conflicts will complicate its ability to extend the BRI across the region.[62]

For its part, Russia is concerned that convulsions in the Middle East could weaken important partnerships. While some observers have framed the reassertion of its influence in Syria as a diplomatic master-stroke, the strategic gains it stands to make over the medium to long term are unclear. Simply achieving a negotiated settlement between Assad and rebel outfits will be a monumental task, let alone rebuilding a country that has suffered more than a decade of civil war. In addition, given how tenuous Russia's military and diplomatic gains have been, it is doubtful that it would be able to achieve a comparable presence in other war-ravaged countries in the region. Mona Yacoubian concludes that Russia will "not seek to replicate its preeminent role in Syria else-where in the Middle East, as such ambitions are well beyond Moscow's capacity. Instead, Russia will engage opportunistically, exploiting per-ceptions of a US withdrawal from the region, while promoting its vision of a 'post-West' world."[63]

One other point deserves mention: having witnessed the toll that America's involvement in the Middle East has taken on its strategic position, it is doubtful that either China or Russia would want to assume a US-style role in the region, even if either country were ultimately to attain the requisite capacity. It is essential, then, not to conflate presence with competitiveness. While the United States has been the predomi-nant external force in the Middle East for most of the postwar era, the strategic dividends that have accrued to it are increasingly dubious. One study estimates that its appropriated and obligated counterterrorism expenditures from 2001 to 2020 (fiscal years) totaled $6.4 trillion.[64] What began as a narrow mission—to target al-Qa'ida and topple the Taliban regime that harbored it—has morphed into a sprawling under-taking that extends well beyond the Middle East and could distort US foreign policy priorities indefinitely; indeed, the accumulated inertia of the United States' involvement in the region has played a central role in thwarting repeated efforts to rebalance to the Asia-Pacific.[65]

The more clarity the United States can bring to its own strategic direction, the more likely it will be to settle upon—and feel at ease with—assessments of China and Russia as serious but constrained com-petitors. The less clarity it is able to attain, the more susceptible it will be to hypervigilance, even alarmism—ascribing strategic vision to tactical improvisation, discerning grand designs in scattershot declarations, and perceiving grave dangers in unremarkable measures—as it appraises their conduct.

The United States' competitive challenge, then, is arguably a psychological one in the first place: will the United States have the self-confidence to prioritize the renewal of its own competitive advantages, training a close eye upon China's and Russia's actions without growing preoccupied with them, or will it determine that it must contest them ubiquitously in order to advance its national interests? If the latter, it risks "falling prey to one of the worst tendencies of many administrations: chasing every emerging threat or opportunity deemed by anyone to be 'vital.'"[66] One of America's key tasks will be to expand the universe of measures it can take to boost its strategic competitiveness independently of what Beijing and Moscow do. The more it can populate that action set, the better positioned it will be to approach them both from a place of confident composure.

The risks of overreaction and overextension are not hypothetical. During the Cold War, the United States fought the Soviet Union across the world—most famously in Vietnam, but also in countries as disparate as Angola and Nicaragua. Some observers conclude that Washington proved to be incapable of distinguishing between the core and the periphery of the postwar order because it feared that its vital national interests were implicated wherever Moscow asserted itself. Odd Arne Westad explains that America's rivalry with the Soviet Union "provided an extreme answer to a question that had been at the center of US foreign policy since the late eighteenth century: in what situations should ideological sympathies be followed by intervention? The extension of the Cold War into the third world was defined by the answer: *everywhere* where communism could be construed as a threat."[67] Christopher Hemmer observes that officials increasingly converged upon a global understanding of vital US national interests, doing so less as a result of objective assessments of strategic shifts than of abstract considerations of perceived credibility:

> If all the United States had to worry about were the material aspects of credibility, there would be no need to expand US security commitments beyond the five areas identified by Kennan as capable of producing military power on an industrial scale ... In NSC-68 [a seminal 1950

blueprint for containment] it is the psychological aspect of credibility that takes center stage and makes a defeat anywhere a defeat
everywhere.[68]

The aforementioned risks—overreaction and overextension—
endure. Osama bin Laden gloated in late 2004 that al-Qa'ida could easily
"provoke and bait" the Bush administration.[69] The 9/11 Commission
estimated that it cost the organization at most $500,000 to execute the
terrorist attacks of September 11, 2001.[70] Those attacks precipitated
a US intervention in Afghanistan that lasted for nearly two decades
and a US intervention in Iraq that lasted for more than eighteen years
and facilitated the emergence of the Islamic State. But the full scope
of America's response extends well beyond those two interventions;
Daniel Byman observed in September 2019 that the United States was
"enmeshed in a series of low-level but grinding, and seemingly endless,
civil wars in the greater Muslim world," fighting terrorists in some
eighty countries.[71]

The rejoinder would seem obvious: the United States prevailed in the
Cold War and, despite having embarked upon a seemingly open-ended
counterterrorism campaign, it remains the world's lone superpower.
But the enormity of power can sometimes conceal the imprudence of
strategy. The United States confronted only one competitor during the
Cold War: the Soviet Union, against which it was relatively on the rise.
And in the early years of the decade 2000–10, during the initial stages
of fighting insurgencies in Afghanistan and Iraq, it was sufficiently
strong for prominent US observers to debate what it should do with the
enormous power it had accumulated over the previous decade. Today,
though, it is in relative decline as it confronts two formidable competitors. Jennifer Lind and Daryl Press note that China and Russia simply
need to focus on "apply[ing] their military and political resources close
to home, whereas Washington must spread its capabilities across the
world if it is to maintain its current status."[72] Considering that an economically inferior rival was largely able to capture US foreign policy
for nearly half a century and that a non-state actor was able to distort
America's strategic outlook with just one low-cost attack, it stands to
reason that China and Russia, with substantial and growing material
assets at their collective disposal, could goad the United States for far
longer, and at a much higher price.

This warning is not intended to justify, let alone encourage, a passive US response to the two countries' actions. It is meant to reinforce a theme of this book: Washington should neither depend upon Beijing and Moscow to define its strategic purpose nor hope that accumulated reactions to their maneuvers will reveal one in due course. It should instead situate its responses to them within a forward-looking frame-work—one that concurrently aims to reposition the United States as a linchpin of collective action and restore the appeal of its domestic example, relying upon a renewed investment in the country's unique competitive advantages.

But Washington will find it difficult to do so if it experiences reflexive pressure to respond to Beijing and Moscow. Resisting such pressure, both self-imposed and externally stoked, will require it to conduct dispassionate net assessments of each country's competitive posture, endeavoring to find a middle ground between complacence and consternation. The next two chapters take up that task.

4

Managing a Resurgent China

A growing number of observers contend that China's resurgence furnishes the ballast US foreign policy has lacked for the past three decades. Josh Hawley, a Republican senator for Missouri and a prominent voice in Congress calling for a more forceful posture toward China, concludes that the country's "bid for domination is the greatest security threat to this country in this century. And our foreign policy around the globe must be oriented to this challenge and focused principally on this threat."[1] Others think that the emergence of an increasingly formidable competitor could help Americans overcome their partisan rancor. "I've always thought Americans would come together," explains David Brooks, "when we realized that we faced a dangerous foreign foe. And lo and behold, now we have one: China."[2] Some of America's well-wishers abroad render comparable judgments. Janan Ganesh ventures that, "[f]or the first time since at least the 1980s, Americans face the kind of economic, ideological, and military challenge that can make domestic antagonism seem beside the point, if not unconscionable."[3]

An Unprecedented Psychological Test

These types of sentiments are eminently understandable in view of China's proportions and the rapidity with which it has achieved them. In the four decades after Washington and Beijing normalized ties, the latter's share of gross world product expanded roughly eightfold, from a little under 2 percent to over 16 percent. In 2020 its gross domestic product reached $14.7 trillion, 70 percent of the United States'.[4] China overtook Germany as the largest exporting country in 2009 and displaced the United States as the largest trading country in 2013. In 2018, 128 out of 190 countries traded more with China than with the United States; 90, remarkably, conducted more than twice as much trade with Beijing as with Washington.[5] Between the onset of the global financial crisis and the end of the 2010s, China is estimated to have accounted for 37 percent of global growth.[6] China loaned some $1.5 trillion to more than 150 countries between 1949 and 2017, exceeding the combined contributions of the World Bank, the IMF, and all Organisation for Economic Cooperation and Development (OECD) creditor countries.[7] While it is difficult to obtain accurate data about the amount of credit Chinese financial institutions have actually loaned—and not simply announced—through the Belt and Road Initiative, few observers dispute that this project is one of the largest development initiatives in the world.

China's military modernization over the past quarter century has also been impressive. In March 1996, after a series of Chinese missile tests and military exercises in the vicinity of the Taiwan Strait, the Clinton administration dispatched two aircraft carrier battle groups to the 110-mile body of water that separates Taiwan from the mainland, prompting Beijing to draw down quickly. Robert Ross observes that America's capacity to force a Chinese retreat without much fear of pushback embarrassed the Chinese Communist Party.[8] Today, by contrast, China has the second-largest defense budget, and there are growing doubts in the US defense community that Washington would be able to defeat Beijing if China were to invade Taiwan.[9] In addition, China has made sufficient progress in constructing and fortifying artificial features in the South China Sea that, according to Greg Poling, "it would be prohibitively costly for the United States to neutralize those outposts during the early stages of a conflict."[10] The Pentagon concluded in a 2020 report that, while China's military had "major gaps and shortcomings," it had surpassed the US military in areas such as shipbuilding, land-based conventional ballistic and cruise missiles, and integrated air defense systems.[11]

China is also increasingly active in the diplomatic realm. In 2010 it acquired the third-largest voting share at both the World Bank and the IMF.[12] A 2019 tally found that it had 276 diplomatic posts, slightly more than the United States.[13] At the beginning of 2021, Chinese nationals were at the helm of four specialized UN agencies: the Food and Agriculture Organization, the Industrial Development Organization, the International Civil Aviation Organization, and the International Telecommunication Union (ITU). China is the second-largest contributor both to the UN's peacekeeping budget and to the UN's overall budget. As it deepens its sway in existing institutions, it also boosts its influence through channels of its own creation, such as the Asian Infrastructure Investment Bank (AIIB).

Appraising China's strides in their totality, one could argue that its greatest challenge to the United States is psychological. Beijing's resurgence worries Washington not only because of the speed with which it unfolds and the number of domains in which it manifests itself but also because of the convictions it challenges: with its single-party authoritarian rule and forceful rejection of the values Washington holds to be universal, China is about as purely distilled an antithesis as one could construct to what many western observers had supposed—and may yet believe—to be the proper course of modernity. The anonymous author of a widely discussed 2021 report titled *The Longer Telegram: Toward a New American China Strategy* warned that China's supplanting the United States as the world's preeminent power would "degrade the American soul, including the innate understanding of who Americans are as a people and what the nation stands for in the world."[14]

The hope that Beijing would take incremental steps in the direction of political liberalization as it became more prosperous has not materialized. Having defied repeated predictions of collapse, communist China is now one of the longest-surviving one-party regimes in history (the Communist Party of the Soviet Union ruled for seventy-four years, and the CCP has ruled for seventy-two). Far from posing an existential challenge to the ruling party, advances in technology have enabled it to consolidate its authority and to establish what may be the most sophisticated surveillance apparatus in the world. In addition, while China has made significant technological progress by stealing intellectual property, it is increasingly becoming an engine of innovation in its own right, undercutting the presumption that authoritarian systems are capable only of replicating the achievements of others.

In dealing with China, the United States confronts a challenge for which there is no self-evident precedent. On the one hand, Beijing is Washington's most formidable competitor, increasingly capable of contesting US national interests and of molding aspects of the postwar order. On the other hand, while talk of decoupling is gaining significant momentum, the level and the complexity of the interdependence between the United States and China mean that attempts to force a rupture would likely do severe damage to the US economy—not only by degrading highly developed linkages but also by cutting off the United States from the engine of global growth. However unlikely substantive bilateral cooperation may be for now, the United States will be unable to advance its own vital national interests without collaborating with China on pressing transnational challenges. Its mission, then, is not to achieve a decisive victory over an existential adversary, but to develop a durable modus vivendi with a complex competitor. Concerningly, though, with their emphasis on "winning" a systemic contest against a country that is assumed to have both hegemonic aspirations and enabling capabilities, discussions of great-power competition discount the necessity of coevolution and disincentivize thinking about policies that could facilitate that process.

Growing US Unease

To understand why China now occupies so central a role in today's discussions of great-power competition, it is helpful to revisit how Washington had hoped Beijing would evolve. The United States had long speculated that China might liberalize at home and become more of a "responsible stakeholder" in world affairs over time, as it integrated itself more into the world economy. For the better part of the past four decades, the two countries proved willing—or at least able—to manage their ideological differences and strategic suspicions by deepening their economic interdependence. Although this undertaking was inherently tenuous—Washington and Beijing had no ready foundation for cultivating trust—it was able to endure for as long as it did not only because there was significant potential for an erstwhile impoverished and isolated China to grow, but also because there was an immense gap between American and Chinese power.

The global financial crisis proved to be a major inflection point in the relationship, convincing at least some Chinese observers of two judgments: first, that the United States was in terminal decline, affording China a window of opportunity to advance its core interests; and, second, that Washington would consequently seek to suppress Beijing's further resurgence. Some US observers expressed anxiety over the appearance of a dysfunctional Washington and worried that Beijing might succumb to hubris in pressing ahead, especially along its periphery. Near the end of the first term of the Obama administration, Jeffrey Bader noted that high-ranking US officials were concerned not only that China sought to overtake the United States but also that Beijing saw the bilateral relationship largely as a zero-sum one.[15]

The United States' unease over China's trajectory intensified with the ascension of a more uncompromising Chinese leader. President Xi initiated a sweeping anti-corruption campaign that centralized his authority and sidelined potential political opponents. He also proved considerably more willing than his predecessor to criticize western ideological precepts while touting China's. In an April 2013 memorandum, the CCP issued a dire warning about "the very real threat of Western anti-China forces and their attempt at carrying out Westernization, splitting, and 'color revolutions.'"[16] And, against the early hopes of some Chinese reformers, President Xi cracked down aggressively on political dissidents, ethnic and religious minorities, and nongovernmental organizations (NGOs).

China also turned more assertive economically. In early 2012 a senior official in the Obama administration mentioned that the president had begun requesting proposals for countering its theft of intellectual property.[17] Just a year later, National Security Advisor Thomas Donilon cited "cyber intrusions emanating from China on an unprecedented scale."[18] The following May, Attorney General Eric Holder unsealed an indictment against five members of the Shanghai-based cyberunit of the People's Liberation Army (PLA), charging them with hacking major companies such as Westinghouse Electric and the US Steel Corporation. Holder's indictment marked the first time the United States had charged foreign government officials with economic espionage.

While China relied upon intellectual property theft to fuel its economic expansion, it also strove to become a more self-reliant center of global growth. President Xi unveiled the Silk Road Economic Belt in a September 2013 visit to Kazakhstan and the Maritime Silk Road in a visit to Indonesia the following month, later merging the two under the banner of the BRI. And in May 2015, pursuing its goal of becoming a global leader in high-end manufacturing, Beijing announced "Made in China 2025," an ambitious initiative aimed at achieving greater self-sufficiency in ten industries that it believes will be central to the evolution of the global economy.

In military and intelligence matters, too, Beijing took steps that sowed alarm in Washington. In September 2015, standing next to President Obama in the White House Rose Garden, President Xi promised that China would not militarize the South China Sea. In May 2016, however, the Pentagon called that pledge into question, noting that China had reclaimed some 3,200 acres in the Spratly Islands and had established facilities that would permit it to sustain a more nimble and consistent military posture there.[19] Separately, the *New York Times* reported in May 2017 that from 2010 to 2012 China had killed or imprisoned between eighteen and twenty of the Central Intelligence Agency (CIA)'s in-country informants, "effectively unraveling a network that had taken years to build."[20]

One could adduce many other pieces of evidence to document China's growing prominence—in world affairs as much as in America's consciousness. By the end of the Obama administration, there was a growing conviction among US observers that the United States needed to recalibrate its approach. Indeed, many began wondering out loud whether Washington had misapprehended Beijing's post-Cold War strategic intentions.

Distrust in the Time of Pandemic

Still, bilateral ties had far from unraveled. The United States and China maintained deep trade and technological interdependence, and they had managed to cooperate in several domains. The Trump administration, however, fundamentally reset US policy, pronouncing that the "engage but hedge" framework that had guided that policy across eight administrations had failed: "For decades," the 2017 national security strategy argued, "US policy was rooted in the belief that support for China's rise and for its integration into the postwar international order would liberalize China. Contrary to our hopes, China expanded its power at the expense of the sovereignty of others." The document contended that "China seeks to displace the United States in the Indo-Pacific region, expand the reaches of its state-driven economic model, and reorder the region in its favor."[21]

Arguing that China had hollowed out America's manufacturing base, especially since acceding to the WTO, and that its technological progress threatened US national security, the Trump administration pursued parallel, though largely unilateral, efforts to challenge Beijing's development: it announced tariffs on Chinese exports that reached a peak average level of 21 percent in late 2019, and it introduced steadily tighter restrictions on Huawei.[22] Departing from the judgment of its predecessors that dated back to the Nixon administration, Trump's framed interdependence not as a stabilizing force in a relationship that had little organic basis for constructive evolution, but as a dangerous mechanism through which Beijing had exploited Washington's misplaced altruism in order to accrue ever greater competitive dividends.

China did little to assuage US concerns. In an October 2017 speech before the 19th National Congress of the CCP, President Xi ventured that his country would move "closer to center stage" in world affairs, declaring that "[n]o one should expect China to swallow anything that undermines its interests."[23] The Chinese National People's Congress voted to abolish presidential term limits the following March, further consolidating the president's domestic authority and cementing external assessments that he had become China's most powerful leader since Mao.

Washington and Beijing briefly interrupted the downward spiral in their relations with the signing of a "phase one" trade deal in January 2020, a victory for members of the Trump administration who had been pressing China to increase its purchases of US goods, become more receptive to US investment, and resume market-oriented reforms. Many observers noted, in addition, that while the administration as a whole had been pushing for greater decoupling between the US and Chinese economies, President Trump himself had often exhibited contradictory impulses—alternatively praising and condemning President Xi, for example, and variously expressing support for and exhibiting caution over accelerated disentanglement.

The arrival of the coronavirus pandemic largely pulled the rug out from under the US–China relationship, as expressions of systemic antagonism came to overshadow the imperatives of competitive coexistence.

The Trump administration argued that China had effectively inflicted COVID-19 upon the world, and members of Congress were properly alarmed to discover how heavily Washington had been relying upon Beijing for basic medicines. China rejoined that the United States was attempting to deflect attention from its own mismanagement of the crisis. The better part of 2020 witnessed a dizzying cycle of mutual retaliations, including expulsions of journalists, closings of consulates, and blacklistings of companies. Beijing lashed out at foreign critics of its pandemic response and moved to consolidate its regional interests in a heavy-handed manner, while prominent US officials began referring to China in more ideological–existential terms. Perhaps most notably, Secretary of State Michael Pompeo spoke of President Xi's "decades-long desire for global hegemony of Chinese communism," warning that, if "the freedom-loving nations of the world" do not "induce China to change," China's leader could "tyrannize inside and outside of China forever."[24]

But the Trump administration was not alone in harboring these sentiments, even if it conveyed them more forcefully. According to a September 2020 tally by Scott Kennedy, the 116th Congress had intro-duced "at least 366 bills with China-related content" since its beginning, 104 having been introduced between May and August 2020 alone.[25] In June 2021, with an eye toward China, the Senate approved a roughly 2,400-page, $250-billion bill, the US Innovation and Competition Act, which would commit some $52 billion to boosting semiconductor pro-duction and approximately $200 billion to stimulating scientific and technological innovation across a range of fields. One assessment called it "the most significant government intervention in industrial policy in decades" and stated that it "reflected a bipartisan sense of urgency."[26] While it remains to be seen how the House will modify the legislation, a more assertive approach to Beijing is likely to be a rare point of continuity in US foreign policy. It is increasingly apparent, too, that the US corporate community, for a long time the staunchest supporter of engagement with Beijing, cannot be relied upon to serve in that role with the same vigor.[27] Public sentiment has followed suit; in March 2021 the Pew Research Center reported that 89 percent of Americans view China as a competitor or an enemy, up from 83 percent in summer 2020, and that 67 percent feel at least somewhat "cold" toward the country, up from 46 percent in July 2018.[28]

A New US "Consensus" on China Policy?

In brief, attitudes toward China have soured among government officials, business leaders, and the general public. What is more, virtually
all observers believe that Washington should adjust its policy in view of
Beijing's trajectory, which is marked by intensifying repression at home
and heightened coercion abroad, and pursue a more selective form
of interdependence. It is important, though, not to confuse hardening sentiment with considered prescription: intensifying distress over
China's resurgence has spotlighted the absence of a clear strategy for
managing that very phenomenon and, more fundamentally, a sober
articulation of what such a strategy should set out to accomplish.

Indeed, the United States has not given itself sufficient time to appreciate what a long-term systemic competition with China would require
of its economy and its society. No less a policymaker-cum-scholar than
Kurt Campbell, the deeply respected Indo-Pacific coordinator at the
National Security Council, has expressed this concern. Beyond being
a central architect of the Obama administration's "rebalance" to the
Asia-Pacific, he has played an important role in shifting the debate
over US policy toward China. In early 2018 he co-authored with Ely
Ratner, now assistant secretary of defense for Indo-Pacific security
affairs, an influential article that called on Washington to reckon with
the assumptions that had underpinned its longstanding approach to
Beijing. But Campbell became concerned that the needed recalibration
was proceeding too quickly; at the 2020 Aspen Security Forum he
warned that the United States is "really plummeting down a staircase
towards an extraordinarily competitive, confrontational set of relations,
which will have consequences that are very difficult to predict, with
extraordinarily little discussion about it."[29] Janan Ganesh puts the point
more bluntly, observing that Washington is "sliding into open-ended
conflict against China with eerily little debate. Politicians who can be
counted on to dispute the color of the sky or the sum of two plus two
are of a piece on the necessity of a superpower duel."[30]

The United States needs to engage in a discussion whose nuance is
commensurate with China's scale. Ganesh Sitaraman concludes that, in
spite of the oft-cited dichotomy of "hawks" and "doves," there are "at
least ten categories in the debate: four on the dovish side, and six on the
hawkish side."[31] The number of taxonomies one could construct affirms

the complexity of the challenge: how should Washington formulate a cohesive strategy toward a country that is both a strategic competitor and a necessary partner? The United States and China are unlikely to achieve a grand bargain or to identify a clear demarcation between hostility and détente. They will have to sustain instead an increasingly challenging, ever-evolving cohabitation.

As noted earlier, a growing number of observers urge the United States to accord singular priority to managing China's resurgence, contending that doing so could have the ancillary benefit of easing America's political divisions. In view of America's relative decline, the appeal of that hypothesis is intuitive. Indeed, Samuel Huntington observed that declinism, even if analytically overwrought, can be useful if it compels Washington to take steps that contribute to its domestic renewal, and therefore to its external competitiveness. But Huntington's optimism was contingent: channeled prudently, anxiety can be a competitive stimulant; harnessed unwisely, it can be a competitive retardant.[32]

Thus, for example, if the United States takes steps that dissuade individuals of Chinese descent from coming and contributing their talents, it risks undercutting its soft power and losing a crucial source of its competitive edge in the development of frontier technologies. If it casts competition with China largely as a zero-sum ideological contest, it risks feeling obliged to match or counter virtually every Chinese action. Such a framing would be a recipe for strategic disorientation and, in time, exhaustion. If it sets out to contain China, it risks unnerving allies and partners that have little desire to participate in a new cold war or otherwise be instrumentalized—trapped in a competitive prism they would find suffocating and patronizing.

The Biden administration is approaching relations with China in a much more disciplined fashion than its predecessor, distinguishing between adversarial, competitive, and cooperative aspects of bilateral ties and noting that the United States "will welcome the Chinese government's cooperation on issues such as climate change, global health security, arms control, and nonproliferation where our fates are intertwined."[33] Ahead of Deputy Secretary of State Wendy Sherman's July 2021 visit to China, a senior administration official stressed that she would affirm the importance of preventing "stiff and sustained competition" from morphing into confrontation and noted that Washington and Beijing would need to fashion mechanisms and understandings to manage that competition responsibly.[34]

But, while US–China relations are likely to be more predictable in the coming years than they were during the Trump administration, strategic tensions are poised to grow more pronounced. The Biden administration observes that China "is the only competitor potentially capable of combining its economic, diplomatic, military, and techno-logical power to mount a sustained challenge to a stable and open international system."[35] And President Xi has instructed CCP cadres to read *On Protracted War*, a collection of Mao's speeches that considers how an emerging power can brace itself for a long-term conflict with a superior one.[36]

The Debate over China's Intentions

In formulating policy toward China, the United States has to assess as accurately as possible, on an ongoing basis and with incomplete information, both its long-term strategic objectives and the material capabilities Beijing would be able to marshal in their service. Foreign Minister Wang Yi observed in September 2018 that "China will not challenge the United States. Still less will China take the place of the United States."[37] Shortly before President Joe Biden took office, Fu Ying, the former Chinese vice foreign minister, stressed that "China does not want to replace US dominance in the world."[38] In his afore-mentioned October 2017 speech, President Xi set forth a number of objectives he believes China should achieve by 2035 and 2049. The first of these dates marks the midpoint between the respective centenaries of the CCP, founded in 1921, and the People's Republic of China, proclaimed in 1949. He envisions that China will have become a global innovation center and will have boosted its soft power significantly by 2035, and that it will have "become a global leader in terms of compos-ite national strength and international influence" by 2049.[39]

Against the backdrop of deteriorating US–China relations and grow-ing Chinese power, the more strenuously Chinese officials assert that Beijing harbors no hegemonic intentions, the more likely US observers may be to conclude that it has precisely those intentions. And, while President Xi stipulates that he envisions China as *a*, not as *the* "global leader," his rhetoric bespeaks significant ambitions for the country's role in world affairs. Indeed, in a speech in commemoration of the CCP's centenary, he characterized China as "a thriving nation that is advancing with unstoppable momentum toward rejuvenation."[40] It is becoming increasingly—and understandably—common for US observers to take China's desire for global preeminence as a given and to discuss the various courses it might chart to achieve that objective. Shortly before the Trump administration left office, the State Department's Policy Planning Staff released a paper in which it concluded that China is intent on "displacing the United States as the world's foremost power and restructuring world order to conform to the CCP's distinctive way of empire."[41]

Still, as a brief but representative inventory of assessments suggests, esteemed observers can interpret China's objectives in different ways. A team of analysts at the RAND Corporation recently concluded that "the CCP-PLA-PRC elite's primary goals remain focused in the domestic arena, on China's periphery, and in the Asia-Pacific."[42] Oriana Skylar Mastro ventures that, while China does not seek to supplant the United States globally, it does aim to "force the United States out [of the Asia-Pacific] and become the region's unchallenged political, economic, and military hegemon."[43] Some observers argue that while China has not yet adopted such a regional objective, sustained US pressure might compel it to do so.[44]

Others believe that China takes a more expansive view of its place in the world. Aaron Friedberg assesses that it seeks to become "the world's leading economic and technological nation and to displace [the United States] as the preponderant power in East Asia."[45] Nadège Rolland contends that the CCP espouses "a vision in which China's leadership is exercised over large portions of the 'global South,' a space that would be free from Western influence and largely purged of the core liberal democratic beliefs supported by the West."[46] Daniel Tobin concludes that it seeks "a single, integrated global order whose interconnectedness is underpinned by China's standards and 'wisdom.'"[47]

One should not accept or dismiss any of these judgments outright since, explains Joel Wuthnow, one would have to be privy to China's internal deliberations to render confident assessments about its intentions. He does not believe that Beijing is "so inscrutable that tentative conclusions about its long-term goals cannot be drawn from information in the public domain." But he cautions that reviewing publicly available materials can yield different judgments; while some careful analysts may conclude that China seeks global dominance, others may reach more tentative conclusions.[48] While observers must consider Chinese leaders' public declarations, they should not assume a one-to-one correspondence between rhetoric and intentions; Jessica Chen Weiss notes that actions often depart from words and that rhetoric is liable to adjust as internal and external realities evolve.[49]

Internal Obstacles to "National Rejuvenation"

For argument's sake, let us stipulate that China has long sought and is increasingly determined to become the world's only superpower and that it aims to occupy that role not within postwar strictures, but in a world order of its own design. By holding the variable of intentions constant at maximum value, we can focus more clearly on the intermediate objectives China would need to achieve on the path to global preeminence; this analysis can give us a fuller sense of the challenges it would confront along the way. Beyond sustaining a baseline of domestic stability, China would have to secure its neighbors' acquiescence to a Sinocentric hierarchy within the Asia-Pacific. It would ultimately have to incorporate Eurasia into an order rooted mainly in China's preferred institutions, rules, and norms. And along the way it would face a formidable litany of hurdles, beginning at home.

Start with demographics. In 2020 China recorded its lowest number of official births since 1961, and its total fertility rate now stands at just 1.3, well below the replacement rate of 2.1.[50] The UN predicts that, while the elderly's share of the country's population will grow from roughly 12 percent in 2020 to 26 percent in 2050, the working-age population, which comprises people between the ages of 15 and 64, will decline by approximately 17 percent (174 million) during that same period. The old-age dependency ratio, which is the ratio between the elderly and people of working age, will increase from 17 percent to nearly 44 percent.[51]

China faces significant economic challenges as well. The country's growth rate had been slowing well before the pandemic; in 2019 it reached its lowest level in nearly thirty years.[52] While China's recovery from COVID-19 has been impressive, the overall cooling trend is likely to resume in 2022 and to go beyond. Indebtedness is another problem;

China's overall debt, roughly equivalent to 141 percent of GDP in 2008, reached about 270 percent in 2020.[53]

The pandemic has introduced additional economic difficulties. It could slow the momentum of China's signature geoeconomic undertaking, the BRI, as many participating countries have applied for debt relief. COVID-19-related logistics disruptions are also likely to intensify the existing efforts of many countries to reconfigure their production processes so as to reduce their dependence on China, especially for vital commodities, for example personal protective equipment (PPE) and components that are used in highly sensitive military technologies. Australia, India, and Japan, for example, have launched an initiative designed to strengthen the resilience of the Asia-Pacific's supply chains. While President Xi has announced a "dual circulation" strategy that aims to blunt the impact of such efforts—"internal circulation" (production designed to boost domestic consumption) taking priority over "international circulation" (production designed to boost exports)—China is presently doubling down on an increasingly inefficient growth model that prioritizes infrastructure-centered investment.

China's innovation journey faces challenges as well. Many observers question whether it will be able to achieve its 2025 goal of 70 percent self-sufficiency in chips—the building blocks of semiconductors that power consumer electronics. In 2019, integrated circuit production in China accounted only for about 16 percent of the country's chip market and, when production by foreign companies is excluded, that figure falls to roughly 6 percent.[54] China imported almost $380 billion of chips in 2020, up from roughly $330 billion the previous year.[55] But it is harder to purchase the expertise required to build advanced chips indigenously.

What is more, while China's subsidization of certain technology sectors has yielded impressive results, the expanding role of the state in the economy could quash potential innovations. It is telling that President Xi intervened personally to stop what would have been the largest initial public offering in history: namely that of Ant, China's dominant financial technology group. The CCP evidently saw Jack Ma—Ant's principal shareholder and China's most famous entrepreneur—as being insufficiently deferential to the state; in an October 2020 speech, Ma had charged Chinese regulators with being overly risk-averse and accused Chinese banks of having a "pawnshop mentality" that undercuts entrepreneurs.[56]

Ecological challenges loom large as well. Yanzhong Huang explains that environmental degradation, especially air pollution, constrains China's growth potential and drives away talent that would be essential to building Beijing into a global financial hub.[57] Amid concerns that the pandemic would slow the country's growth, the government approved the building of more coal power plant capacity in the first half of 2020 than it approved in 2018 and 2019 combined, a statistic that suggests that its road to greener growth will be fraught.[58] And the flooding that struck Zhengzhou in July 2021 previews the kinds of difficulties China will confront as it tries to enhance the resilience of its vast system of urban infrastructure.[59]

While the CCP has proven impressively adaptive in managing domestic crises and sustaining public support, its increasingly aggressive crackdown on activists and NGOs betrays considerable insecurity. According to government figures, China's annual expenditures on public security roughly doubled between late 2012 and 2019, reaching $211 billion—more than its official defense spending.[60] Also, ostensibly under the auspices of an anti-corruption campaign, President Xi has made a growing number of influential enemies, prioritizing the consolidation of his power over the preservation of the CCP's flexibility. Richard McGregor warns that, because he is "so firmly in charge of the party, with no clear rivals and no known succession plan, he is also setting the stage for a full-blown crisis of leadership in the future."[61]

Beyond its borders, China is struggling to induce Taiwan's submission. It had once hoped that it could de facto absorb Taipei through increasing economic integration, thereby achieving reunification without having to resort to military force. That gambit appears to be backfiring. For starters, nationalism in Taiwan is growing, not declining. Between 1994 and 2018, while the percentage of the public identifying as only Taiwanese increased from 20 percent to 54.5 percent, the percentage identifying as only Chinese decreased from 26 percent to less than 4 percent. Part of the explanation lies in evolving expectations: "A generation of young Taiwanese, who like to say they were 'born independent,' have never thought their homeland could be subsumed into the People's Republic of China the way Hong Kong was in 1997."[62]

Under Tsai Ing-wen, moreover, Taiwan is asserting itself proactively on the world stage. In her May 20, 2016 inaugural address, she vowed to pursue the New Southbound Policy, which would reduce Taipei's economic dependence on Beijing and strengthen its own relations across the Asia-Pacific. Shortly after being reelected in January 2020, President Tsai made clear that Taiwan would not be intimidated: "We don't have a need to declare ourselves an independent state," she told an interviewer. "We are an independent country already and we call ourselves the Republic of China, Taiwan."[63] Taipei has seen its international stature rise, buoyed in part by its impressive response to the pandemic. In March 2020 the American and Japanese ambassadors to the UN drafted a démarche that called for Taiwan to be granted observer status at the World Health Organization (WHO). The document was supported by their counterparts from Australia, Canada, France, Germany, New Zealand, and the United Kingdom.

China continues to intensify its pressure on Taiwan, increasing its incursions into Taipei's air defense identification zone and intoning more sternly that its quest to achieve "national rejuvenation" is predicated upon reunification. But Taiwan is bolstering its defenses and capitalizing on growing concerns among advanced industrial democracies over China's conduct. At their April 2021 summit, President Biden and his Japanese counterpart, Prime Minister Yoshihide Suga, referenced the Taiwan Strait in a joint statement—the first time leaders from Washington and Tokyo have done so since 1969.[64]

In Hong Kong, meanwhile, the persistence of the pro-democracy movement is a growing thorn in the CCP's side. In November 2019, approximately 70 percent of eligible voters in Hong Kong cast their ballots in district council elections and delivered a stinging rebuke to China: pro-democracy candidates won 389 of 452 seats, up from 124 four years earlier, while pro-mainland candidates won only 58, down from 300.[65] Hong Kong police detained 15 prominent pro-democracy figures in April 2020, including the media tycoon Jimmy Lai; the lawyer Martin Lee, widely considered the father of Hong Kong's democracy; and Figo Chan, a young activist who played an important role in mobilizing protests against an extradition bill proposed and then withdrawn in 2019. China has implemented legislation that would jeopardize the "one country, two systems" arrangement, which theoretically guarantees Hong Kong's semi-autonomous status through 2047. On the pretext of defending "national security," the new law gives Beijing wide latitude to criminalize not only the activities of the pro-democracy movement but also the exercise of basic rights.

The CCP does not appear to have weighed seriously the possibility that Taiwan and Hong Kong would continue to defy its wishes. The very coercion it had hoped would pacify them has constrained its freedom of prudent maneuver. If China were to back down, the CCP might well suffer a significant loss of domestic legitimacy. But the risks of proceeding are just as significant, if not more. If China were to invade Taiwan, it would risk devastating retaliation from Washington, significant damage from Taipei's increasing "porcupine" defenses, and crushing sanctions. In addition, with Beijing preoccupied, Washington and Delhi could leverage their combined naval assets in the Indian Ocean to choke off energy supplies that flow to China through the Strait of Malacca.[66]

If China continues its crackdown on Hong Kong, it will undermine a vital financial hub upon which it continues to rely and will make it more politically costly for advanced industrial democracies to countenance trade and investment agreements with Beijing. It will also suffer more diplomatic embarrassments; the United Kingdom has offered $59 million to help resettle Hong Kong residents, a move that could set a precedent for other western countries to follow. Beijing's only intermediate option is to sustain pressure on Taiwan and Hong Kong indefinitely. Conditioning one's relations with others on the presumption of their indefinite pusillanimity and eventual acquiescence is a risky bet.

China's Self-Encircling Diplomacy

Beyond its immediate periphery, China encounters even greater challenges to its strategic ambitions. For starters, it confronts a set of militarily and economically formidable democracies that, although they have not yet moved to form an explicitly countervailing coalition, are strengthening their own defense capabilities and enhancing their security cooperation with one another. And the CCP's coercive COVID-19-era diplomacy has undercut Beijing's standing well beyond the Asia-Pacific. To appreciate the imbalance between its economic heft and its strategic acumen, one need only consider how propitious an opportunity it had to enhance its reputation at the outset of the pandemic.

China confronted withering criticism over its initial response. The CCP targeted the doctors and journalists who tried to sound the alarm—most prominently Li Wenliang, who succumbed to the virus in February 2020—and imposed severe restrictions on public movement, at one point locking down some 60 million citizens in Hubei Province alone. By March, though, it had managed to turn the narrative tide in its favor, having largely contained the first wave of the pandemic, and shifted its focus to shipping PPE and dispatching teams of doctors to numerous countries in distress. The United States, meanwhile, was struggling to manage the spread of COVID-19 and, in a marked departure from its postwar tradition, playing only a minor role in the world's efforts to flatten the curve. Claudia Major spoke for many alarmed observers: "What will this mean in five years for great-power competition? In ten years will we say, 'This is the moment that China rose and the US declined,' or will the US rebound?"[67]

Arvind Subramanian noted several measures that China could have taken to bolster its global standing while Major's question was top of mind—for example, waiving all debt it was owed, offering liquidity to countries that were hemorrhaging capital, and enhancing the developing world's access to its market.[68] Even if it had taken none of those steps, simply tending to its own recovery, it would likely have avoided much of the opprobrium it would soon bring upon itself. But China's seeming narrative advantage over the United States would be short-lived. Chinese ambassadors to many African countries were summoned after racist incidents against Africans in Guangzhou elicited global attention. A steady stream of reports began to surface about defects in Chinese PPE shipments. In early April, the Chinese government announced that there were no new reported COVID-19 fatalities inside China for the first time since the beginning of the outbreak, an announcement that elicited what would prove to be an enduring skepticism about the veracity of official published data. The government reacted angrily, embarking on a two-front course of "wolf warrior" diplomacy. The first front aimed to put critics of China's pandemic response on the defensive: high-level diplomats demanded that recipients of Chinese PPE express their gratitude publicly, criticized the responses of western countries, peddled conspiracy theories about the origins of the virus, and imposed sanctions on several exports from Australia after Canberra requested an independent inquiry into those origins.

The second front involved a heightened assertion of China's regional interests. As noted earlier, China passed "national security" legislation that calls into question whether Hong Kong will be able to preserve the last vestiges of its semi-autonomous status. It began buzzing Taiwan's territorial airspace on a regular basis and increasing preparations for a potential attack on the island. It launched an incursion across its disputed boundary with India and de facto seized territory Delhi claims as its own. And it further pressed dubious maritime claims in the South China Sea and East China Sea.

The continuation of this two-front diplomacy has proven self-defeating. The Five Eyes countries—Australia, Canada, the United Kingdom, the United States, and New Zealand—are expanding their collaborative agenda, and Japan has expressed an interest in joining the network. The members of the Quad are intensifying their security cooperation, defying longstanding predictions that the grouping would fail to gain momentum. Washington and Delhi signed a pact to share geospatial intelligence in October 2020; it is the last of three "foundational" agreements the United States signs with close military partners (the other two involve reciprocal logistics support and secure military-to-military communications). The following month, to offer just one further example, Japan and Australia signed an agreement to facilitate the execution of joint military exercises.

Even entities such as the Association of Southeast Asian Nations, normally more guarded in their judgments, have begun adopting stronger positions. In February 2020 Rodrigo Duterte, the president of the Philippines, ordered the termination of the Visiting Forces Agreement with the United States. In June and, again, in November of that year, though, the department of foreign affairs in Manila postponed the abrogation of that agreement, and in July 2021 Washington and Manila renewed it. In July 2020 Malaysia's permanent mission to the UN declared that China's maritime claims in the South China Sea were illegal.[69] And in September of that year, the day after the Chinese foreign minister called the United States "the most dangerous factor that damages the peace in the South China Sea," Vietnam's foreign minister rejoined that Hanoi welcomed Washington's "constructive and responsive contributions to ASEAN's efforts" to uphold peace and order in that body of water.[70] To offer one last illustration, in August 2021 the United States and Indonesia conducted their largest joint training exercise to date, one that involved 3,000 troops.[71]

Another telling example is NATO, which only first cited the "challenges" posed by China's resurgence in December 2019.[72] By June 2020, Secretary General Jens Stoltenberg had concluded that this resurgence was "multiplying the threats to open societies and individual freedoms, and increasing the competition over our values and our way of life."[73] And in June 2021, for the first time in its history, the alliance formally noted the challenges presented by China's military modernization.

A similar shift is occurring across Europe. In May 2020, the European Union's top diplomat called China a "systemic rival that seeks to promote an alternative model of governance," conceding that Brussels had been "a little naïve" in its dealings with Beijing.[74] He urged the European Union to develop "a more robust strategy for China, which also requires better relations with the rest of democratic Asia."[75] And the European Union's competition chief, noting a lack of reciprocity in Brussels's economic relations with Beijing, stressed that the European Union needs to be "more assertive and confident about who we are."[76] Foreign Minister Wang visited five European countries in September 2020—France, Germany, Italy, the Netherlands, and Norway—and President Xi held a virtual summit with EU leaders soon after. China found itself on the defensive, though, facing pointed questions about its crackdown on Hong Kong, its maritime claims in the South China Sea, and its restrictions on European companies that try to access the Chinese market. While a veritably transatlantic approach to China's resurgence may not come to fruition, closer alignment between Washington and Brussels is emerging.[77]

China's diplomacy could also challenge its technological ambitions. In July 2020 the United Kingdom pledged to remove all Huawei equipment from its 5G networks by 2027, reversing a January 2020 decision that would have given the company up to a 35 percent share in "non-core" components of those networks, and France announced restrictions that would effectively phase out the company by 2028. Perhaps most notably, since it possesses Europe's largest economy, Germany passed legislation in April 2021 that would make it much harder for Huawei to play a role in building out the country's 5G networks.

Leading Chinese international relations scholars, including Shi Yinhong, Yan Xuetong, and Zhu Feng, have concluded that Beijing's increasingly strident diplomacy could backfire.[78] And Reuters reported that, in April 2020, a Ministry of State Security-affiliated think tank presented a report to President Xi and other top Chinese officials that concluded that unfavorable global sentiment toward China had reached its highest level since the CCP's brutal crackdown on protesters at Tiananmen Square in 1989.[79] At least for now, the leadership does not appear to be heeding such warnings.

In a famous 2005 essay outlining how China would achieve a "peaceful rise," Zheng Bijian observed that China would "strive for peace, development, and cooperation with all countries of the world," beginning with its neighbors; he explained that Beijing's economic development would contribute to "the shaping of an East Asian community that may rise in peace as a whole."[80] Today, contrary to those predictions, China's relations are increasingly strained—not only with many of its neighbors but also with the United States and a growing number of European countries.

It has been quite striking, in fact, to observe how much China is evidently willing to undercut its own diplomatic outreach. Whether it believes that it has achieved a sufficient threshold of centrality in world affairs to warrant the deference of other countries, or that it must signal unflinching resolve in the pursuit of an increasingly capacious set of national interests that it deems vital, or that the strategic utility of US alliances and partnerships is diminishing, both its foreign policy and the accompanying rhetoric are growing increasingly assertive. Intuition suggests that China would slow down the pace of its resurgence, and perhaps even cap its own trajectory, if it does not cultivate a baseline of trust abroad. But perhaps it has concluded that, if it can continue expanding its share of the global economy and mastering the technologies that increasingly power global development, it will be able to secure new relationships far afield and, in due course, lessen the recalcitrance of those countries that are most concerned about its ambitions—namely its Asian-Pacific neighbors. If this hypothesis proves correct, Beijing may not need to match the diplomatic network in whose establishment and sustainment Washington has invested such great effort.

For now, though, it strains credulity to believe that China will be able to assume ever greater centrality in world affairs if it engenders ever greater distrust. Arguing that "China must display humane author-ity in order to compete with the United States," Yan Xuetong observed in 2011 that "the core of competition between China and the United States will be to see who has more high-quality friends."[81] Beijing's current course will likely inhibit the formation of such friendships, as President Xi has departed significantly from the restraint that Deng Xiaoping preached and has exhibited little sign of recalibrating. In addi-tion, the very conduct that isolates China abroad bolsters the CCP's domestic support, posing an acute dilemma for the leadership; Michael Schuman explains that the leadership "has crafted a narrative of China as a victim of foreign predation whose time has come to stand tall once again on the world stage (under the firm guidance of the party). That almost requires Beijing to take a hard stance in foreign disputes—any-thing less might be perceived as unacceptable weakness."[82]

The implications are at once worrisome and reassuring. If China is willing to incur significant reputational costs in conducting its foreign policy, it is unclear how much the United States can singlehandedly do to deter it. At the same time, Beijing has affirmed that it is its own greatest challenger: despite its intensifying fulminations against US foreign policy, it is chiefly encircled by the suspicions its own actions have cultivated—and continue to deepen.[83] However vaulting China's long-term objectives may be, its strategic myopia will likely undercut their pursuit.[84]

China's Sputnik Moment

This recitation of China's competitive liabilities may appear to invite passivity. Near the turn of the century, the director of studies at the International Institute for Strategic Studies concluded that "the country that is home to a fifth of humankind is overrated as a market, a power, and a source of ideas . . . Only when we finally understand how little China matters will we be able to craft a sensible policy toward it."[85] The author adduced an impressive wealth of evidence in support of this judgment. In retrospect, of course, it seems preposterous. Considering how much progress China has made in the intervening two decades, sur-passing perhaps even the expectations of its own leadership, why should one assume that present obstacles will thwart its continued resurgence? The framework of great-power competition rightly cautions against complacence borne of triumphalism. But alarmism borne of defensiveness is equally unlikely to position Washington for a long-term cohabitation with Beijing. The United States needs to exhibit a more calibrated disposition, of temperance borne of confidence.

While the deterioration of China's diplomatic standing belies the oft-heard proposition that its leaders are unequaled strategists, the scale and momentum of the country's resurgence warn against predictions of its coming disintegration, especially when considered alongside the CCP's adaptiveness. Recall that the Soviet Union's economy was never bigger than about two fifths of the United States'. In addition, partly to insulate itself from western economic pressure, Moscow pursued a largely autarkic course of development during the Cold War. That it was able to compete with Washington for nearly half a century despite its relative impoverishment and self-imposed isolation should give pause to those who counsel containment against China, whose economy is both far larger in relative terms and vastly more integrated.

The United States can undoubtedly cause China significant headaches through unilateral actions. In mid-2018 the Trump administration initiated a campaign of tariffs that contributed to a sharp decline in Chinese exports to the United States. Roughly two years later, in May 2020, the Department of Commerce announced a provision whereby any foreign chip producer that wishes to sell semiconductors to Huawei using US-made parts would have to apply for a special license; the assumption was that the department would deny most such applications, if not all. Commerce further squeezed China that September by imposing sanctions on the country's biggest chipmaker, Semiconductor Manufacturing International Corporation.

Yet it is doubtful that unilateral US pressure can stifle China's technological development indefinitely.[86] Importantly, it was not until Beijing initiated its self-sabotaging diplomacy during the pandemic that Huawei began experiencing sustained setbacks. Before then, many of America's allies and partners complained that the Trump administration had not presented compelling evidence that the CCP was using Huawei to conduct large-scale espionage. As for the president, sometimes he appeared to be at odds with the broader thrust of his own administration. In February 2019, less than a month after the Justice Department charged Huawei with attempting to steal intellectual property from T-Mobile and circumventing US sanctions on Iran, the president suggested that he would consider dropping the charges in order to facilitate a trade deal between Washington and Beijing. Near the end of 2019, Huawei announced that it had posted record profits despite US pressure.[87] Even as late as April 2020, the *Wall Street Journal* was reporting that "close allies like the UK and Germany have balked, telling the Trump administration that their own internal cybersecurity agencies can monitor Huawei equipment and keep it secure."[88]

While Huawei now finds it harder to gain traction in advanced industrial democracies, a study carried out at the Center for Strategic and International Studies found that between 2006 and April 2021 it closed seventy agreements with governments or state-owned enterprises in forty-one countries, primarily in Latin America, sub-Saharan Africa, and the Asia-Pacific.[89] Besides, to companies in competitor and in friendly countries alike, Washington's efforts against Huawei signal that dependence upon US technology could be a liability.[90] By virtue of having to become more self-reliant, Huawei may turn out to be more resilient in the medium to long run. US export controls, too, may have the unintended consequence of strengthening China's overall innovative capacity.[91]

It is true, of course, that China has been striving to boost its economic autonomy for some time. The Asian currency crisis of 1997–8 and the global financial crisis of 2008–9 persuaded Beijing not only that it could not rely upon Washington to be a prudent macroeconomic steward but also that it needed to rely more upon domestic consumption. Still, it is not apparent that China regarded an accelerated decoupling from the United States as a national security imperative before the Trump administration: Bob Davis and Lingling Wei observe that Beijing saw "the trade battle as its version of America's Sputnik moment—a foreign threat that requires the country to redouble its technological efforts."[92] China is rapidly working to cultivate alternative markets and to bypass supply chains that go through the United States.[93]

The Core of the World's Central Competition

If China has indeed had its Sputnik moment and Washington and Beijing are girding themselves for a long-term struggle, what is the essence of their competition?

There is, of course, a military dimension. According to the 2020 Pentagon report (see n. 11), the PLA is bolstering its capacity to "counter an intervention by an adversary in the Indo-Pacific region and project power globally."[94] Observers are especially concerned about the rapid buildup of the People's Liberation Army Navy (PLAN). According to Thomas Shugart, a former US Navy submarine warfare officer, the PLAN launched almost 600,000 tons of new warships between 2015 and 2019. The US Navy, in turn, launched almost 400,000 tons, only 60 percent of which are allocated to the Asia-Pacific.[95] In September 2020, Secretary of Defense Mark Esper announced that the navy would construct a fleet of 355 ships, manned and unmanned, to make the United States' "future naval force" more capable of delivering "lethal effects from the air, from the sea, and from under the sea."[96]

Military competition between the United States and China is likely to intensify, especially in the Asia-Pacific, where anxiety over contingencies involving a Chinese attack on Taiwan or an encounter between US and Chinese vessels in the South China Sea is mounting. If one only juxtaposes Washington's and Beijing's aggregated military capabilities, one may assess that the former's deterrence capacity is eroding. But China's route to achieving regional military dominance is much more fraught if one includes America's allies and partners—especially given that many of them are increasingly worried about China's conduct. Denny Roy ventures that, "[e]ven without the United States, the region is not so outweighed by China that resistance to Chinese domination would be futile."[97] What is more, explains a recent RAND Corporation study, the PLA remains largely untested: "The combat inexperience, persistent corruption, and incomplete nature of its reorganization all provide ample reasons to doubt the PLA's ability to achieve its vaunted goals."[98]

There is also an increasingly pronounced ideological dimension to US–China competition. In advance of the 20th National Congress of the CCP in 2022, President Xi continues to consolidate his power, eroding the norms of collective leadership and stable succession that Deng endeavored to entrench. In July 2020 he initiated a purge of China's domestic security apparatus, and the individual who is tasked with enforcing it compared it to the Yan'an Rectification Movement of 1942–5, which consolidated Mao's control of the party.[99] President Xi similarly relies on greater external assertiveness to strengthen his political authority at home, thereby creating a cycle from which it could prove difficult to extricate himself.

Some observers contend that ideology is not incidental to a strategic competition between the United States and China, but central. According to Tanner Greer, Chinese leaders "are engaged in an 'ideological struggle' with the values of a hostile liberal order. The stakes of this struggle could not be higher: They believe that the future of the global order and the survival of their regime is at stake."[100] If this judgment is true, it is important to assess China's ideological competitiveness. On the one hand, its economic heft allows it, if not exactly to seed its ideology in less developed countries, at least to make them more receptive to authoritarianism. David Shullman warns that, "[f]rom Cambodia to Serbia to Uganda, China is offering large-scale training on how to manipulate public opinion, censor and surveil journalists and civil society activists, and implement CCP-style cybersecurity policies."[101] And Sheena Chestnut Greitens notes that COVID-19 could create a significant demand for the high-tech surveillance equipment China has used to contain the pandemic within its own borders.[102]

On the other hand, Jessica Chen Weiss observes that "Beijing has projected a parochial, ethnocentric brand of authoritarian nationalism," such that President Xi's discussion of "the China dream" embodies "a self-centered CCP rhetoric that is likely to prevent Chinese political concepts from gaining universal appeal."[103] Indeed, the more scrutiny China faces, the more disquiet it elicits. It confronts growing condemnation abroad for the mass internment of Uighurs in Xinjiang, for the expanding program of coerced labor in Tibet, and for the construction of an artificial intelligence (AI)-powered panopticon-style system of surveillance. It imposes diplomatic and economic penalties on countries that award literary prizes to Chinese dissidents, criticize China's human rights record, permit visits from the Dalai Lama, prevent Huawei from playing a role in building out their 5G networks, or otherwise act in ways that offend China's sensibilities. The continued expulsion of foreign journalists and censorship of think tanks such as the Center for Strategic and International Studies furnish additional evidence that China is unwilling—if not unable—to abide growing criticism with temperance. These are not the actions of a country that has confidence in the intrinsic allure of its ideology—or, perhaps more importantly, that is preoccupied with external perceptions.

Even if China takes itself to be engaged in an ideological struggle with the United States, there are at least three reasons why
Washington should not respond accordingly. First, if the CCP's very
existence poses an intolerable threat, the United States cannot be safe
while the regime in China remains in power; the United States would
jeopardize its national security were it to pursue coevolution with an
existential adversary. Elbridge Colby and Robert Kaplan explain that,
"in great-power competition, insistence on ideological concordance
or total victory is a fool's errand—and quite possibly an invitation to
disaster."[104] Second, targeting the CCP would likely make the Chinese
people rally more closely around their leaders, thereby limiting the
prospects for Beijing's political evolution.[105] Indeed, some research
suggests that escalating hostility to China from the United States would
only heighten nationalism in the Chinese public.[106] If, however, as
suggested earlier, the CCP's present diplomacy threatens to undercut
China's strategic prospects, why should Washington not take actions
that stoke nationalist fervor in Beijing? The answer is a temporal one:
while the kind of nationalism President Xi is promulgating will probably continue to damage Beijing's stature over time, actively inflaming
it from the outside might compel the CCP to engage in face-saving
provocations that increase the possibility of short- to medium-term
security crises.[107] The third reason why the United States should avoid
embarking upon an ideological campaign is that it might end up isolat-
ing itself. Evan Medeiros and Ashley Tellis note that "most US allies
and partners are not interested in regime change in Beijing . . . They
want to limit Beijing's assertive behavior abroad, but they have little
desire to undermine the Chinese government at home."[108]

China's Narrative Momentum

Even as the military and ideological dimensions of strategic competition between Washington and Beijing become more pronounced, they
are unlikely to predominate. To determine which axes are likely to take
center stage, it is helpful to examine the four main sources of China's
influence—none immutable but each significant and all, collectively,
redoubtable.

First, there is economic performance undergirded by technological
progress. A little more than a decade ago, China played a vital role in

engineering the world's recovery from a downturn that originated in the United States. It was the first major power to come out of recession after the onset of the pandemic. Its global exports reached a record high in 2020, despite the Trump administration's imposition of tariffs and the economic devastation wrought by the spread of the coronavirus.[109] And its economy has defied decades of gloomy prognostications.

Indeed, the world is now even more economically dependent upon China than it was before COVID-19. The larger Beijing's economy grows, the more difficult it will be for companies outside the mainland to cut themselves off entirely, even as they take insurance measures to mitigate vulnerabilities in their supply chains. Henry Farrell and Abraham Newman argue that China's economy and the global economy are like "Siamese twin[s], connected by nervous tissue, common organs, and a shared circulatory system"—a vivid metaphor that illustrates both the difficulty and the peril of attempting to force a rupture.[110]

While the US corporate community may not be as strong a ballast for sustaining US–China ties as it was in the 1990s and in the subsequent decade, it is unlikely to support an intensified push to divorce the two countries' economies. In September 2020, some 3,500 US-based companies—including household names such as Home Depot, Target, and Tesla—filed lawsuits against the Trump administration for imposing tariffs on Chinese exports.[111] And in August 2021 almost three dozen influential US business groups urged the Biden administration to revamp trade talks with China and reduce those penalties.[112] Nor is there much evidence that the rest of the world seeks to decouple from China; Nicholas Lardy reports, in fact, that "China's share of global foreign direct investment in 2020 reached an all-time high of one quarter."[113]

To enhance its ability to grow independently, China is moving aggressively to boost indigenous innovation. Li Keqiang, the current Chinese premier, stated in May 2020 that one of the CCP's top priorities would be to invest some $1.4 trillion in advanced technologies through 2025, with a particular focus on 5G networks, so as to underpin "the internet of things."[114] In September of that same year, the government announced an initiative to cultivate "ten strategic emerging industrial bases with global influence, 100 strategic emerging industrial clusters with international competitiveness, and 1,000 strategic emerging industrial ecosystems with unique advantages."[115] Ryan Hass and Zach Balin note that roughly a third of the world's AI-involved companies operate in China, and some of them—such as Alibaba, Baidu, and Tencent—are globally competitive.[116] While Beijing still lags behind Washington in terms of innovative capacity, the technological sophistication of its exports is growing.[117]

A second source of China's influence is its deepening involvement in global governance. Beijing is certainly pursuing initiatives outside the postwar order, including the AIIB, the BRI, and Made in China 2025. But it also plays a greater role in obscure but crucial multilateral fora within that system. Between 2016 and 2019, for example, Chinese companies contributed all twenty proposals the ITU received for standards to govern the development of surveillance technology.[118] The Chinese government provides yearly stipends of up to $155,000 to companies that are pushing to develop international standards around the use of emerging technologies.[119]

Nevertheless, in many cases China simply capitalizes on self-inflicted US errors. By abandoning major multilateral agreements, the Trump administration often ceded critical leverage to China without Beijing's having to invest much effort, if any. Take the Trans-Pacific Partnership (TPP), which would have been the biggest regional trade accord in history had it come to pass, as it would have accounted for some two fifths of GWP and one third of world trade. Through mid-2013 or so, China had tended to frame the deal as part of a US-led containment campaign. But, as it seemed progressively likely that the agreement would come to fruition, the government changed its tune, stating that it might be amenable to joining negotiations. Unfortunately, though, the United States announced its intent to withdraw from the agreement shortly after Donald Trump was inaugurated. The other eleven participants in the TPP negotiations pressed on, signing the Comprehensive and Progressive Agreement for Trans-Pacific Partnership in March 2018. In the meantime, the successful conclusion of negotiations over the Regional Comprehensive Economic Partnership (RCEP) leaves the United States further excluded from the Asia-Pacific's economic architecture.[120]

The Trump administration also abandoned the 2015 Paris climate accord, giving China the opportunity to cast itself as a more responsible environmental actor than the United States, even though it is the largest producer of carbon emissions and is revamping its push to generate coal power plant capacity. Paradoxically, China's sheer scale has ensured that, in responding to its own pollution crisis, it has also emerged as a global leader—if not the world's foremost leader—in clean energy innovation.[121] In September 2020, President Xi pledged that China would achieve peak emissions before 2030, the date set forth in the 2015 agreement. More notably, he stated the country's intention to achieve zero net carbon emissions by 2060.

Separately, explains Kristine Lee, after the Trump administration withdrew from the UN Human Rights Council, China largely neutralized that body's criticisms of China's human rights abuses.[122] More recently, in April 2020, a week after the administration stated that it was temporarily suspending funding for the WHO, China pledged an additional $30 million to the organization. The administration announced that it was withdrawing from the organization near the end of May, a move observers warned would make the WHO more beholden to Beijing, even though Washington has contributed far more; the United States provided nearly 15 percent of its funding in 2018–19, whereas China provided less than a quarter of 1 percent.[123] Vijay Gokhale, India's ambassador to China from January 2016 to October 2017, rhetorically asked why Beijing would undertake to dissolve the current order if, by virtue of the United States' abdication, it could emerge as the system's de facto underwriter.[124]

A third way in which China gains influence is by exploiting fissures in US society and touting itself as a model of domestic competence. That effort is not new, of course. Beijing criticized Washington's macroeconomic stewardship after the global financial crisis. And in August 2011, with Congress struggling to agree upon a course of action to rein in the country's debt, Standard and Poor's (S&P) downgraded its long-term credit rating for the United States by one notch, prompting China to renew its call for a global financial system less dominated by one reserve currency. But Beijing's critiques have become more pointed, especially under President Xi. On the eve of the 19th National Congress of the CCP, Xinhua opined that "[e]ndless political backbiting, bickering, and policy reversals, which make the hallmarks of liberal democracy, have retarded economic and social progress and ignored the interests of most citizens."[125]

The year 2020 offered China ample grounds for schadenfreude. The CCP seized upon the death of George Floyd at the hands of Minneapolis police to deflect attention from China's intensifying crackdown on Hong Kong. A spokesperson for the Chinese Foreign Ministry tweeted "I can't breathe" in response to her American counterpart's call for the international community to hold the CCP accountable.[126] David Wertime observed that Beijing turned to "longstanding tropes in Chinese government propaganda and the state-led curriculum dating back to the rule of Mao Zedong: that the US is unsafe, chaotic, and beset with racial strife."[127] A bitter presidential election gave Chinese officials more fodder. In October, the International Crisis Group took the unprecedented step of issuing a report on the potential for election-related violence in the United States.[128] And President Trump stoked alarm at home and abroad when he declined to commit to a peaceful transition of power if he were to lose his reelection bid. The *Washington Post* observed that the Chinese media aimed to portray the United States as "a politically crumbling edifice."[129]

But perhaps nothing has done more to damage America's global reputation in recent years than its initial response to the pandemic. A lethargic reaction to the coronavirus on its arrival, poor coordination between national and subnational government actors, and the politicization of mask wearing and social distancing contributed to a situation in which the world's sole superpower seemed hapless. The United States reported 200,000 new COVID-19 cases for the first time on November 27, 2020, just over three weeks after it had reported 100,000 new cases for the first time. In early 2021, two weeks before Joe Biden was sworn in as president, the country recorded yet another grisly milestone: over 4,000 coronavirus deaths in one day. China, on the other hand, recovered quickly from the pandemic and, while some observers question how accurate its official figures on infections and deaths are, the government does appear to have largely contained the spread of the virus within the country's borders (though the Delta variant casts doubt on the viability of its "zero tolerance" approach to containing the virus).

One of the most influential documents of the Cold War, NSC-68, explained that the United States had to "lead in building a successfully functioning political and economic system in the free world. It is only by practical affirmation, abroad as well as at home, of our essential values, that we can preserve our own integrity, in which lies the real frustration of the Kremlin design."[130] COVID-19 has led some observers to wonder whether Beijing is more functional than Washington.

These three sources of influence—China's economic and technological progress, its growing role in global governance, and Washington's domestic dysfunction—collectively furnish a fourth, one that is arguably the most potent: narrative momentum. Robert Gilpin once observed:

> Whereas power refers to the economic, military, and related capabilities of a state, prestige refers primarily to the perceptions of other states with respect to a state's capacities and its ability and willingness to exercise its power . . . the fact that the existing distribution of power and the hierarchy of prestige can sometimes be in conflict with one another is an important factor in international political change.[131]

This distinction suggests that, even if Beijing continues to lag behind Washington in "power," it could go a long way toward weakening America's network of alliances and partnerships if it were to overtake the United States in "prestige." In the communiqué it issued after the Fifth Plenum, held in October 2020, the CCP referred to a "profound adjustment in the international balance of power."[132] While the phrase had appeared in previous CCP proclamations, never before had it featured in one of such high-level importance. And, at the beginning of 2021, President Xi adopted a triumphant tone in an address to provincial- and ministerial-level officials: "The world is undergoing profound changes unseen in a century, but time and the situation are in our favor."[133]

Drawing upon these four sources of influence, China seeks to entrench parallel narratives with a reinforcing effect: Beijing is irreversibly gaining strength, steadily moving to redress a global strategic balance that has unjustly been US-centric for too long, while Washington is quickly losing ground, anxiously seeking to buttress a configuration of geopolitics and affirm a conception of governance whose inadequacies will only grow more apparent. If it succeeds in gaining traction for those messages, it could persuade some of Washington's friends to subordinate their concerns over Beijing's long-term strategic intentions to assumptions of its eventual economic dominance. One of the United States' essential tasks, then, will be to push back against the aforementioned narratives; left unchallenged, they could engender more risk-taking behavior from China, elicit more defensive maneuvers from the United

States, and therefore create more room for miscalculations that could generate security crises.

An Asymmetric Approach to a Limited Competitor

If the preceding discussion has at times appeared conflicted, it is because there is no self-evidently sound way in which to "subtract" China's competitive liabilities from its competitive assets. Given this methodological challenge, it is unsurprising that observers reach different conclusions about its long-term strategic prospects. The extent of their disagreement can nevertheless be quite striking. Some depict Beijing as an inexorably ascendant superpower, guided by a farsighted and technocratic elite. Others portray it as a fatally misguided upstart, driven by an impetuous and hubristic ruler.

The United States would be unwise to predicate its policy on either of these assessments. The extent of China's integration into the global economy and the adaptiveness of the CCP suggest that it is likely to prove an enduring challenger. But Beijing confronts formidable difficulties at home, in its neighborhood, and further afield that collectively call into question the supposition that it will eventually succeed Washington.[134] While the scale and scope of its resurgence dictate that it should influence America's effort to forge a more resilient post-pandemic order, the phenomenon is not so daunting that it should determine the parameters of that undertaking. Jude Blanchette observes that China is neither two feet tall nor ten feet tall, but instead "six-foot-nine. That is a size that poses significant challenges but does not—or should not—overwhelm our ability to conceive of strategy."[135]

Forecasts that China will absorb and assimilate much of the rest of the world en route to global hegemony discount the potency of the resistance it presently confronts and will increasingly encounter. The more vocally it criticizes the current order, the more it spotlights the parochialism of its own conception (an inchoate one at best, since abstractions such as "community of common destiny for mankind" do not lend themselves to clear interpretations). Elizabeth Economy observes that "China's leadership globally is largely confined to those issues where its interests are easily advanced, such as economic development through the BRI or security cooperation to prevent terrorist attacks or democratic revolutions through the Shanghai Cooperation Organization."[136]

If China proves incapable of cultivating a baseline of trust beyond its borders, it will effectively have forsaken all but one strategic pathway: achieving a gravitational economic pull so inescapable that even its fiercest critics eventually come to the view that their national interests are better served by accommodating Beijing's conception of world order than by acting upon their own anxieties. While one cannot disclaim this outcome, one can reasonably question its plausibility. Audrye Wong finds that the strategic returns thus far to China's geoeconomic initiatives have been underwhelming.[137] And even if, as seems likely, its GDP surpasses the United States' in absolute terms in the next decade, its per-capita GDP will lag behind for several more. In addition, Beijing will find it difficult to overtake Washington without achieving a comparable power projection capacity and developing an alternative order that compels advanced industrial democracies to abandon the existing one. Were aggregate economic size alone more decisive, the power transition between the United Kingdom and the United States would probably have occurred in the late nineteenth century; the latter did not emerge as the world's foremost power, though, until after World War II.

As for the United States, it maintains a range of impressive and in some cases singular competitive advantages. Its working-age population is set to grow by more than 16 million between 2020 and 2050—a roughly 8 percent increase.[138] Despite ongoing speculation that the US dollar might lose its centrality in global financial markets, recent years have only entrenched its status as an unrivaled reserve currency. The United States also remains the world's leading technological power. Martin Wolf notes that, in addition to being home to fourteen of the world's twenty most valuable companies and ten of the world's twenty leading universities, it maintains a commanding position in venture capital investment—thanks in good measure to its continued ability to recruit extraordinary talent from around the world.[139] The United States is the world's largest producer of both oil and natural gas. It is the only country capable of projecting military power into every corner of the world. Its sprawling set of alliances and partnerships remains unrivaled.[140] And, while the postwar order it helped establish is creaky, it, too, is far-reaching.[141]

Where the framework of great-power competition might recommend a China-centric US foreign policy, the preceding analysis encourages the pursuit of one that is simply China-influenced. The former considers how Washington can manage Beijing's resurgence; the latter considers how selective competition with Beijing can inform a US campaign of self-renewal.

The United States should work to reduce its reliance upon China for medical supplies, for inputs that go into its highly sensitive military technologies, and for other commodities that are essential to defending its vital national interests. The Biden administration has conducted a thorough review of the United States' supply chain vulnerabilities and is building upon the efforts of the Trump and Obama administrations to fortify the country's defenses against hacking campaigns by CCP-sanctioned actors. Washington should also increase foreign military financing for member countries of ASEAN, especially those that are embroiled in maritime disputes with Beijing, so that they feel more empowered when they resist China's attempts to impede freedom of navigation in the South China Sea. Given that between a fifth and a third of world trade is estimated to transit through this body of water, their efforts to push back become essential.[142] In addition, while China aims to cast itself as a dedicated champion of human rights, the United States should join its allies and partners to spotlight more pro-actively and consistently the abuses that China is committing at home and abroad, be they assaults against religious and ethnic minorities or crackdowns on protesters in Hong Kong. It should also make clear to China that it regards the freedom of speech of American citizens, companies, and campuses as sacrosanct, and that any diplomatic overture on Beijing's part that amounts to an attempt to restrict that freedom would be a nonstarter.

In the main, though, the United States should pursue an asymmetric strategy in order to reverse China's narrative momentum—pushing back against China where necessary but focusing primarily on investing anew in its own competitive advantages, while allowing China's increasingly counterproductive diplomacy to advance US national interests. A strategy oriented too narrowly toward responding to Beijing's actions would consume Washington's attention and signal anxiety. A US-focused, China-influenced alternative, by contrast, would free up strategic bandwidth and project confidence.

Realistic Expectations of Allies and Partners

One of the United States' greatest competitive advantages is, of course, its diplomatic network—which is unparalleled and, at the moment, underused. The Biden administration has encouragingly rejoined the Paris climate accord, the UN Human Rights Council, and the WHO. It has also made the resuscitation of the Joint Comprehensive Plan of Action—or some version of the deal—a core foreign policy priority. Going forward, it should consider entering talks with the eleven member countries of the CPTPP, to see whether they would be amenable to Washington's joining. The United States is conspicuously absent from that agreement as well as from the RCEP and, since negotiations over the Transatlantic Trade and Investment Partnership have stalled, it is unclear that Washington has much of a trade agenda.

But the United States needs to do more than simply reengage where the Trump administration disengaged. It needs to think more creatively and ambitiously about how it enlists its allies and partners, forges new multilateral trade agreements and upgrades existing ones, promotes technology-intensive infrastructure in developing and underdeveloped swaths of the world, and participates in conferences that will help determine how countries and non-state actors use frontier technologies. The more embedded the United States is within both established fora and ad hoc coalitions, the better positioned it will be to resume its role as a central catalyst of collective action—a role that will grow more important as transnational challenges increase in number and scale.

China's resurgence will, of course, be an important topic in the United States' conversations with its allies and partners, and Washington's success in courting advanced industrial democracies has been impressive: it is increasing intelligence-sharing efforts with other members of the Five Eyes network, deepening security cooperation with other members of the Quad, collaborating with Brussels to press for greater market access in China, working with allies and partners to reduce their collective reliance upon Chinese 5G infrastructure, and drawing greater attention to Beijing's human rights abuses.

But the United States should not conflate growing alignment with strategic consonance. Alan Beattie explains that, while "a common threat" can "induce solidarity," if one were to map out the eleven combined member and guest countries in attendance at the 2021 G7 summit, the "Venn diagram of the G7+4, showing sets of countries prepared to take action on various issues, would exclude leading players each time—and leave some nations outside the universal set altogether."[143] And, even as advanced industrial democracies increasingly note their ideological differences with China—for instance Mario Draghi, Italy's prime minister, stated after the summit that China "does not share the same vision of the world that the democracies have"— few of them feel comfortable defining their foreign policies through a China-centric prism.[144] It was reported in May 2020 that the United Kingdom had floated the establishment of an informal D10 that would comprise the G7 member countries plus Australia, India, and South Korea. Tellingly, though, London shelved the proposal ahead of the summit, when France, Germany, and Japan expressed concerns about "appearing openly hostile to Beijing."[145]

A recent task force concludes that "the significant, even dominant role that security concerns play in the American approach to China leads various issues (notably economic and technological) to be 'securitized' (to be viewed through a security lens)," whereas "Europe has focused on commerce, human rights, the environment, and 'soft security' issues."[146] In the Asia-Pacific, of course, geography leaves US allies and partners with little choice but to view China's resurgence through more of a security lens than their European counterparts. Still, they are increasingly fearful of being entrapped by an escalating US–China rivalry that will weigh most heavily upon their region.

The upshot is that balancing against China is more likely to comprise a patchwork of incremental, disparate efforts than a program of sweeping, unified resistance. If Washington bases its strategy toward Beijing upon the emergence of a cohesive coalition, it is likely to be disappointed. Indeed, even countries with significant apprehensions about China's resurgence can be expected to react unfavorably if they believe that Washington largely regards them as instruments of strategic competition with Beijing. When asked to comment on the perception that many western observers see India as a counterbalance to China, Subrahmanyam Jaishankar, India's external affairs minister, replied: "I find the idea of being someone else's pawn in some 'Great Game' terribly condescending . . . I'm in it because of my own ambitions."[147]

In addition, recent years suggest that the United States will have only limited success if its efforts focus primarily on thwarting Chinese-led initiatives. Consider what happened when the Obama administration tried to undercut support for the AIIB. When the United Kingdom announced that it intended to participate in the new venture, a senior official stated that Washington was "wary about a trend [in London] toward constant accommodation of China, which is not the best way to engage a rising power."[148] The AIIB ended up with fifty-seven founding members, including many of the United States' closest allies, for at least two reasons. First, even countries that share its concerns over China's strategic ambitions want to decide for themselves, on a case-by-case basis, whether it is in their national interest to support an initiative from Beijing. Second, not all undertakings bearing China's imprimatur are—or should reflexively be construed as—inimical to global development: "Many of the AIIB's early joiners may have been seeking to advance their bilateral interests with China, but they also clearly saw the broader value of doing so in a context that could be viewed as pro-development."[149] The Asian Development Bank (ADB) estimated in early 2017 that its forty-five developing member countries would collectively need to invest $1.7 trillion per year between 2016 and 2030 to sustain growth, eliminate poverty, and mitigate climate change.[150] The AIIB now has more than one hundred member countries, and it has partnered with the ADB and the World Bank to finance infrastructure projects.

A similar line of reasoning applies to China's flagship geoeconomic project: that there are numerous legitimate critiques of the BRI does not obviate the scale of infrastructure needs across the developing world. In May 2020, Secretary of State Michael Pompeo threatened that the United States might "simply disconnect" from allies and partners that sign up for the initiative.[151] Those kinds of ultimatums are unlikely to gain traction; an early 2021 tally found that some 140 countries had entered into more than 200 BRI cooperation agreements.[152] Nor, importantly, are they necessary, considering that the BRI has been more improvised than scripted to date and that it is experiencing growing fiscal challenges and geopolitical obstacles.[153] The United States would be better served by leveraging its comparative advantages in international development, "including cutting-edge technologies, world-class companies, deep pools of capital, a history of international leadership, a traditional role in setting international standards, and support for the rule of law and transparent business practices."[154]

The United States and the United Kingdom have initiated a conversation about building high-end infrastructure projects in the developing world, and the European Union has entered into comparable discussions with India and Japan. These disparate dialogues could, in time, form "a kaleidoscope of coordinated bilateral and multilateral partnerships between the European Union and US and Indo-Pacific nations."[155] Perhaps most ambitiously, the G7 countries have unveiled a Build Back Better World initiative that aims to harness private-sector financing to spur infrastructure investment in the developing world through four focus areas: climate change, health security, digital technology, and gender equity. While intended as a response to the BRI, it encouragingly does not seem intent on trying to replicate China's undertaking.

To offer a final example, that there are numerous legitimate critiques of Huawei does not obviate the scale of connectivity needs across the developing world. In February 2020, White House economic advisor Larry Kudlow announced that the Trump administration was working with AT&T, Dell, and Microsoft to develop a 5G infrastructure from scratch.[156] So far there are only three companies that offer that type of infrastructure, comprising the full package of software and hardware needed to construct a new 5G network: Huawei and its two European competitors, Ericsson and Nokia. Washington may not be able to cultivate a national champion that can credibly rival Huawei, even though America's prospects for competing in the global 5G space appear more auspicious than they did near the end of the Trump administration.[157] David Sanger concludes that, even if the United States were to continue its crackdown, "China will dominate 40 percent or more of the world's telecommunications networks."[158]

Many lawmakers and observers have articulated proposals that could help the United States and its friends go beyond stifling Huawei and offer compelling alternatives of their own. The Innovation and Competition Act would allocate $1.5 billion to a Public Wireless Supply Chain Innovation Fund designed to support efforts aimed at the creation and usage of Open Radio Access Network 5G networks. And the United States and Japan have agreed to collaborate on a $4.5 billion effort to develop both 5G and 6G mobile networks.

While the United States should continue its conversations on building out infrastructure and connectivity globally, it should not make the counterbalancing of China the organizing principle of its interactions with allies and partners. The fulcrum should instead be the advancement of a more resilient order, one that is more capable of managing not just great-power tensions but also transnational challenges. The United States' friends will be more enthusiastic about contributing to a forward-looking venture—one that does not, in principle, exclude China—than about serving as the instruments of a reactionary agenda. Melvyn Leffler observes that during the Cold War "the United States took actions—such as the Marshall Plan and the reconstruction of West Germany—that could be justified on their own terms, for reasons other than containment."[159]

Today it similarly behooves Washington to take actions that can be justified without citing Beijing's resurgence. Indeed, the reflexive invocation of China to justify all manner of measures does not demonstrate competitive acumen; it betrays growing anxiety. Jude Blanchette observes that, when President Xi and his advisors "articulate their vision, it's not an America strategy. It's 'this is the role China wants to play in the world over the next 10, 20, 30, 40, 50 years.'"[160] Similarly, the United States should have not "a China strategy," but a compelling vision, of which the management of China's resurgence is but one component. After all, intensifying strategic competition with Beijing has simply placed in sharper relief a set of external and internal imperatives that Washington should have been pursuing more assiduously in the first instance.

The Need for Domestic Renewal

While the United States must reposition itself abroad, per the previous section, it must concurrently revitalize itself at home, beginning with its economic and technological investments. Federally funded research and development fell from 1.86 percent of GDP in 1964 to 0.62 percent in 2018.[161] In August 2020 the Trump administration announced that federal agencies and private-sector partners would pledge more than $1 billion over five years to establish twelve research institutes—seven focused on AI and five focused on quantum information sciences.[162] Meanwhile the Innovation and Competition Act would direct $81 billion to supporting the National Science Foundation and $10 billion to establishing new technology hubs across the United States.[163]

But innovation does not occur in a vacuum; it depends on people. The United States is losing its appeal as a magnet for international students—partly because colleges and universities in other countries continue to make strides, but also because Washington has taken a series of measures in recent years that make it feel less welcoming. A March 2020 report found that America's share of international students had fallen from 28 percent in 2001 to 21 percent in 2019 and that new international student enrollment had declined by nearly 11 percent since 2016. "Institutions continue to report," it noted, "that prospective international students and their families are concerned about US federal policies and rhetoric on immigration, along with apprehensions of personal safety and tense race relations."[164]

Should those concerns become entrenched, they could undercut America's long-term competitiveness vis-à-vis China, not only dissuading prospective foreign-born students and researchers but also unnerving those who currently work in the United States. Ishan Banerjee and Matt Sheehan note that China has the largest proportion of leading AI researchers, "but a majority of these Chinese researchers leave China to study, work, and live in the United States."[165] Whether this trend will continue is unclear. Consider the case of Zhu Songchun, a leading expert in computer vision who received his doctorate from Harvard in 1996 and joined the Departments of Statistics and Computer Science at the University of California, Los Angeles in 2002. It was reported in September 2020 that he would return to China to direct Peking University's Institute for Artificial Intelligence. William Overholt worries that "years from now we may look back on the exodus of scientists like [Zhu] as comparable to the expulsion in the McCarthy era of a nuclear expert who went on to become the father of China's nuclear weapons program."[166] As the US government scrutinizes Chinese and Chinese American scientists more closely through programs such as the Department of Justice-led China Initiative, initiated under the Trump administration, more observers express concern over their potential impact on the attractiveness of US educational institutions and America's reputation for openness.[167] That scrutiny also raises questions about the boundary between the narrow targeting of criminal activity and overreaching crackdowns on appropriate research, especially as many scientists have been wrongly charged.[168]

As the last chapter discusses, restoring innovative competitiveness is just a part of the incremental, painful work the United States will have to do to renew the power of its own example. James Goldgeier and Bruce Jentleson explain that COVID-19 has spotlighted many of the challenges that undercut the appeal of US governance: "Economic equality has been declining for more than 40 years, while 'deaths of despair' are rapidly rising. Systemic racism tarnishes the country's image abroad as a champion of democracy, justice, and the rule of law."[169] The United States' allies and partners will rightly ask how it can contribute to revitalizing the postwar order if it proves incapable of managing its domestic challenges more effectively. Noting "the widespread view that in key domains, the United States . . . does not have the competence to be trusted," Samantha Power, now head of the US Agency for International Development, argues: "Restoring American leadership . . . must include the more basic task of showing that the United States is a capable problem solver once more."[170]

The Inescapability of Cohabitation

The aforementioned agenda is daunting. Encouragingly, though, the United States can go a long way toward enhancing its strategic competitiveness on its own, independently of what China does. Shortly after President Biden took office, Secretary of State Antony Blinken listed a number of steps Washington could take to that end, observing that they all are "actually within our control. These are things we can do. These are decisions we can make."[171] In addition, China is charting a diplomatic course that seems bound to compound its isolation among precisely the other major powers whose trust will be essential to its continued resurgence. Perhaps even more telling than the growing cooperation between China's neighbors is the hardening of attitudes that is occurring in Brussels. In March 2021 the United States, the European Union, the United Kingdom, and Canada jointly sanctioned Chinese officials involved in human rights abuses in Xinjiang. China responded by sanctioning not only prominent members of the European Parliament but also high-profile European think tanks—a decision that has prompted Brussels to reconsider whether it should ratify a major investment agreement with Beijing. Indeed, China's expanding abuses against Uighurs and its intensifying repression of Hong Kong, among other acts, are prompting Europeans to rethink the overall contours of their dealings with China.[172]

This combination of realities—that the United States can substantially bolster its strategic competitiveness vis-à-vis China regardless of what Beijing does, and that China continues to compound its own encirclement—suggests that Washington should regard Beijing's resurgence as a formidable, yet manageable challenge. What, then, should American policy toward China ultimately attempt to accomplish? Washington must work toward the achievement and maintenance of a condition that accommodates the ineluctability of growing tensions as much as it appreciates the imperative of sustained cooperation.[173] The most immediate precondition is the avoidance of a military confrontation, which would imperil both the possibility of long-term coexistence between the United States and China and the stability of a global order that is already laboring under enormous stress. Despite the self-evident need for sustained and transparent communication between the militaries of the world's two foremost powers, Washington and Beijing have proven unable to strengthen that channel for a variety of reasons.[174] As observers are increasingly concerned about contingencies that could arise from a Chinese attack on Taiwan or a clash between US Navy and PLAN vessels in the South China Sea, there is an urgent need to establish crisis management mechanisms.

A longer-term precondition for competitive cohabitation is mutual acceptance, however begrudging: Washington and Beijing must appreciate that neither can relegate the other to a marginal position in world affairs or decouple its economy fully from that of the other. In the Asia-Pacific, where competition between the two is most intense, while China will prove to be an increasingly estimable counterweight to the United States, it is unlikely that it will displace Washington entirely—not only because it is surrounded by countries with large economies and advanced militaries but also because its conduct is driving them further into America's security orbit. Of particular note is India, which, while continuing to prize its strategic autonomy and recognizing the necessity of a détente with China, feels a heightened urgency to upgrade ties with the United States. Although most observers do not label Delhi a great power, its booming economy and formidable military capabilities are likely to pose a growing challenge to whatever regional objectives Beijing may harbor. Jeff Smith ventures in fact that "[b]y mid-century India may be China's and America's only geopolitical peer."[175]

Hervé Lemahieu and Alyssa Leng assess that the Asia-Pacific's future "is likely to be defined by asymmetric multipolarity. When neither the United States nor China can establish undisputed primacy in Asia, the actions, choices, and interests of middle powers will become more consequential."[176] Indeed, neither Washington nor Beijing would appear to appreciate how much the Asia-Pacific's evolution has proceeded, and can continue, in spite of them. Evan Feigenbaum notes that Japan, Malaysia, and ASEAN have been instrumental in boosting its economic and institutional integration and that "contemporary Asian regionalism . . . has deep historical roots and many non-Chinese champions."[177] Strategic tensions between the United States and China play a critical role in the Asia-Pacific's evolution, but not a determinative one.

This conclusion holds well beyond the region. Whereas the Cold War ended with the dissolution of one of the contenders, it is highly unlikely that the intensifying competition between the United States and China will culminate in either one's collapse. It is more probable that the two countries will, as they must, maintain a tense, fluid balance. Such an outcome seems even more likely when one considers the agency and calculations of other countries, factors that one risks discounting by imposing a G2 overlay upon world affairs or by applying power transition theory. A 2020 study overseen by Samuel Brannen, now deputy assistant secretary of defense for plans and posture, predicted that "the highest likelihood outcome for world order in the decade ahead" would be "a loose multipolarity. Under any outcome, the relative strength of both the United States and China would be diluted or balanced by the influence and independent foreign and security policies of India, Japan, Germany, France, the United Kingdom, and others."[178]

The word "independent" is essential. While observers often contend that third powers will eventually have to "choose" between Washington and Beijing, those powers are increasingly avowing their desire to avoid such a choice—and, in some cases, expressing skepticism that the choice does or must exist. Lee Hsien Loong, Singapore's prime minister, observes that Asian-Pacific countries "fervently hope not to be forced to choose between the United States and China."[179] The German government states that "[n]o country should . . . be forced to choose between two sides or fall into a state of unilateral dependency.

Freedom of choice regarding membership of economic and (security) policy structures is crucial for Indo-Pacific countries."[180] An especially forceful statement in this vein comes from Scott Morrison, Australia's prime minister: "Our actions are wrongly seen and interpreted by some only through the lens of the strategic competition between China and the United States. It's as if Australia does not have its own unique interests or its own views as an independent sovereign state. This is just false."[181]

As they recalibrate their respective approaches to middle powers, the United States and China would both do well to appreciate the reputational damage they have incurred in recent years. Those powers are alarmed by the degree of incompetence that Washington exhibited in responding to the pandemic, at least initially, and the results of the 2020 presidential election make clear that there is a significant possibility of another "America First" leader. Thus, even those allies and partners that breathed a sigh of relief when President Biden was elected must contend with concerning possibilities: a renewed multilateralism could once more give way to a coercive transactionalism, and US initiatives to facilitate the emergence of a more resilient postpandemic order could prove ephemeral. China, meanwhile, whatever its motivations—anxiety, opportunism, hubris, or some combination thereof—has comported itself in a manner that will make it difficult for it simply to recover the diplomatic standing it possessed at the end of 2019, let alone to mold the external environment Zheng Bijian believes will be essential to its continued resurgence. While observers sometimes portray China as a master grand strategist that thinks decades into the future and patiently waits for the day when the United States is too hobbled by internal dysfunction to obstruct its path to preeminence, China's own self-constraining diplomacy belies such depictions.

Beyond accepting the necessity of cohabitation, the United States and China must restore a willingness to entertain cooperative possibilities. That the pandemic has intensified bilateral strategic distrust bodes ominously, not only for relations between the two countries but also for the world's capacity for collective action.[182] It will be difficult enough for Washington and Beijing to concede the necessity of coevolution, let alone to pursue it in good faith, for each believes in its own exceptionalism and regards the other as an antithetical interloper. The United States frames China as the principal disruptor in world affairs, seeking to export a regressive model of internal governance. China contends that the United States harbors unfounded pretensions to universal values and discounts the centrality Beijing enjoyed in world affairs before the Industrial Revolution. Neither is inclined to see the other as a reliable partner in the quest for a sustainable balance between competitive and cooperative dynamics. Nor does either have a play-book upon which to draw. Yet they have little choice but to create one: only by subordinating their presumptions about historical singularity to discussions of a sustainable order can they advance their shared vital national interests.

Assessing Russia's Conduct and the Sino-Russian Entente

While most discussions of great-power competition assign greater weight to China's resurgence, Russia is a formidable player in its own right. It has the world's largest landmass, which encompasses eleven time zones, the largest proven reserves of natural gas, and the largest stockpile of nuclear weapons. It also has the fourth-largest defense outlays, the ninth-largest population, and the eleventh-largest gross domestic product. Finally, it is a permanent member of the UN Security Council. Russia thus endures as a central actor in world affairs, even if it is a shadow of what the Soviet Union once was.

The Debate over Russia's Greatness

Observers disagree, however, over a number of analytical questions, three of which readily come to mind. First, is Russia a great power? Second, is it a declining power? Third, how prominent a role should Washington accord Moscow in its strategic outlook?

On the first question, Michael McFaul, who served as US ambassador to Russia from 2012 to 2014, notes that Moscow "has reemerged . . . as one of the world's most powerful countries—with significantly more military, cyber, economic, and ideological might than most Americans appreciate."[1] While it is "inattentive to some of the means required to sustain a great-power status," conclude

William Courtney and Howard Shatz, "Russia is clearly a great power."[2]

Others disagree. Mark Galeotti argues that, "in any objective terms, Russia is not a great power."[3] Zack Cooper concurs: "Moscow no longer qualifies as a 'great power.'" He observes that Russia has "a declining population. Russia also has . . . a GDP per capita that ranks 74th globally. Sure, Russia has nuclear weapons, but so do Pakistan, North Korea, and Israel."[4]

On the second question, Joseph Nye answers in the affirmative, remarking that "Russia can only be an international spoiler. Behind the adventurism, it is a country in decline."[5] Anton Barbashin agrees, albeit stressing that the process may be protracted: "Russia is in decline the same way . . . Rome was before and during Aurelian's rule. It is inevitable, but it might take a while."[6]

Again, others disagree. Kathryn Stoner warns that depictions of a declining Russia are obsolete: "Russia isn't just formidable in cyberspace. It is globally resurgent in ways that we can't afford to dismiss, from Crimea to Syria to sub-Saharan Africa, Venezuela, the Arctic, Europe, and beyond."[7] Simon Saradzhyan and Nabi Abdullaev note that "the view of Russia as a declining power has persisted in the 21st century, though most of its adherents . . . have not revealed how they define the country's decline, over what period of time, and relative to what countries."[8]

Turning to the third question, finally, Michael Kofman argues that Russia "will not decline as a threat to the United States in any appreciable way in the near or medium term . . . Moscow is an enduring great power and should continue to be a major factor in US strategy."[9] Dmitri Trenin and Thomas Graham caution Washington against devaluing Moscow's importance amid its growing focus on Beijing, noting that the United States and Russia "remain the only two powers—by virtue of geographical location or strategic reach—that can impact the entire territory of the Eurasian supercontinent that along with North America constitutes the core of the modern world."[10]

Others contend that the United States would be misguided if it were to accord China and Russia comparable roles in its foreign policy. Elbridge Colby stipulates that great-power competition "essentially means China. Russia is a distant second."[11] Mark Montgomery and Eric Sayers argue that "the magnitude of the challenge posed by a

China with the world's second-largest economy far exceeds that of Russia."[12]

There is also some debate over Russia's long-term strategic objectives, though the continuum is narrower than in the case of China's. While many observers assess that Beijing seeks to overtake Washington in global preeminence, few, if any, believe that Moscow harbors such an ambition. Still, some contend that Russia aims to reconstruct its former Soviet empire. President Putin considers the post-Cold War settlement to be a grave injustice, famously lamenting that the Soviet Union's collapse was "a major geopolitical disaster" of the twentieth century.[13] In a February 2007 speech at the Munich Security Conference, he decried the prospect of a unipolar world and assigned to Washington much of the blame for global instability, intoning that the United States "has overstepped its national borders in every way. This is visible in the economic, political, cultural, and educational policies it imposes on other nations."[14]

Even if Russia does hope to reestablish an empire that encompasses the former Soviet Union's territory, it would be hard-pressed to do so. NATO has steadily expanded its membership since the end of the Cold War, and Moscow is now flanked on its immediate west by three members—Estonia, Latvia, and Lithuania. President Putin stated in mid-2015 that "only an insane person . . . can imagine that Russia would suddenly attack NATO."[15] It is more plausible that Moscow would seek to annex additional territories in non-NATO European countries with significant ethnic Russian populations.

Many observers of Russian foreign policy are of the view that its principal objectives are, first, to establish an informal but clear sphere of influence, which could theoretically furnish a buffer against external security challenges, and, second, to achieve recognition as a great power. Seva Gunitsky argues that this second objective—sometimes referred to as a desire for *derzhavnost* (great-power status)—is central to Russia's ambitions; it "essentially means both being a great power and being recognized as such by others."[16] Some observers venture, tellingly, that Moscow need not contribute to the postwar order's modernization to realize that goal. Indeed, Russia could affirm its importance by declining to participate in that effort. Nikolas Gvosdev explains that Moscow conceptualizes the belief in its "indispensability" in "negative terms—namely, that the absence of Russian help, even if that assistance is small in comparison to what others are providing, will preclude success."[17]

Strategic Opportunism

Few observers would deny that Russia has demonstrated a considerable capacity to challenge US national interests. In January 2017, along with Turkey and Iran, it initiated the Astana peace process in Syria, where Assad clings to power over a devastated country. In December of that same year, it concluded a deal to sell two batteries of its S-400 missile defense system to Turkey, which has the second-largest army of NATO member countries. Alongside enduring tensions between the United States and Europe over the provision of collective defense and the management of tensions with Russia, frictions between Washington and Ankara are an increasingly glaring challenge for NATO. Despite an initial threat of US sanctions as well as reservations that many fellow EU members continue to maintain, Germany will proceed with the completion of Nord Stream 2, a roughly 760-mile pipeline that will supply Russian natural gas to Europe. Similarly, despite intense US pressure, India agreed in October 2018 to buy five S-400 batteries from Russia. The reach of intrusions such as the SolarWinds hack—widely attributed to Russia, but believed to have been launched from inside the United States—indicates how difficult it will be to establish, let alone reinforce, norms around cyber restraint. To offer one last example, Moscow is contributing to the global recovery from COVID-19 in a way that few observers had anticipated, an outcome that gives it potential strategic leverage in recipient countries. Theresa Fallon contends that the Sputnik V vaccine might enable it to shift its reputation from that of "a pariah state after the annexation of Crimea" to that of "a vaccine provider and 'liberator' from the pandemic."[18]

The extent to which these lines of effort constitute a strategic vision, though, is less clear. It is notable that President Putin used to speak more ambitiously when outlining his vision for Russia's place in world affairs. A little over a decade ago, he called for the establishment of "a Eurasian Union," which he imagined as "a powerful supranational association capable of becoming one of the poles in the modern world and serving as an efficient bridge between Europe and the dynamic Asia-Pacific region."[19] But western sanctions, a net decline in oil prices, and military adventurism have collectively limited Russia's capacity to serve in this intermediary role. At least right now, on balance, its strategic prospects do not appear especially auspicious.[20] Its relationship with the United States continues to deteriorate. Its ties with the European Union, while perhaps not as poor, are increasingly strained. And its attempt to "pivot" eastward has yielded mixed results, leaving it increasingly dependent upon its ties with China to certify its great-power status.

The previous chapter noted that assessments of China's foreign policy tend to oscillate between extremes. Some observers depict China as a calculating and ruthless juggernaut that bends the arc of history in its favor; others cast it as an impatient and insular power that will eventually prove unable to reconcile the character of its governance to the realities of globalization. One encounters equally unhelpful dualities in appraisals of Russia's conduct: on the one hand, a strategic grandmaster whose tentacles are stealthy yet ubiquitous; on the other, a decaying power whose maneuvers are clumsy and disjointed.

Robert Person contends that "we should neither minimize nor mythologize Putin's strategic abilities. Rather, we should recognize that he is a strategic opportunist."[21] Russia has proven nimble in asserting influence despite a continued decline in its relations with the United States and increasingly fraught ties with the European Union. Still, one should distinguish between agility and foresight. If one accepts Samuel Huntington's proposition that the mark of a great power is its capacity for self-renewal, then Moscow has significant foundational work to undertake. The *Financial Times* reported in early 2021 that real disposable income in Russia had fallen for five out of seven years between 2014 and 2020 and that Moscow's per capita GDP was 30 percent lower than it had been in 2013.[22] Russia has not implemented the kinds of economic reforms that would bolster its private sector, enhance its innovative capacity, or slow the pace of capital outflows. Nor does it appear to have made sufficient preparations for the world's transition away from hydrocarbons.[23]

Compounding its domestic woes, it has created headaches for itself abroad. For starters, its 2014 incursion into Ukraine has made an enemy of the very country whose deference Moscow has long seen as essential to its position as a great power. Whatever cultural significance Crimea may have to President Putin, it is proving to be an economic burden. And in Central Asia, which is Moscow's putative background, Beijing is increasingly overtaking it as the principal source of trade and investment.

Moving further afield, a widespread narrative holds that Russia, having exploited the Obama administration's concern over further US entanglement in the Middle East so as to insinuate itself, is now a decisive diplomatic player in that region. A more plausible appraisal is that Moscow is struggling to safeguard Soviet-era partnerships. While its support for Assad has enabled it to test new weaponry and to gain more of a foothold in the Middle East, Syria has incurred such sweeping devastation over the past decade that Russia's intervention could prove to be an economic liability; indeed, Robert Ford, the former US ambassador to Syria, believes the Russians "have a large dead albatross hung around their necks."[24] In Libya, similarly, while Russia is an important external actor, it is hardly the only one; it has worked to bolster warlord Khalifa Haftar, but Turkey has supported Haftar's opponents in the Tripoli-based Government of National Accord. Anxieties that Russia will emerge as a kingpin in the Middle East if and as the United States rebalances toward the Asia-Pacific are overwrought. If it is far-fetched to believe that the United States can control a region that is riven by so many overlapping sources of instability—civil wars in Syria, Libya, and Yemen; an Islamic State that continues to wreak havoc; and volatile oil prices—it should strain credulity at least as much to imagine that a far less powerful country could achieve such control.

Similarly, when weighing assessments that Russia is stealing a march on the United States in, say, sub-Saharan Africa or Latin America, it is essential to identify the baseline from which Moscow seeks to bolster its footprint and to consider the range of obstacles it might confront. The complexities of contemporary geopolitics should disabuse any country of the belief that it can singlehandedly dominate a given region, let alone achieve global hegemony. In brief, if it is analytically unjustified and diplomatically imprudent to dismiss Russia's impact, it is at least as counterproductive to exaggerate it; neither condescension nor aggrandizement is advisable. The tendency toward the latter seems to have grown in recent years, Moscow's interference in America's 2016 presidential election having played a pivotal role in elevating Putin's apparent influence: "There wasn't an election he didn't hack, a border he wouldn't violate, or an American ally he couldn't manipulate."[25]

Russian attempts to propagate disinformation go back roughly a century, and there is every reason to believe that they will become more sophisticated. Exposing them will continue to be an essential task for the United States. So, too, though, will be maintaining a sense of perspective. Given how widespread the assumption is among US observers that the Russian government or government-supported actors are behind disinformation campaigns that divide Americans, Moscow would probably not have to expend much extra effort to inflame societal fissures within the United States; indeed, it might not have to do anything. Joshua Yaffa explains that the Kremlin "merely needs to gently stir the informational pot. Or to let others think that it has ... If the goal is disruption and confusion, then being seen to affect outcomes is as good as actually affecting outcomes."[26] It is difficult, if not impossible, to isolate the causal impact of Russian disinformation efforts on the phenomenon of political polarization in the United States. But the *perceived* impact arguably matters far more: "Regardless of the potency of its measurable output," observes Jon Allsop, "Russia has undoubtedly planted itself in the American psyche as a big threat."[27] Indeed, a recent report notes that in 2017 the Kremlin-backed Internet Research Agency initiated "a sustained effort to exaggerate the specter of its interference."[28] If Moscow can take up permanent residence in Washington's consciousness, it will have registered a significant achievement in its quest to amplify existing US divisions.

That accomplishment would further distract the United States from the proximate sources of its cacophonous information environment. Richard Stengel, former undersecretary for public diplomacy and public affairs, contends that most of the disinformation to which Americans are exposed is generated domestically. More concerningly, he notes that that disinformation is in high demand.[29] Complicating matters, the open marketplace of ideas, which is so integral to democratic societies, is also an efficient transmission belt for disinformation. This reality creates a dilemma for the United States: is there any way to bolster the resilience of that marketplace without compromising its essence? Emily Bazelon ventures that the chief challenge to democratic discourse comes not from government censorship but from "the mass distortion of truth and overwhelming waves of speech from extremists that smear and distract."[30]

Even if the United States were able to implement a technological solution that blocked the entry of all foreign-generated disinformation, it is doubtful that America's internecine political infighting would disappear. Fiona Hill laments that "[t]he Russians don't have to do a thing." She warns that, "[i]f we can't heal our own divisions, then we're going to be exploited from here to eternity, and our allies will be turning away in horror."[31] Hill's conclusion raises a distressing question: if Americans of different ideological persuasions increasingly come to regard one another as mortal enemies rather than fellow travelers even without Russia's having to exert any further effort, how sustainable are US democracy and its core institutions? The United States will undermine its path to domestic renewal if it uses the specter of external subversion to avoid a reckoning with largely self-inflicted divisions.[32]

An Incremental Escape from the Security Dilemma

Though it may be counterproductive to overstate the success of Russia's foreign policy or the impact of its disinformation operations, it is unsurprising that Washington is not greatly inclined to cooperate with Moscow. Russia has hived off territory along its periphery, most recently when it annexed Crimea in 2014. In April 2021 it stoked US fears of a flare-up in the conflict between Moscow-backed separatists and Ukrainian forces by massing 80,000 to 100,000 troops along its border with Kiev. It interfered in America's 2016 and 2020 presidential elections, seeking not so much to privilege particular points of view as to incite Americans on different sides of contentious issues to attack each other more forcefully. It supports disintegrationist elements within the European Union, hoping to dilute the strength of transatlantic ties still further. It bolsters a vicious regime in Syria. And, to cite just one further reason for US disillusionment, it was strongly implicated in the murder of the opposition leader Boris Nemtsov in February 2015 and in the extraterritorial poisonings of Sergei Skripal in March 2018 and Alexei Navalny in August 2020.

Russia nurses its own grievances. It contends that Washington humiliated Moscow in the aftermath of the Cold War by treating it as a defeated pariah rather than a still great power, and it maintains that the United States continues to speak about Russia's material assets and strategic outlook in derogatory terms. It also alleges that Washington reneged on early 1990s promises to halt NATO's expansion, argues that the bombing of Kosovo by NATO forces in 1999 contravened international law, and believes that the United States is trying to destabilize Russia by supporting "color revolutions" and other democratic movements.

Against this backdrop, Charles Ziegler concludes that the two countries are now in a deeply entrenched security dilemma.[33] Few observers have high hopes for amicable US–Russia relations, even as some hope that Washington and Moscow may eventually find common cause in counterbalancing Beijing.[34] For now, the question is whether they can prevent their ties from deteriorating indefinitely and establish a foundation that facilitates modest cooperation.

Considering that the United States and the Soviet Union were able to register cooperative achievements despite regarding each other as existential adversaries—they inked arms control agreements, established hotlines and other arrangements to prevent encounters between their military forces from escalating, and even pooled resources to fund research into a smallpox vaccine—it should not be beyond the capacity of Washington and Moscow to do so today, especially given that their strategic competition does not rise to a comparable level of intensity. Indeed, the United States and Russia have partnered on several occasions in recent years, negotiating New START; stabilizing the Northern Distribution Network, which supplied US troops in Afghanistan; and working with the other members of the UN Security Council to move the Joint Comprehensive Plan of Action across the finish line. Today, even if one believes that cooperative possibilities are few or that pursuing them is a fool's errand, the United States will continue to depend upon Russia to achieve its own national interests:

> We must avoid the risk of inadvertent nuclear war, achieve the responsible use of both space and cyberspace, enhance European security by diminishing the chance of military conflict, manage China's rise, and take steps to address the destabilizing effects of climate change. If we limit our attention to the Russia challenge, then we will obscure or overlook these other stakes and deny ourselves the chance to improve US national security by making progress on them.[35]

It is encouraging, then, that President Biden and President Putin agreed to reinstate their respective countries' ambassadors and underscored the importance of "strategic stability" at their June 2021 summit, committing to continued discussions around arms control and cyber restraint. While those outcomes might seem minor at first blush, they acquire greater significance within the context of a great-power relationship in free fall. Serge Schmemann wrote before the summit that "simply getting together and demonstrating a readiness to give real diplomacy a chance . . . would be mission accomplished."[36] Even incremental steps to stabilize bilateral ties and lay the groundwork for further dialogue are welcome—and essential.

Russia as "Hurricane" and China as "Climate Change"

The extent to which the United States will succeed in placing its relationship with Russia on a more predictable footing will depend in part on the trajectory of Russia's relationship with China. If Moscow assesses that it is more likely to cement its great-power status by strengthening ties with Beijing than by pursuing a détente with Washington, it may not invest as much in strategic stability with the latter. If, however, it comes to believe that an increasingly asymmetric relationship with Beijing has rendered it intolerably vulnerable to economic coercion, it might recalibrate its present course. The latter scenario seems unlikely for now; on the contrary, Washington is expressing growing concern over the progression of Sino-Russian ties.

Indeed, the 2017 national security strategy and the 2018 national defense strategy often present China and Russia in tandem—a juxtaposition that makes sense at first blush. While the two are far from being ideological clones, both are authoritarian bulwarks that consider the diffusion of democratic governance a challenge to their sovereignty. Both believe that the Soviet Union's dissolution birthed an unfairly lopsided strategic balance—one that, while less skewed three decades on, is still too US-centric. Both regard US alliances as instruments of containment. Both think that the global financial system relies too heavily upon the greenback. And the list of shared grievances could easily be extended.

But, because the challenge that Russia poses to US national interests is substantially different from the one presented by China, it is important for Washington not to group them together—even as it notes similarities between their worldviews and monitors trends in their collaboration. A growing number of observers fear that Beijing can and will emerge as a peer competitor to Washington on its own. That assessment suggests that the growing US focus on great-power competition would likely exist even if Russia were to disappear. It is uncertain that the reverse would obtain: if China were to disappear, Washington would be unlikely to consider Moscow, on its own, a sufficiently potent competitor to warrant that kind of focus, even as managing relations with Russia would remain an essential element of US foreign policy. As Fyodor Lukyanov explains, "the clash between Moscow and Washington is not central to the international system, which is polycentric, chaotic, and diverse."[37]

Despite enduring concerns over the possibility of an armed confrontation between American and Russian military forces, especially in the Baltics, defense planners are shifting their attention to China. Before General James McConville assumed his role as US army chief of staff, his transition team advised him that China would overtake Russia as the more pressing competitor to the United States between 2028 and 2035 and accordingly recommended that the army "[deter] Russia in the near term with a 'good enough' force in Europe, while investing in the long-term requirements against the larger threat in Asia."[38]

In addition, Moscow has far less capacity than Beijing to win global influence through trade and investment partnerships. Nor is there much evidence that Russian ideology has widespread global appeal, or that Moscow seeks to export a particular vision of world affairs. When it adduces America's domestic woes as evidence of democratic decay, it cannot credibly cite its own internal performance as a compelling alternative. China, by contrast, can increasingly do so, on account of several factors: the rate of growth it continues to achieve despite continued prognostications of a hard landing or a sustained slowdown; the resilience it has demonstrated in weathering two of this century's greatest systemic shocks—the global financial crisis and the pandemic; and the extent to which it drives global innovation. Even if the governance that China practices has little chance of boosting its ideological appeal significantly beyond its own borders, the performance it registers does.

On balance, while Russia is a major power with ample capacity to contest US national interests, it is unlikely to prove a systemic rival.

China is more likely to do so, because its economic heft and techno-logical capacity enable it to make inroads even in countries that have serious and growing misgivings about its strategic intentions. It is for this reason that some observers compare Russia's foreign policy to "a hurricane," while China's looks more like "climate change": the former characterization bespeaks discrete disruptions while the latter connotes overarching challenges.[39] Those analogies also point to dif-ferences in how the two countries work to contest the United States. In February 2020 a member of the Federal Bureau of Investigation's Foreign Influence Task Force assessed that "Russia wants to watch us tear ourselves apart, while it seems that China would rather manage our gradual economic decline over the course of generations."[40] A little over a year later, the Office of the Director of National Intelligence (ODNI) issued a report on foreign interference in the 2020 presidential election, offering additional insights into the distinctions between the two countries' respective efforts. Moscow, it explained, likely "assess[es] that continued influence operations against the United States pose a manageable risk to Russia's image in Washington because US–Russia relations are already extremely poor." China, by contrast, "did not view either election outcome as being advantageous enough for China to risk blowback if caught [deploying interference efforts]."[41]

Geopolitical climate change is a formidable problem, as are geopo-litical hurricanes, though patient, confident US diplomacy is capable of managing both. Prevalent conceptualizations of great-power competi-tion run the risk of overstating the challenges that China and Russia individually pose to US national interests. They also risk intensifying one of the phenomena US observers have long regarded as potentially most inimical to those interests: a sustained expansion of Sino-Russian ties.

The Improbability of Wedges

Zbigniew Brzezinski posited in 1997 that, for the United States, "the most dangerous scenario would be . . . an 'antihegemonic' coalition united not by ideology but by complementary grievances. It would be reminiscent in scale and scope of the challenge once posed by the Sino-Soviet bloc, though this time China would likely be the leader and Russia the follower."[42] Many Eurasianists fear that a Sino-Russian entente would be more powerful than the sum of its constituents and express concern that Moscow's support could amplify Beijing's capacity to emerge as a peer competitor. Indeed, a recent report concludes that their symbiosis "will be most problematic in the way that it increases the challenge that China poses to the United States," especially inasmuch as it bolsters Beijing's deterrence capacity in the Asia-Pacific and amplifies China's narrative about the failings of democratic governance.[43]

Sino-Russian relations gained significant momentum after Russia's incursion into Crimea, for Moscow had to contend not only with western sanctions but also with turbulence in global energy markets; the price of crude oil plummeted from roughly $120 per barrel in June 2014 to under $60 at the end of the year and, despite rebounding briefly, it fell to around $40 by the end of 2015.[44] Moscow felt compelled to strengthen economic ties with Beijing. Beijing, in turn, discerned an opportunity to secure concessions on imports of energy and arms.

But the Sino-Russian rapprochement began in earnest a quarter-century earlier. Because Washington's opening to Beijing had largely been predicated upon its desire to counterbalance Moscow, the disintegration of the Soviet Union weakened a pillar of the emerging US–China relationship and created new possibilities for cooperation between China and Russia. The end of the Cold War, of course, was a humiliating episode for Russia, which underwent economic and social upheaval throughout the 1990s. The outcome also unnerved China, whose leadership continues to study the confluence of factors that led to it. Near the end of 2000, Evan Feigenbaum observed that China and Russia "share a deepening conviction that a principled stand against certain core American strategic concepts will give them the high ground against the United States."[45]

Two decades on, the United States' relationship with China is at its lowest point since the two countries initiated normalization in 1979, and the United States' relationship with Russia is at its lowest point since the end of the Cold War. At the beginning of 2019, a report by the ODNI assessed that Sino-Russian alignment had reached its highest level since the mid-1950s, warning that "the relationship is likely to strengthen . . . as some of their interests and threat perceptions converge, particularly regarding perceived US unilateralism and interventionism and Western promotion of democratic values and human rights."[46] Concerningly, both US–China relations and US–Russia relations continue to deteriorate.

The fatalistic interpretation of this reality is that those declines were inevitable; as the United States awakened to the realities of great-power competition and pushed back more forcefully against efforts by Beijing and Moscow to subvert the postwar order, it would inevitably trigger retaliation. Had Washington been more attuned to their synergy in the immediate aftermath of the Cold War, the thinking goes, it might have been able to slow the development of that phenomenon. In truth, some level of Sino-Russian convergence would probably have occurred regardless of what course of foreign policy the United States had pursued in the 1990s; the degree of preponderance that Washington had inherited through the implosion of its erstwhile antagonist gave both countries a powerful structural incentive to pursue closer ties.

Still, it behooves the United States to consider how its present orientation might provide additional succor to those ties: there is an intrinsic tension between a framework that explicitly presents China and Russia as America's two chief competitors and a hope that Washington can drive a wedge between the two. Angela Stent warns that "the twin US policies of sanctioning Russia and pursuing a trade war with China have pushed the two countries closer together."[47] There is also a risk that Washington will adduce the progressing entente between Beijing and Moscow as evidence that it needs to adopt further confrontational policies toward both. Such a decision, though, would impart greater momentum to Sino-Russian relations, compounding US insecurity.

Observers occasionally encourage the United States to try to pry apart the two countries. They venture that Washington might be able to execute a variant of the "triangular diplomacy" pursued by the Nixon administration during the 1970s. At that time Washington was indeed favorably positioned to orchestrate such a maneuver, not only because it was far more powerful than either Beijing or Moscow but also because there was an alignment of strategic interests: the United States discerned an opportunity to buttress its campaign of containment, while China, bristling at the Soviet Union's depiction of it as an inferior, relished the prospect of bolstering its perceived power—what Gilpin called prestige.

Today, though, both Beijing and Moscow increasingly believe that Washington is a superpower in structural decline and that it seeks to slow the shift to a more multipolar system while it still has a preponderant share of global power. The strength of that shared conviction would militate against attempts to hive one country off from the other. As a senior Biden administration official observed in June 2021, both countries "are highly attentive to efforts to create tension or to split them, and they are very focused on what . . . both perceive is the larger, menacing problem, and that is the United States."[48]

Begin with China. It has not sought a military alliance with Russia. Nor has it hesitated to stoke Moscow's anxieties—whether by sending migrant workers into Russia's sparsely populated Far East, by asserting itself economically in Central Asia, or by stealing military-focused Russian intellectual property. Even so, it has no strategic interest in weakening its relationship with a reliable supplier of energy and arms. Indeed, the more the economic imbalance between China and Russia favors the former, the more leverage China will have to secure favorable terms on those imports.

For its part, Russia would have to make at least two assessments: that an increasingly asymmetric economic relationship with China had become a net strategic liability; and that there was a plausible path to a détente with the United States that could, over time, develop into a durable and constructive relationship. It does not appear to have reached either conclusion. Some observers of US–Russia relations had initially thought that the Trump administration's arrival might encourage Moscow to contemplate a recalibration of its approach to Washington. President Trump himself, after all, was in favor of relaxing tensions with Russia, and he seemed to enjoy a personal rapport with President Putin. But he faced strong pushback from Congress, as well as from prominent members of his own administration. Nor could he overcome structural tensions between Washington and Moscow—tensions that are growing in number and severity.

Were Russia to pursue a warmer relationship with the United States in the interest of counterbalancing China, it would confront a double risk. First, Washington's apprehensions about Beijing might not prove sufficient to counteract its suspicions of Moscow. Second, China could punish Russia for defying its senior partner. Although its calculus may change over time, Moscow presently has little incentive to endanger its ties with the motor of global growth and the linchpin of global trade.

Nor does President Putin seem inclined to jeopardize a deepening entente that is arguably his foremost strategic achievement.[49]

Until perhaps President Putin's aforementioned speech at the Munich Security Conference, it seemed that Russia might still envision a future primarily dependent on, or at least related to, reintegration with the West, however much it inveighed against US efforts to promote democracy and against NATO expansion. But it seems to have gradually come to the view that it can more effectively cement its status as a central power by riding the coattails of China's resurgence, putting aside the indignities of an increasingly asymmetric partnership. Consequently, most observers of Sino-Russian relations are skeptical that the United States will be able to loosen the two countries' embrace. Stephen Hadley and Paula Dobriansky predict that turning Russia against China would be "difficult if not impossible to execute in practice."[50] A team of scholars at the Carnegie Endowment for International Peace goes further, asserting that "any notion that the United States could drive a wedge between the two countries . . . represents magical thinking."[51]

A Limited Entente

Even so, Sino-Russian relations are not guaranteed to go from strength to strength. For starters, the two countries have a troubled history. Some accounts of their difficulties begin in the late 1850s, when a declining Qing Dynasty was midway through two struggles. It was trying to suppress a rebellion of the Taiping Heavenly Kingdom—a conflict that left some 20 million dead from war, starvation, and disease and may well rank as the deadliest civil war in history. At the same time, it was struggling to repel incursions from the British and the French empires during the Second Opium War. The 1858 Treaty of Aigun gave Russia the lands on the left bank of the Amur River—lands totaling some 600,000 square kilometers—that the 1689 Treaty of Nerchinsk had designated as Chinese territory.

A century later, rising tensions between the Soviet Union and China triggered their famed split, which nearly culminated in war in 1969. Mao rejected Nikita Khrushchev's criticisms of Joseph Stalin and saw in his promulgation of "peaceful coexistence" with the West an attenuation of Moscow's revolutionary resolve. Khrushchev found Mao to be petulant and reckless and accused China of initiating a border clash with India in 1959 in order to thwart the possibility of a détente between Washington and Moscow. Jeremy Friedman explains that, while the Soviet Union and China shared a commitment to dismantling what they decried as a capitalist–imperialist nexus, they advocated different approaches:

> For the Soviets, the cause of replacing capitalism with socialism would always remain their top priority, and anti-imperialism mattered insofar as it served that greater purpose. For the Chinese, on the other hand, having had more direct experience with the trials and tribulations of imperialism, anti-imperialism remained the guiding focus of the revolutionary process, and socialism was seen as a tool with which to shift the global balance of power through economic development and autarky.[52]

Today, although China and Russia are increasingly vocal in denouncing western-style democracy (and, in China's case, extolling one's own model of governance as well), there are limits to the normative appeal of their entente, in part because their own foreign policies are more transactional than ideological. Whether one considers its COVID-19 "vaccine diplomacy" campaign, the trade and investment agreements it has signed in recent years, or its attempts to build out 5G networks, Beijing seeks to translate its economic heft and technological momentum into enduring influence with countries across the ideological spectrum. Russia, too, interacts with a wide array of countries, aiming to leverage its energy resources and military assets. Indeed, two of its key foreign policy achievements in recent years involve two of the world's leading democracies: the Nord Stream 2 natural gas pipeline is boosting energy ties between Russia and Germany; and the delivery of S-400 units to India that began in late 2021 is strengthening defense ties between Moscow and Delhi. With its Sputnik V vaccine, moreover, Russia contributes to inoculation efforts across Latin America and Africa, and even in Europe. There is a difference between attempting to make strategic inroads on the basis of ideological conviction, as the Soviet Union did during the Cold War, and hoping that transactional diplomacy will create more breathing room for authoritarian norms. If one believes that Sino-Russian relations have growing ideological potency, democratic underperformance offers at least as plausible an explanation as authoritarian appeal.

The two countries also have significantly different approaches to the postwar order. Russia is not embedded to nearly the same degree as China, although it wields important leverage by virtue of being a permanent member of the UN Security Council. It seems to have concluded that it can more effectively accrue influence by exposing the frailties of the order than by contributing to its modernization. It is true, of course, that Beijing does not confine itself to exercising influence within a system that it often avows to be obsolescent. But it is, in parallel, intensifying efforts to achieve greater stature within the postwar order. It is also notable that, while China and Russia hail their partnership in the abstract, they do not reflexively support each other's specific policies; Beijing has yet to endorse Moscow's annexation of Crimea, for example, and Moscow has yet to endorse Beijing's expansive claims in the South China Sea. This calculated reticence belies their outward affinity. Indeed, some observers of Sino-Russian relations aver that China regards Russia's diplomacy as ineffectual on the whole, even blundering, whereas Russia maintains that it is a primarily western power despite its increased focus on the Asia-Pacific. Raffaello Pantucci notes that, in private conversations with US interlocutors, Chinese officials say: "These bloody Russians, look at what they've done in Ukraine—it's a disaster." Russian officials counter: "We don't really trust these Chinese. After all, we're really Europeans."[53]

There are certainly synergies, deliberate and unintentional, between the two countries' conduct. Some reports suggest that China has employed Russian-style disinformation tactics during the pandemic.[54] And, while China will not necessarily endorse Russian military forays, say, in Russia's near abroad or in the Middle East, it can leverage those disruptions to pursue trade and investment opportunities in support of the Belt and Road Initiative.[55] The question is whether growing alignment can ultimately create a sustainable Sino-Russian architecture that counterbalances the postwar order. Thus far there is a considerable gap between the actual impact of the two countries' entente and its theorized potential; Bobo Lo ventures that it is unclear "whether the Sino-Russian partnership can develop into a more cohesive and influential force in international politics, or whether the current modus operandi between Beijing and Moscow—bilateral cooperation along-side separate foreign policies—will continue indefinitely."[56]

One reason why the entente may not evolve beyond its present configuration is the principally negative character of the relationship: it is defined more by that which it opposes than by that which it espouses. While it vocally denounces what it believes to be a US-dominated order, the parameters of the more multipolar, less normatively western system it would prefer remain vague (and even many close US allies and partners would not object to the first element, greater multipolarity). Another constraint could come from Russian anxiety, even resentment. John Pomfret observes that, while bilateral relations have steadily pro-gressed, "Russia has also chafed under the impression that it is now the junior partner in its relations with Beijing . . . Chinese called Russia 'big brother' [in the 1950s]. Now they jokingly call it 'big sister.'"[57] China's GDP was roughly four times as large as Russia's in 2010 ($6.1 trillion vs. $1.5 trillion). It was more than eight times as large by the end of the decade ($14.3 trillion vs. $1.7 trillion).[58] While China recovered quickly from the pandemic, Russia entered into a recession. There is some evidence that this disparity has heightened Moscow's unease over its relationship with Beijing. Early on during COVID-19, Andrew Higgins observed that the crisis had dented "China's image as a benign force from which Russia can only reap benefit. This is slowly being eclipsed by anxiety over China's new, unwelcome role as a source of disease, agonizing uncertainty, and frustrated hopes."[59] And two papers by prominent Russian observers—one by Sergey Karaganov, another by Sergey Dubinin and Yevgeni Savostyanov—have called on Moscow to formulate a more balanced foreign policy, one that should reflect both the unlikelihood of a constructive relationship with Washington and the threat of growing supplication to Beijing.[60]

Thus far Russia appears to have accommodated itself to the reality of its subordinate status. Yet Beijing understands well Moscow's desire to be seen as a great power, and Chinese officials speak of Sino-Russian relations in increasingly soaring terms. In June 2019 President Xi him-self went so far as to exclaim that President Putin is his "best friend and colleague."[61] If, however, China eventually dispenses with such flattery—whether because the economic asymmetry between Beijing and Moscow surpasses a certain threshold or because relations between the two presidents' successors are not as friendly—Russia might not see fit to accept this status quietly. Artyom Lukin ventures that, while Sino-Russian relations may well deepen over the short to medium run, it is possible to imagine a longer-run scenario in which China overreaches and offends Russia's sensibilities: "The post-Xi generation of the Chinese elite could well develop a superiority complex toward Russia and refuse to treat it as an equal partner . . . If Moscow, out of its great-power pride, insists on full political equality with China, that could rupture the Russia–China axis."[62] While Russia accords singular priority to upgrading its relationship with China, it is also boosting defense ties with India and Vietnam, two countries that have territorial disputes with Beijing.

A Chronic Condition

Most observers intuitively appreciate the strategic import of deepening Sino-Russian relations, but distilling the essence of this partnership can be challenging. Here are just some of the phrases used to characterize it: "Faustian bargain," "uneasy truce," "axis of convenience," "friendship by geopolitical necessity," "opportunistic mésalliance," "morganatic marriage," and "axis of authoritarians."[63] Today's Sino-Russian relationship may not have the potency of an alliance. But it is no longer burdened by the rigidity of such an arrangement either. Sergey Radchenko notes that the two parties are now "free to disagree, something that was certainly lacking in the 1950s, when any disagreement was perceived as China's challenge to the Soviet authority."[64] Dmitri Trenin adds that they "continue to prefer the 'never-against-each-other-but-not-always-with-each-other' formula for Sino-Russian ties. This formula conveniently combines reassurance with flexibility . . . and eschews the tricky issue of hierarchy."[65]

Even though the relationship defies simplistic formulations, it proceeds with a clear momentum. In July 2017 the two countries' navies conducted a joint exercise in the Baltic Sea for the first time. In September 2018, marking another first, China participated in Russia's annual Vostok military exercise. In December 2019, pursuant to their May 2014 agreement, the two countries opened a pipeline that is scheduled to deliver 38 billion cubic meters of natural gas to China annually by 2024. A year later they conducted a joint patrol mission over the East China and Japan Seas—just two months after President Putin had stated that "it is quite possible to imagine" a military alliance between the countries.[66]

There is probably little that the United States can do in the short term to slow the progression of Sino-Russian ties. There are, however, steps it should consider taking that could have a salutary effect in the medium to long term. First, it should avoid giving the impression that it views Beijing and Moscow as a unified entity—especially in high-profile documents such as the NSS and the NDS, which play an important role not only in shaping the remits of agencies across the government but also in conveying to international audiences the broad brushstrokes of US foreign policy thinking and priorities. The more Washington stresses that juxtaposition, the more it risks intensifying the very entente whose progression it has long sought to slow.

Second, without indulging in any wishful thinking about the possibility of a "new model" of great-power relations with Beijing or about the prospect of a reset with Moscow, Washington should affirm that it is not resigned to an indefinite deterioration of ties with either of them. It should discuss with each a set of incremental confidence-building measures whose cumulative weight could pave the way for considering parallel, reciprocal steps to ease strategic tensions. It should impress upon China and Russia the extent to which an ongoing trilateral dialogue will be essential to the fulfillment of their respective vital national interests. And, finally, it should avail itself of opportunities to embed bilateral diplomacy within multilateral undertakings, which the toxicity of US–China and US–Russia relations is less likely to derail. One reason why agreements such as the JCPOA are so important is that they affirm the ability of great powers to subordinate bilateral frictions to geopolitical opportunities—an ability that, if harnessed, can give them encouraging points of reference when they do turn to bilateral tasks.

Third, while forgoing crude attempts to drive a wedge between the two countries, the United States should not hesitate to acknowledge Russia's concerns over China's long-term strategic intentions. Nadège Rolland ventures that, while China will look for ways to assuage those concerns in the short to medium term, it anticipates that "the accommodation of Russia's needs and fears will only be a transitional phase during which China needs to bide its time: in the long run, Russia will have become a toothless former superpower, surrendering the stage for Beijing to fully assert its own influence over Eurasia."[67] Washington should encourage Moscow to see improved ties with the West as an escape hatch of sorts that can prevent it from becoming overly beholden to Beijing's strategic dictates.[68] It should also remind Russia that China has done little to ease Moscow's concerns. Beijing is now the predominant economic power in Central Asia, a region that Russia considers to fall within its proper sphere of influence, and the withdrawal of US forces from Afghanistan could give China greater room to contest that orbit. Meanwhile, even though conjectures that China will eventually colonize Russia's Far East are overwrought, there is some evidence that Moscow is looking to preempt such an outcome and that, perhaps in part as a result of cultural prejudice, some Russian residents of that region are wary of China's growing economic footprint there.[69]

Although the Sino-Russian entente is likely to remain a chronic condition for US foreign policy, the United States need not regard it as an insuperable threat. While ties between China and Russia are indeed becoming more multifaceted and sophisticated, it is unclear whether they can represent themselves as an authoritarian axis possessing widespread ideological appeal. Nor can one readily discern how they would operationalize their preferred vision of world order, assuming they even have such a conception. In April 1997, China's and Russia's presidents declared: "No country should seek hegemony, practice power politics, or monopolize international affairs."[70] That the two countries' current leaders could easily have penned such a statement today suggests that their relationship remains more rooted in articulations of what they condemn than in affirmations of what they champion. If the United States demonstrates anew its ability to address its own socioeconomic fissures, it could help counter the narrative of authoritarian ascendance. And if it works more assiduously with its allies and partners to construct a more resilient post-pandemic order, it could place China and Russia on the defensive; whereas Beijing and Moscow are presently fixated on the deficiencies of the current architecture, they might instead feel nervous about losing global influence if they do not support that affirmative undertaking.

6

Seizing America's Great-Power Opportunity

At no other point since the end of the Cold War has the United States had a more urgent imperative—or a more compelling opportunity—to reimagine its role in world affairs: amid a devastating pandemic that spotlights the deficiencies and challenges the foundations of the postwar order, many of its friends question whether it can serve as a stable power, let alone as an exemplar of democracy. And, in turn, this imperative-cum-opportunity has given rise to a newly vigorous debate over the grand strategies and overarching concepts that should shape US foreign policy.

With some notable exceptions, recent years have solidified a broad, bipartisan assessment that great-power competition should be the dominant framework.[1] There is great appeal—narrative, analytical, and prescriptive—in succinct conceptualizations such as "containment" and "global war on terrorism," which seek to bring a chaotic world into sharper focus. And great-power competition does spotlight a core set of strategic dynamics: China's resurgence, Russia's disruptions, and Sino-Russian relations are all increasingly salient.

China is narrowing America's margin of military preeminence in the Asia-Pacific. It is the most formidable economic and technological challenger the United States has confronted. And the more the Chinese Communist Party demonstrates its effectiveness in managing domestic crises and overseeing robust growth, the more it could undercut the attractiveness of America's democratic example. Russia, while a pale shadow of the Soviet Union, has overcome the economic trauma it endured in the 1990s, and its armed forces have improved substantially since its brief conflict with Georgia in 2008. Its ongoing hacking campaigns demonstrate that its cyber offensive capabilities are growing apace, and it benefits from a widespread presumption in Washington that Moscow is either conducting or abetting many of the disinformation campaigns that divide Americans. And even if its military forays into countries as disparate as Ukraine and Syria may not accrue long-term strategic dividends, they underscore a capacity to undercut US national interests.

Few observers would disagree that America's relations with China and Russia are growing more competitive. Ties between Washington and Beijing are at their lowest level since normalization, and they continue to deteriorate. Ties between Washington and Moscow are at their lowest level since the end of the Cold War, and they, too, continue to deteriorate. While global stability will require both relationships to evolve into durable forms of competitive cohabitation, there is unfortunately little reason to believe that either one is headed for a détente in the short term.[2] In addition, US observers increasingly fear that deepening Sino-Russian ties could create a formidable authoritarian stronghold that spans Eurasia.

The management of intensifying strategic tensions with China and Russia, then, will be essential to the conduct of US foreign policy. But centering America's role in the world around that undertaking is problematic, above all because it risks subordinating affirmative planning to defensive reactions. It is important to reiterate here a distinction this book has attempted to stipulate—namely between great-power competition as phenomenon and as framework, as description and as prescription. Great powers do compete, of course, and relative US decline means that China and Russia can contest US national interests more forcefully. In the absence of further specification, though, the observation that strategic tensions are intensifying does little to illuminate how the United States should navigate them. It instead pressures Washington to challenge Beijing and Moscow comprehensively and continuously, making it believe—or perhaps fear—that it can sustain a certain baseline of strategic competitiveness only by engaging in an all-consuming struggle. But this kind of contestation is unlikely to restore the degree of preeminence Washington enjoyed in the immediate aftermath of the Cold War, or to mobilize a coalition of allies and partners that exhibit a uniformly urgent approach to great-power competition. William Burns, now director of the CIA, explains that the United States will no longer have a "singular unifying purpose of competition" or a "singular unrivaled position of strength."[3] US foreign policy should proceed not from irretrievable imbalances or implausible futures, but from dispassionate appraisals such as Burns's.

The more Washington bases its foreign policy upon responses to Beijing's and Moscow's present actions and inferences about their future conduct, the more it will cede to them the strategic initiative. China and Russia are acutely aware of the psychological burden the United States bears. Any leading power would, of course, experience anxiety while observing its relative decline. In America's case, that inbuilt distress is compounded by two factors: the conviction with which it avows its own exceptionalism; and the reality that its two chief competitors challenge its conception of modernity—a conception that the end of the Cold War seemed to have vindicated.

In her account of the peaceful transition between London and Washington, Kori Schake notes that "Great Britain was the society most like America in the nineteenth and early twentieth centuries, sharing related populations, common history, similar language, political philosophies that emerged from the European enlightenment, and cultures easily accessible to the broad population."[4] But as she chronicles, the passage was highly fraught and contingent, notwithstanding this impressive degree of cultural affinity. We are unlikely to witness a power transition between the United States and China—or, more expansively, between the West and a Sino-Russian condominium. Still, the comparative absence of that affinity in Washington's relationships with Beijing and Moscow will further complicate the task of managing those two powers.

The United States should fully anticipate that China and Russia will pursue with greater vigor two existing efforts: discrediting its reputation for competent governance; and goading it into contesting them ubiquitously, even when vital US national interests are not implicated— and perhaps especially then. They would like its allies and partners to conclude—and, ultimately, the United States itself to accept—that it is a terminally declining power, internally riven by democratic excess and externally disoriented by strategic anxiety. Washington will have to exercise restraint in face of their baits and prioritize its central task: to invest anew in its unique competitive advantages, articulating a vision that is anchored more in the world it seeks to realize than in the competitors it seeks to thwart. The rest of this final chapter offers eight principles that the United States should keep in mind as it seeks to reposition itself abroad and rebuild itself at home.

Eight Principles to Inform US Foreign Policy

PRINCIPLE 1   Prioritize the renewal of the United States' unique competitive advantages

I swam competitively as a kid. When I joined one of my hometown teams, our coach gave all the new young swimmers some advice that, in retrospect, applies far beyond the pool. She told us to look left and right every now and then during our races to get a sense of where we were in relation to the other swimmers. Yet she warned us that, if we looked left or right every time we came up for air, we would get distracted and lose our forward momentum. Every swimmer has a different style, she continued, so she encouraged us all to focus on developing our own styles each day, working on weaknesses that surfaced but not trying to transform ourselves into other swimmers. While finalizing the draft of this book, I came across an observation made by a champion swimmer that reminded me of my coach's wisdom: Mike Wenden, who won two gold medals for Australia at the 1968 Mexico City Olympics, explained that, "[i]f you let one of your competitors distract you from your focus on yourself, then [that competitor has] won the battle and now ha[s] the edge on you. The very best competitors are the ones who can resist distractions."[5]

Imitation may be the sincerest form of flattery, but it is arguably among the poorest guides to strategy. Insofar as the United States gets distracted, it risks not only undertaking maladroit attempts at emulating its competitors but also signaling to allies and partners that it has lost confidence. Its best bet for positioning itself favorably in relation to China and Russia is to reinvent itself continuously, focusing in the main on harnessing its competitive advantages more fully. This conclusion is not a veiled call for the United States to be insular; it should observe how other countries, allies and competitors alike, are adjusting to their own domestic challenges and external environments, and, if there are lessons it can readily incorporate as it navigates its own difficulties, it should do so. Still, it should resist the temptation it will invariably feel at times to "out-China" China (say, at building brick-and-mortar infrastructure in the developing world) or to "out-Russia" Russia (say, at conducting disinformation operations).

It will be especially challenging, yet imperative, to ignore such temptations in managing a resurgent Beijing, whose economic momentum continues to defy longstanding predictions of stagnation, even of collapse. The United States should respond to this phenomenon by becoming a more dynamic version of its best self. Thus, in a commentary that warns Washington against efforts to replicate Beijing's "military–civil fusion" strategy, which appropriates for government purposes those private sector innovations the CCP deems to have national security utility, John Thornhill observes that one of America's core advantages "lies in invention, innovation, and fierce economic and political competition. That is its greatest national security asset that should never be lost."[6] Similarly, while US infrastructure is indeed in urgent need of repair, the United States would be remiss to follow China's playbook: "China's leapfrogging—practically to bullet trains from bicycles—may have limited direct application to improving American infrastructure. The two nations have different needs and diametrically opposed political systems, starting with carte blanche for Chinese leaders to order up construction."[7] To offer one last example, Federal Reserve Chairman Jerome Powell rightly cautions Washington against rushing to deploy a central bank digital currency simply because Beijing's experiment is generating some interest: "It is far more important to get it right than it is to do it fast. The currency that's being used in China is not one that would work here."[8]

There is a more prosaic reason for Washington to pursue an asymmetric strategy, one whose principal thrust is to refresh core US competitive advantages: the United States has limited leverage to shape how China and Russia behave, particularly when it acts alone and those two countries believe that certain of their vital national interests are at stake. The United States does, however, have full control over what it does and does not do.

While some of its competitive advantages are largely inbuilt, for instance its geography, few are guaranteed to last; the United States must work to preserve them. One such advantage is immigration, which has been essential to US innovation in the postwar era. Just consider the fight against COVID-19. One of the world's most efficacious vaccines resulted from a partnership between Pfizer, whose CEO was born in Greece, and the German biotechnology company BioNTech, two of whose star scientists are children of Turkish immigrants to Germany. Another leading vaccine was created by Moderna, whose co-founder and chairman was born in Lebanon to Armenian parents. With their reliance upon mRNA instead of DNA, these breakthroughs could revolutionize vaccine development.

The *Lancet* forecasts that, while China will eclipse the United States in overall economic size by 2035, the latter will have the world's largest gross domestic product again in 2098. It warns, however, that "liberal immigration policies . . . have faced a political backlash in recent years, which threatens the country's potential to sustain population and economic growth."[9] A growing body of evidence, quantitative and anecdotal, suggests that the United States' relative ability to attract immigrants may be diminishing.[10] Of particular concern is the impact of Trump-era restrictions on Chinese students and researchers, who play a vital role in maintaining the country's edge in frontier technologies.[11] Remco Zwetsloot remarks that, in technological competition, "[t]he only thing the US has that China doesn't seem to replicate easily is the ability to attract and retain international talent, whether through universities or through the labor market."[12] His observation underscores how essential it is for the United States to retain this ability.

But immigrants do far more than revitalize the US economy; they affirm the power of the country's narrative, which is rooted in a symbiosis: as the United States enables individuals from around the world to reinvent themselves in their search for greater opportunities, they, in turn, help it reinvent itself in its quest to draw the realities of its politics closer to the rhetoric of its creed.

Another central US advantage is the dollar, which has endured many crises one might reasonably have expected to test its credibility, most recently the pandemic. But several factors could undercut its perch over time. The United States' increasing use of sanctions and other instruments to "weaponize interdependence," for example, worries competitors and friends alike.[13] As China, Russia, and various European countries (and others, too) seek ways of circumventing the dollar with increasing purpose and determination, it stands to reason that their efforts will gradually bear fruit, even if in a limited way. The United States' balance sheet is another concern. Many leading economists expect that US interest rates will remain low indefinitely, and the long-held assumption that ballooning debt would hamper economic growth has diminishing traction.[14] Still, cautions Brian Riedl, "[i]t takes a lot of hubris to risk your solvency on the assumption rates stay unusually low forever."[15] If and as China's economic heft continues growing, one would expect the Chinese renminbi to make strides, even if not in direct proportion. Finally, the rising interest in and proliferation of digital currencies could weaken the dollar's grip.

There could be a substantial lag between a decline in relative US economic heft and a diminution in the dollar's status. Even though the United States' GDP overtook the United Kingdom's in the late nineteenth century, the greenback did not displace the pound as the dominant currency until the 1950s.[16] And there are no plausible rivals to the dollar on the horizon for now. History tells us, though, that no reserve currency retains its status forever.

To offer one final example, the United States benefits enormously from the postwar order's existence. It is important, of course, not to take a blinkered view of that system. Recent interrogations of the "liberal world order" demonstrate that the term is historically fraught and analytically blurry.[17] The United States often made common cause with autocracies in contesting the Soviet Union. While the order became more encompassing over time, it was mainly established by western powers and designed to advance their national interests. What is more, the stability it provided was strained at best; while many observers characterize the Cold War as "the long peace," that period of almost half a century witnessed proxy wars, civil wars, and genocides that exacted a devastating global toll. Today we also know that Washington and Moscow came to the precipice of nuclear calamity on several occasions. In brief, the establishment of a geopolitical order does not imply the existence of orderly geopolitics.

The inadequacies of the present system are sufficiently great in number and acute in character that simply attempting to reboot it would be misguided. So, too, though, would be discarding it; for all its evident frailty, the extent to which it has diffused makes it difficult for other arrangements to get off the ground. However strong a gravitational pull its economy comes to exert, Beijing will find it hard to overtake Washington as the world's leading power if it is unable to construct a compelling alternative and recruit a durable roster of willing participants. Moreover, the postwar order contains many building blocks that encode US influence, ranging from the Bretton Woods institutions to America's longstanding alliances and partnerships. The question is how to rearrange and repurpose them so as to enhance global stability and address transnational challenges more adequately.[18] Finally, without indulging in hyperbole about the postwar order's normative enlightenment, one can acknowledge the significant gains in health and prosperity that that system has facilitated—or at least with which it has been associated. Importantly, outside the United States, the principal beneficiary of its entrenchment has been the United States' foremost competitor, China while Fu Ying has critiqued it as exclusionary and antiquated, she concedes that it "has made great contributions to human progress and economic growth."[19] John Ikenberry accordingly cautions the United States against

> reorient[ing] its grand strategy entirely toward great-power competition. The United States would be forfeiting its unique ideas and capacity for leadership. It would become like China and Russia: just another big, powerful state operating in a world of anarchy, nothing more and nothing less ... In the twentieth century, it alone among the great powers articulated a vision of an open, postimperial world system. More than any other state, it has seen its national interest advanced by promulgating multilateral rules and norms, which amplified and legitimized American power.[20]

PRINCIPLE 2   **Regard the power of America's domestic example not as a supplement to external competitiveness, but as a precondition for it**

John Gaddis argues that the United States prevailed against the Soviet Union because its democratic system was resilient and adaptive: "The country can be no stronger in the world than it is at home. This was the basis for projecting power onto the world scene. We've lost that at home right now."[21] If one were to collapse while running a mile, a physical trainer who encouraged that individual to sign up for a marathon would be irresponsible. If a country seems incapable of addressing its domestic challenges, even its well-wishers abroad would hesitate to support its stewardship of world affairs. There is a good reason why all passengers aboard an aircraft are told to secure their own oxygen masks before trying to assist others should the cabin pressure drop.

The United States has often come under harsh scrutiny for its response to internal crises, among them Hurricane Katrina in 2005 and the macroeconomic downturn of 2008–9. But its initial mismanagement of the pandemic has arguably inspired more consternation abroad than any other phenomenon in this century: the world's only superpower has registered the worst response to the pandemic, at least as measured by absolute numbers of infections and fatalities. Fintan O'Toole commented: "Over more than two centuries, the United States has stirred a very wide range of feelings in the rest of the world: love and hatred, fear and hope, envy and contempt, awe and anger. But there is one emotion that has never been directed towards the US until now: pity."[22]

A country's ability to manage internal crises is only one element in the example it sets for the rest of the world. Another is the capacity it displays over the longer term to heal its socioeconomic fissures, narrowing the gap between the realities it embodies and the ideals it professes. In mid-2020, when the pandemic, a recession, and protests against racial injustice were all convulsing the country, Tom McTague captured a widespread sentiment:

> Even in previous moments of American vulnerability, Washington reigned supreme. Whatever moral or strategic challenge it faced, there was a sense that its political vibrancy matched its economic and military might, that its system and democratic culture were so deeply rooted that it could always regenerate itself. It was as if the very *idea* of America mattered, an engine driving it on whatever other glitches existed under the hood. Now, something appears to be changing. America seems mired, its very ability to rebound in question.[23]

Skepticism of such assessments is understandable, in part because observers within and outside the United States have often questioned the viability of its democracy and the likelihood of its renewal, only for a US renaissance to unfold. The 1960s and the 1970s were an especially vexing time in America's postwar history: they witnessed a spate of high-profile assassinations—John F. Kennedy and Medgar Evers in 1963, Malcolm X in 1965, Robert Kennedy and Martin Luther King, Jr. in 1968; four days of race riots after Dr. King's murder; the killings of four students and the wounding of nine others at an antiwar rally at Kent State University in 1970; growing discontent over involvement in Indochina; the resignation of Richard Nixon in 1974; and a spell of stagflation that lingered into the early 1980s.

In 1975, amid this turbulence, Michel Crozier, Samuel Huntington, and Joji Watanuki co-authored a famous Trilateral Commission report titled *The Crisis of Democracy*, in which they warned that public confidence in democracy and its enabling institutions was declining in Western Europe, the United States, and Japan. The concerns that Huntington expressed in his section of the report have a renewed resonance now: "If American citizens don't trust their government, why should friendly foreigners? . . . The turning inward of American attention and the decline in the authority of American governing institutions are closely related, as both cause and effect, to the relative downturn in American power and influence in world affairs."[24] And in 1979, shortly before President Jimmy Carter gave what came to be known as his "malaise speech," his pollster Patrick Caddell urged him to address the public's "crisis of confidence." Years later, Caddell observed that, "for the first time, we actually got numbers where people no longer believed that the future of America was going to be as good as it was now. And that really shook me, because it was so at odds with the American character."[25]

A core quality of that character, one that has helped the United States reinvent itself throughout numerous periods of domestic trial, is introspectiveness, however halting. Race relations offer a compelling and newly salient example. In early 1947 President Harry Truman observed: "We are learning what loud echoes both our successes and our failures have in every corner of the world . . . When we fail to live together in peace, the failure touches . . . the cause of democracy itself in the whole world."[26] Michael Klarman notes that "Americans did not have to worry about what foreigners thought of their racial practices" during the interwar period; despite having the world's largest economy, the United States was not, after all, the world's leading power and, accordingly, did not elicit commensurate scrutiny. He explains how, nevertheless, after World War II, "as Americans and Soviets competed for the allegiance of a predominantly non-white third world, US race relations acquired international significance."[27] In response to propaganda from Moscow, Washington did not deny the existence of systemic racism within its borders. Instead it rendered Supreme Court decisions such as *Brown vs. Board of Education* (1954), *Bailey vs. Patterson* (1962), and *Loving vs. Virginia* (1967) and passed bills such as the Civil Rights Act (1964), the Voting Rights Act (1965), and the Fair Housing Act (1968), all of which expressed both a willingness to acknowledge its own imperfections and a commitment to redressing them. Each of these accomplishments dealt a blow to Soviet narratives about US democracy.

Today, as China faces growing criticism over its mass internment of Uighurs, it is disingenuously looking to repeat the Soviet Union's ploy. When Beijing adduces Washington's moral blemishes as evidence of hypocrisy, the United States should respond in three ways. First, it should continue to spotlight the range of human rights abuses that occur in China. The latter initially denied, for example, that it ran camps in Xinjiang, but it eventually had to acknowledge their existence in the face of overwhelming evidence. Its insistence that the camps offer "vocational training" is widely derided. The run-up to the 2022 Winter Olympics demonstrates, moreover, that China's human rights record is more and more of a liability—not only diplomatically but perhaps also economically. Second, the United States should continue to call attention to the reality that its civil society vigorously and continuously criticizes the actions of the government and the police. As National Security Advisor Jake Sullivan stated at a high-profile diplomatic summit between US and Chinese officials in March 2021, "a confident country is able to look hard at its own shortcomings and constantly seek to improve."[28] The space for comparable discussions in China, by contrast, is small and shrinking. Third, the United States should strive to address its own moral shortcomings, as it has always done, however imperfectly.

Noting the extent to which America's #MeToo movement and ongoing reckoning with racial injustice have inspired comparable movements far beyond its borders, David Pilling observes that, "despite its evident traumas and failings, the US continues to act as a moral and political touchstone for much of the world."[29] China's crimes against Uighurs have triggered widespread condemnation but, crucially, have not elicited an attendant sense of disappointment; few individuals look to Beijing as a moral exemplar or believe that the CCP would permit civil society to initiate a sustained, free-flowing conversation on the regime's human rights abuses. The same holds for Russia and its repression of political dissidents and Chechens. If the rest of the world were to stop looking to the United States for moral inspiration, one could reasonably conclude that relative US decline has entered into an even more critical phase.

PRINCIPLE 3   Do not use external competition as a crutch when undertaking internal renewal

Dominic Tierney notes that "threats are more effective unifiers than opportunities . . . Psychologists have found that people are more motivated by dangers where there is a responsible agent (like the Soviet Union) rather than impersonal dangers (like global warming)."[30] America's experiences during the twentieth century demonstrate that it can channel competitive anxiety in the service of national renewal; consider the scientific and technological achievements it recorded in responding to Germany during World War II and to the Soviet Union during the Cold War. Against that backdrop, a resurgent China and a revanchist Russia would collectively seem to furnish an opportunity for the United States to revisit a tested playbook and overcome its strategic drift. Evan Osnos explains: "To some in Washington . . . the prospect of reprising the Cold War—the last major conflict that Washington won—offers the familiar comfort of an old boot."[31]

Wearing that boot again could be risky, though, for several reasons. First, one cannot extrapolate from a country's past record the manner in which it will respond to today's competitive pressures. Second, the United States was on an ascending trajectory in previous competitions. Today it is in relative decline. Third, as the preceding chapters have attempted to argue, neither China nor Russia seems poised for a Soviet-style collapse, numerous competitive frailties notwithstanding. The maintenance of a strained cohabitation and the quest for a certain victory call for very different kinds of diplomacy. Fourth, the United States will find it difficult, if not impossible, to achieve its own vital national interests if its relations with Beijing and Moscow degrade ever further into antagonism. A separate point deserves mention: the United States should not require an external impetus to discipline its foreign policy, much less to address wide-ranging domestic challenges. Nor should it overstate the extent to which China and Russia are responsible for those challenges. While both countries will continue to exploit America's domestic dysfunction as evidence of the limitations of democracy, it is ultimately up to US policymakers to redress it.

It is sensible enough to regard competitive anxiety as one instrument in a fully stocked toolkit for self-rejuvenation. Noah Smith observes that, "while it would be nice if we didn't need international rivalry to drive technological progress, at least its return gives us one more reason to be optimistic about innovation and research in the coming decade."[32] It would be dangerous, though, to rely upon that anxiety as the principal lever. If "America's best hope of retaining some cohesion in the coming decades is a mighty China," policymakers and the public should be concerned.[33] Were this judgment true, it would imply that the United States lacks an intrinsic motivation, if not the capacity, to address its domestic challenges; it has to be prodded. The judgment might even suggest that Americans are incapable of forging a shared identity unless they can identify a country whose influence and ideology they find objectionable. The United States should not depend upon juxtapositions with China or Russia to articulate a creed that reverberates globally. If only the emergence of a seeming antagonist or the search for a plausible one can prevent Americans from drifting further into ideological tribalism, the resilience of their polity, the health of their institutions, and the prospects for their country's competitiveness will all be in doubt.

Even if one believes that the Soviet challenge contributed to greater internal cohesion, growing political polarization casts doubt upon the hypothesis that a resurgent China will have a comparable effect.[34] Besides, a confident country should be capable of defining itself on the basis of its aspirations at least as much as on the character of its competitors. Shortly after the fall of the Berlin Wall, Flora Lewis observed that a "steady course in the world and a steady concern for continuing failures on delivering America's promise to its citizens need attention. One great struggle for the minds of men has been won. It must be followed not by a search for a new enemy but by putting the fruits of triumphant ideas into practice."[35] More than three decades on, the United States confronts two formidable competitors, and the ideological precepts it once regarded as triumphant are contested. But Lewis's basic point still obtains.

It is also important to recall the corrosive effects that external competitions can have on domestic politics. The United States detained over 120,000 Japanese Americans in internment camps after the Japanese attack on Pearl Harbor. After Mao's ascent to power, Republicans and Democrats attempted to frame each other as being weaker on China— and, as competition with Moscow intensified, to do the same vis-à-vis the Soviet Union. As for the chilling, far-reaching effects of Senator Joseph McCarthy's attempt to uncover disloyalty in the ranks of US government officials, these are well documented.

Similar risks present themselves today. At a time when the United States is witnessing a disturbing surge in violence and discrimination directed against members of the Asian American and Pacific Islander community, Washington must not allow its intensifying competition with Beijing to shroud that community in a cloud of suspicion or to make prospective Chinese students and researchers from abroad feel unwelcome.[36]

PRINCIPLE 4   Frame internal renewal as an explicit objective of US foreign policy, not as a desired byproduct

Many preliminary analyses of the 2016 presidential election stressed that discussions of US foreign policy in Washington too often traffic in abstractions that seem disconnected from Americans' lived experiences. "For years," one such analysis observed, "the foreign policy establishment has preached the importance of sustaining the US-led, rules-based international order—an exhortation that, at best, was meaningless to most Americans. At worst, it smacked of soulless globalism."[37] As British historian Timothy Garton Ash quips, "[n]o one's heart ever beat faster at the sound of the rules-based international order."[38] While "great-power competition" may have a sharper edge, gaining popular support will still prove challenging. Richard Fontaine observes: "Survey after survey shows that while concerns about China are gradually rising, the vast majority of Americans are relatively unconcerned with great-power competition and much more focused on other threats."[39] The head of the Center for Strategic and Budgetary Assessments corroborates this assessment: "During the early Cold War, a series of minor shocks followed by a major one—the Korean War—convinced not just American leaders but the American public at large that the United States had entered a period of great-power competition . . . Such a consensus on modern great-power competition, although potentially emerging, has yet to take hold."[40]

The American public does not favor "isolationism," if that position is taken to mean a fundamental rejection of engagement with and contributions to external affairs.[41] Americans are, however, increasingly wary of using military power abroad, having witnessed the disappointing results of US interventions in Afghanistan and Iraq, the emergence (and now resurgence) of the Islamic State, and the broader Middle East's descent into chaos after a series of revolutions swept through the region in the early 2010s. An August 2020 survey by the Eurasia Group Foundation found that, "[w]hen 'engagement' is split into military and non-military components, only three in ten Americans favor liberal hegemony. Most Americans do support engagement of some sort—but US foreign policy leaders should think twice before claiming that the American people are on board with the elite consensus they promote."[42]

Engagement is likely to elicit greater public support if it contributes to the mitigation of America's socioeconomic challenges. In September 2020, reviewing a wealth of recent polling data, Bruce Stokes concluded: "Voters want the next US president to focus first on domestic issues—overcoming the pandemic, digging the country out of a deep economic hole, calming racial tensions, and reversing inequality."[43] A few weeks later, the Carnegie Endowment for International Peace released a report by a bipartisan group of distinguished authors, all of whom had had high-level roles in the US government (several of them are now serving in the Biden administration). Drawing upon hundreds of interviews with state and local community leaders in Colorado, Nebraska, and Ohio, they found

> no evidence [that] America's middle class will rally behind efforts aimed at restoring US primacy in a unipolar world, escalating a new Cold War with China, or waging a cosmic struggle between the world's democracies and authoritarian governments. In fact, these are all surefire recipes for further widening the disconnect between the

foreign policy community and the vast majority of Americans beyond Washington, who are more concerned with proximate threats to their physical and economic security.[44]

Policymakers should neither hope nor expect that the public will support a protracted, steadily more expansive competition with China and Russia, even if they believe its strategic virtues to be self-evident.[45] Instead, Americans will be increasingly likely to ask what contributions US foreign policy is making to improving their day-to-day material welfare: "In times of scarce resources, US foreign policy choices ought to continuously demonstrate their utility, which means focusing on the problems that matter to Americans."[46]

The Biden administration is right to focus on promoting "a foreign policy for the middle class," even if it proves unable to justify all its particular foreign policies under that heading. A study by Carter Price and Kathryn Edwards found that, while growth in per capita GDP and growth in total taxable income roughly tracked each other between 1945 and 1975, after 1975 the trajectories began to diverge in favor of the top 10 percent. The authors estimated that, had that divergence not occurred, the bottom 90 percent would have earned $47 trillion more in taxable income between 1975 and 2018.[47] The Center on Budget and Policy Priorities reports that "the share of wealth held by the top 1 percent rose from just under 30 percent in 1989 to 38.6 percent in 2016, while the share held by the bottom 90 percent fell from 33.2 percent to 22.8 percent."[48] Between March 18, 2020 and October 15, 2021, as the pandemic devastated much of the American public, the combined wealth of US billionaires increased by roughly $2.1 trillion.[49]

Other troubling evidence points to a disconnect between US engagement abroad and the welfare of the American people. Noting that life expectancy in the United States only increased by three years between 1990 and 2018, David Leonhardt observes: "There is no other developed country that has suffered such a stark slowdown in life spans."[50] Over 3.3 million Americans died in 2020, the highest number in recorded US history, and life expectancy registered its largest one-year decline since World War II.[51]

In view of such realities, Americans will be increasingly likely to ask how US foreign policy is enhancing their resilience in the face of transnational challenges, beginning with pandemic disease. COVID-19 has demonstrated the United States' unacceptable level of dependence upon other countries for supplies of essential medicines. But it has also clarified the extent to which the United States must maintain a baseline of cooperation with China. How many American lives might have been saved, and how much economic devastation might the United States have avoided, if the two countries had collaborated at the outset to identify the origins of the coronavirus and to find best practices for reducing transmission? It is sobering to consider that more Americans have succumbed to the coronavirus than died in battle in all of America's wars between 1775 and 1991.[52] And as singular as COVID-19 has been, pandemics are likely to occur more frequently as urbanization accelerates; both intrastate and international travel increase; and humans engage more heavily in activities such as deforestation, which bring them into contact with disease-carrying animals.[53]

The effect of climate change on Americans' welfare is also becoming more pronounced. In the aftermath of the February 2021 winter storms that triggered blackouts across the country, the *New York Times* warned that, as this phenomenon "brings more frequent and intense storms, floods, heat waves, wildfires, and other extreme events, it is placing growing stress on the foundations of the country's economy."[54] One study estimates that, given the current trajectory of global warming, by 2050 the United States' GDP could be up to 7 percent smaller than it would be in a no-climate change world.[55] The decade 2011–20 was the hottest one on record, and the next decade is likely to be even hotter. Cooperation with China—and, to a lesser extent, with Russia—will be essential to the mitigation of climate change.

While transnational challenges increasingly threaten Americans' safety and prosperity, they do not occupy a commensurate place in US national security discussions. Michael Mazarr notes the discrepancy between the present focus of those discussions—"the ability to flow war-winning levels of military power to distant corners of the globe to contend with potential aggression in highly demanding, localized contingencies directly adjacent to potential adversaries"—and the reality that "[t]he leading perils to Americans now come from sources other than foreign armies or major wars."[56] Even as it continues to prepare for and guard against scenarios that could escalate to great-power military confrontation, US foreign policy should accord a more central role to addressing "nontraditional" security threats.[57]

PRINCIPLE 5 Enlist allies and partners in affirmative undertakings

One of the United States' greatest competitive assets is its network of allies and partners. The United States properly continues urging them to play a more active role in managing their own defenses, as it seeks to render its own global security presence more sustainable and to promote greater symmetry and interoperability in its relationships. Republican and Democratic administrations alike have stressed that Washington should not be expected to take care of its friends' security indefinitely. Former Secretary of Defense Robert Gates famously warned non-US members of NATO in 2011 that "there will be dwindling appetite and patience in the US Congress . . . to expend increasingly precious funds on behalf of nations that are apparently unwilling to devote the necessary resources or make the necessary changes to be serious and capable partners in their own defense."[58] The former head of South Korea's Special Warfare Command acknowledges that he does not "expect another 70 years of unilateral support. We need to be more independent, just to be a good ally."[59] In a similar vein, the French president Emmanuel Macron has asserted that Washington will respect Paris only if Paris is to achieve sovereignty over its own defense.[60]

But the United States should strike a balance. The Trump administration rightly highlighted the need for greater burden-sharing, but because it often berated the United States' friends publicly—and even threatened them in some cases—it compelled them to consider not only how they can better insulate themselves against the vagaries of US foreign policy but also how they can reduce the centrality of ties with Washington in their strategic outlooks. When the United States presses its allies and partners to do more to assure their own security, it should make it clear that it is doing so because it wants its relationships to prove more durable and dynamic, not because it views those relationships as an imposition.

The more China's military capabilities develop, the more incumbent it will be upon its neighbors to deter further destabilizing conduct on its part. In its 2020 defense strategic update, Australia pledged to spend roughly $186 billion on defense over the coming decade, nearly 40 percent more than it had earmarked in 2016.[61] Japan approved its largest ever defense budget in December 2020, avowing to "strengthen its defense capability at speeds that are fundamentally different from the past."[62] In addition, the country's July 2021 defense white paper stated that it would cooperate with the United States, Australia, India, the United Kingdom, France, Germany, Canada, and New Zealand to promote its vision of a "free and open Indo-Pacific"; importantly, the document marks the first time that Japan has explicitly linked the maintenance of cross-strait stability to its own security.[63] While India is unlikely to abandon its posture of strategic autonomy, it is pursuing stronger defense ties with the United States, and doing so much more openly and vigorously than before. An "Asian NATO" is unlikely, but the United States should encourage the Quad's newfound momentum. Although South Korea is not a part of that grouping, it is a linchpin of regional security; it is encouragingly poised to spend an additional $275 billion on defense between 2021 and 2025.[64]

The United States should work with its Asia-Pacific allies and partners to uphold freedom of navigation and to challenge any coercive conduct on China's part. A key element of this second undertaking, of course, will be strengthening Taiwan's psyche; beyond deterring threats to the island's security, the United States and its regional friends should strengthen their economic ties with Taiwan, advocate for its greater representation in international institutions and diplomatic fora, and reject the alleged inevitability of its reabsorption into the mainland.[65]

Similarly, the more Russia's military capabilities grow, the more its neighbors should assume responsibility for deterring it from further revanchism. Non-US NATO defense spending began increasing after Moscow's incursion into Crimea, and this trend continues, although it is unlikely that all NATO members will fulfill the pledge they made at the September 2014 Wales Summit to increase their defense spending to 2 percent of GDP by 2024. Transatlanticists have widely criticized the 2 percent figure as an arbitrary benchmark, noting that it confuses defense spending with alliance contributions. Some members, for instance Greece, surpass that threshold but do little to project force beyond their borders, while others, for instance Denmark, do not yet meet it but have nonetheless made notable contributions to NATO operations. While the United States understandably wishes that other members would increase their defense expenditures at a faster clip and prioritize the development of capabilities that are more interoperable with the ones that the United States has deployed in the Baltics, it should applaud steady improvement rather than decrying insufficient progress.

As it continues these burden-sharing conversations, the United States must widen the scope of its dialogues with allies and partners. Even if they appreciate why Washington is focused on great-power competition, they may not find the framework relevant to themselves. Nor will they take kindly to the implication, even if unintended, that their perspectives and decisions matter less because they are not "great" powers. Kathleen Hicks explains that "rivalry among the United States, China, and Russia is important to geopolitics, but so is the degree to which other 'great powers,' some with nuclear weapons, seek alternative paths, potentially together. France, Germany, India, and Japan are powers in their own right, for example."[66]

In March 2021 the National Committee on American Foreign Policy held a series of roundtables with participants from the United States, the United Kingdom, Australia, Canada, the European Union, India, Japan, and South Korea to discuss the potential for shared approaches to the Asia-Pacific. "Participants strongly felt," explained rapporteur Rorry Daniels, "that the Quad must have a framing that does not reinforce binary choices about great-power competition to be attractive in the region."[67] Even as Canberra, Delhi, and Tokyo strengthen their military and diplomatic ties with Washington, they cannot readily detach their economies from Beijing's. They worry, moreover, that an indefinite deterioration of US–China relations would further jeopardize the security and undermine the prosperity of the region they call home.

A comparable picture emerges in Europe. Drawing upon a late 2020 survey commissioned by the European Council on Foreign Relations of more than 15,000 participants from eleven European countries, Ivan Krastev and Mark Leonard observe that "[m]any people in America now see the prospect of a new Cold War as giving their foreign policy a new focus. But Europeans are asking themselves exactly the opposite question: 'What is the point of being a European if the Cold War has returned?'" They further note that a substantial number of those polled regard European sovereignty "not [as] a grand entry into international politics but an emergency exit from the bipolar world of tomorrow. It is an application for early retirement from great-power competition."[68] Walter Russell Mead likewise cautions Washington against overstated hopes of strategic alignment with Brussels: "[T]here are issues, like climate change and the crackdown on illicit finance, on which transatlantic cooperation can be expected to grow . . . But overall, Russia is too weak and China is too far away to frighten Europeans into a policy rethink."[69] Shortly after President Biden took office, the *New York Times* explained that European leaders "hardly view" Beijing "as an enemy" and that Moscow "remains a nuclear-armed neighbor, however truculent, and has financial and emotional leverage of its own."[70]

On balance, the United States will have to accept that even longstanding allies and partners will not always confirm its threat perceptions, share its policy priorities, or abide its strategic preferences. The Regional Comprehensive Economic Partnership (RCEP) is notable for having brought China, Japan, and South Korea under the auspices of a single free trade agreement (FTA) for the first time, and those three countries are pressing forward on a FTA among themselves. Even though Beijing's conduct has placed its investment accord with Brussels on shaky ground, China has now overtaken the United States as the European Union's largest trading partner, and European corporate executives are pushing back against calls for decoupling.[71] Germany, meanwhile, is proceeding with the Nord Stream 2 pipeline and looking to deepen its cooperation with Russia on climate change. And Delhi, while taking an increasingly forceful stand against Beijing, is boosting defense ties with Moscow. As the United States tries to renew its friendships in the post-Trump era, Kori Schake offers this advice: "Having allies requires sacrifices grounded in common values; it does not mean that other democratic countries must in every case do what the United States wants."[72]

While the G7, US–EU, and NATO summits that took place in 2021 demonstrate that advanced industrial democracies are increasingly vigilant about the competitive challenges posed by China and Russia, these gatherings also affirm that the United States will find it hard to sustain its core relationships if it frames them too narrowly around the task of competing with those two countries. One might rejoin that US foreign policy during the Cold War was intrinsically oppositional: Washington cast itself as the antithesis of Moscow. Crucially, though, it contested the Soviet Union within a larger, forward-looking project of constructing a postwar order. It will be essential for the United States to compete with China and Russia in a comparable way, not only because there are now more transnational challenges that demand great-power cooperation but also because Washington is less likely to have success by courting allies and partners on an ideological basis.

Indeed, despite concerns that authoritarianism is becoming more attractive, we are not seeing the crystallization of liberal and illiberal blocs so much as the emergence of a messier geopolitics, one whereby countries try to maximize their freedom of strategic maneuver by establishing relationships on an issue-specific basis—dealing with like-minded countries whenever possible, but interacting with others as they deem necessary. Frances Brown and Thomas Carothers warn that many friends of the United States "would balk at signing on to an American-led global democracy push if it is centered on countering Beijing and Moscow. These countries have been bruised by past episodes where Washington conflated its geostrategic agenda with a democracy agenda—most recently in the global war on terrorism—and are wary of signing on to any sequel of that approach."[73]

Selective, circumscribed competition with China and Russia has a better chance of winning support than an all-encompassing, maximalist conception—as does a US foreign policy that focuses more on the vision Washington wishes to pursue than on the outcomes it seeks to avoid. Shortly after Joe Biden was elected president, the European Commission released a paper in which it concluded that the United States and the European Union "have a once-in-a-generation opportunity to design a new transatlantic agenda for global cooperation" that can buttress "a post-corona world." Calling climate change and biodiversity loss "the defining challenges of our time," the document exhorted Washington and Brussels to "advance global common goods, providing a solid base for stronger multilateral action and institutions." The paper did not ignore China and Russia; it noted that reinvigorated transatlanticism would be "essential in a world where authoritarian powers seek to subvert democracies, aggressive actors try to destabilize regions and institutions, and closed economies exploit the openness our own societies depend on."[74] But, appropriately, its focus was far more expansive. The United States and the European Union should consider what they can do together to advance a more resilient post-pandemic order—referencing China and Russia where necessary, but ideally not having to use those two countries as a basis for shared undertakings.

A similar point holds for the Quad, whose ability to transition from abstract grouping to geopolitical concept may be limited if it is rooted principally in the counterbalancing of China's resurgence. It is encouraging that the four member countries are expanding their remit, for example by working to boost supplies of COVID-19 vaccines to Southeast Asia and playing a more active role in shaping norms around frontier technologies.[75]

To expand the scope of its cooperation with allies and partners—and, more broadly, to regain trust as a catalyst of collective action—Washington must bolster the ecosystem of actors that shape its foreign policy. Many of the United States' friends may be reluctant to make common cause with it, as they fear that another "America First" administration could take power in 2025 or 2029 and undercut, if not reverse, any commitments the Biden administration makes to them. That Donald Trump secured roughly 11 million more votes in 2020 than he did in 2016—and, in so doing, made significant inroads into traditionally Democrat-leaning voting blocs—suggests that there is a broad constituency for political figures who embrace his worldview, even if they do not have the former president's force of personality. While the United States will not be able to eliminate fears about its capriciousness, it can temper them somewhat if it accords a greater role in its foreign policy to subnational actors, whose internationalist inclinations largely endure, no matter the administration in power. Anne-Marie Slaughter notes that the United States

> has a wide array of philanthropies, businesses, civic organizations, universities, and faith groups that are deeply embedded in global networks; this is a hallmark of the openness of US society and its diversity. If properly integrated with government initiatives to tackle global problems, these networks will be relatively impervious to the efforts of any future president to withdraw from the world.[76]

PRINCIPLE 6   Appreciate the limits to America's unilateral influence

Developing wider foundations for its alliances and partnerships will become more important as the influence Washington can wield on its own declines. Recognizing the reality of that decline will in turn be essential—as will abandoning nostalgia for an imagined past. To conclude that the United States has squandered its preeminence is doubly problematic: beyond suggesting that there was once a time when Washington could substantially dictate the course of world affairs, it implies that Washington could go a considerable way toward reclaiming that leverage through force of will and clarity of vision.

It is true, of course, that the United States emerged from World War II with a preponderance of material power, but that imbalance resulted from an outcome that was unlikely to endure and would have undermined US national interests if it had: Europe's and Asia's wartime devastation. In addition, as a trio of developments would soon demonstrate, the oft-heard assertion that Washington exercised hegemony in the postwar era is ahistorical. On August 29, 1949, the Soviet Union detonated an atomic bomb, thereby ending America's nuclear monopoly. Having occurred more than three years before the CIA had forecast (the agency doubted that Moscow would produce its first bomb before mid-1953), this event sowed alarm within the Truman administration.[77] Just a month later, Mao proclaimed the creation of the People's Republic of China after his communist forces decisively defeated Chiang Kai-shek's Kuomintang forces. And in December 1950 his peasant army dealt US forces a shocking defeat in the Battle of Chosin Reservoir, causing consternation in the United States at the prospect of a worldwide communist offensive.

A reasonable interpretation of these three developments is that, the enormity of its power notwithstanding, the United States faces acute limitations to the outcomes it can achieve and the setbacks it can prevent. But many US observers adduced the three developments as evidence of a foreign policy that was impotent at best and incompetent or even treasonous at worst. In a seminal December 1952 article, Scottish historian Denis Brogan expressed bewilderment at such conclusions and devoted particular attention to the alleged "loss" of China:

> The Chinese Revolution, an event of immense importance, is often discussed as if it were simply a problem in American foreign and domestic policy and politics. The Communist triumph in China is discussed as if it were simply the result of American action or inaction, the result of the mistakes, and worse than mistakes, of General Marshall, Secretary Acheson, President Roosevelt, and the Institute

of Pacific Relations; and as if the Communists or the Russians would not have "captured" China had American policy been represented and controlled by Representative Judd—or even, perhaps, by Senators Cain and Jenner.[78]

The intervening decades have witnessed countless more setbacks, starting with the Korean War, which ended in stalemate and registered nearly 34,000 US battle deaths. The most recent example is the failed intervention in Afghanistan that saw the Taliban return to power, after almost twenty years of US involvement that produced more than 2,400 combat deaths on the American side. In between were the Bay of Pigs, the fall of Saigon, the overthrow of the Shah of Iran, the Battle of Mogadishu, and the emergence of the Islamic State, to name just a few other developments.

Any appraisal of the United States' foreign policy will include some litany of this kind. The approach is limited, though, not only because it overstates the extent to which any unfavorable outcome implicates that policy but also because it discounts the emergence of salutary trends that have developed over time. In the second half of the twentieth century, the roster of democracies increased significantly, the world experienced a massive expansion in prosperity, and the United States cultivated a network of alliances that remains unrivaled. In addition, the order that Washington helped build and develop after World War II flourished even after the principal pretext for its establishment—the advance of Soviet influence—no longer obtained.

If one believes that the present deterioration of US relations with China and Russia will continue apace, one should expect the United States to experience many more of the kinds of setbacks noted earlier. Washington will undermine its strategic equipoise if it interprets every one of them as a consequence of US weakness or ineptitude. Erica Borghard warns that, "[i]f American grand strategy rests on 'winning' every interaction in the so-called great-power competition, policymakers are left with a brittle strategy that forces unpalatable choices between capitulation and escalation."[79] It is tempting, but ultimately unrealistic to imagine that the United States could have prevented China's militarization of the South China Sea or Russia's incursion into Crimea, for example, without taking steps that would have risked a military confrontation. To chastise it for "allowing" unfavorable outcomes to occur is to indulge the illusion of omnipotence that Brogan so trench-antly critiqued.

The United States should focus more on assessing the overall trajectory of its strategic position vis-à-vis China and Russia than on fixating on the outcomes of individual competitive episodes. To assess that trajectory properly, it must ensure that self-examination does not morph into self-flagellation. The status Washington enjoyed between the early 1990s and the onset of the global financial crisis was highly aberrant. Even if it had avoided self-inflicted strategic errors, the "rise of the rest," the growing heft of non-state actors, and the proliferation of transnational crises would have cumulatively reduced its margin of preeminence. A resurgent China and a revanchist Russia, then, are not avoidable consequences of misguided US diplomacy as much as they are expected outcomes of relative US decline. Going forward, the United States will increasingly have to grapple with an uncomfortable question: what level of influence can it allow its competitors to achieve? Or, perhaps less presumptuously, how will it adapt if and as their influence extends beyond its comfort threshold? Rana Mitter observes:

> Even as many Western countries seek to define the ways in which China's current behavior is illegitimate, they avoid a more difficult question. What are legitimate aims for China in its own region and the wider world? China is a large, powerful state that has the world's second-biggest economy. A state of that size cannot be expected to participate in the global order solely on the terms of its rivals—not least because some of China's recent success owes much to Western failure.[80]

Mitter's proposition also applies to Russia, even if not as urgently.

Washington can play a significant role in shaping the external environment in which Beijing and Moscow operate, especially if it embeds its approach to strategic competition within a forward-looking effort to address transnational challenges alongside its allies and partners. Ultimately, though, it has assured control of only two phenomena: the decisions it makes and those it does not.

PRINCIPLE 7   Pursue cooperative possibilities that can temper the destabilizing effects of great-power competition

The term "postwar order" is so deeply embedded and instinctively invoked in mainstream discourse that one can forget its aspirational significance: the UN was established with the overriding objective of avoiding another world war. The most fundamental goal of today's great powers must be to prevent the competitive dynamics inherent in their relations from culminating in an armed conflict. Paul Kennedy observed in August 2013 that, if they "prevent any actions that might lead to a world war, we should all be happy. Their job is simply to hold firm the iron frame that keeps the international system secure."[81]

There are many factors that should theoretically diminish the probability of an armed confrontation. When territorial conquest plays less of a central role in world affairs, the strategic objectives of initiating conflict are less evident. The United States, China, and Russia are all aging rapidly, and recent scholarship suggests that graying countries are less prone to militarism.[82] The existence of nuclear weapons also continues to exert a deterrent effect. Sadly, though, the experience of tragedy does not curtail the capacity for folly: one fears that the pillars of Paul Kennedy's metaphorical iron frame are creaking, if not crumbling.

Indeed, a growing number of observers believe that the likelihood of great-power war is increasing. Paul Musgrave warns that the latest iteration of the Nagorno-Karabakh conflict, which occurred in late 2020, "provides yet another reason to worry that the world is entering a new phase of more violent conflict—including major wars."[83] And Christopher Layne speaks for many others when, with reference to the United States and China, he predicts that, "without a change in direction, war between them in the coming decades is not only possible but probable."[84]

A nascent branch of scholarship suggests, in addition, that we perhaps take an overly sanguine view of the fact that there has been no third world war. Bear Braumoeller explains that "what we see in the historical record and the data . . . isn't so much a constant movement toward a less conflictual world but rather an irregular series of shifts from more conflictual periods to less conflictual ones and vice versa, based largely on which international orders existed at the time."[85] A recent study argues that the diminishing frequency of interstate wars "would need to endure for at least another 100 to 150 years before it could plausibly be called a genuine trend."[86] Tanisha Fazal and Paul Poast observe that, on account of improvements in medicine and sanitation, the number of those injured in battle has increased significantly in relation to the number of those killed over the centuries; therefore, if one focuses only on the latter figure, one is likely to underestimate the full toll of armed conflict. Fazal and Poast also note that, because the two world wars were singularly deadly, observers tend to assume that an armed confrontation must produce a comparable number of fatalities if it is to qualify as a great-power war. But the two scholars challenge this supposition by citing conflicts before World War I (the Franco-Austrian War, the Austro-Prussian War, and the Franco-Prussian War) and after World War II (the Korean War and the Vietnam War) that pitted great powers against each other without producing casualties on the scale of either world war.[87]

Of most immediate concern is the potential for an armed confrontation between the United States and China. The erstwhile guardrails that circumscribed the competitive dynamics between them—official dialogues between government officials, economic interdependence, and people-to-people exchanges, for example—exert diminishing force. Unlike the United States and the Soviet Union during much of the Cold War, present-day United States and China have few mechanisms in place to deescalate military encounters. Because they do not have a clear sense of each other's red lines, operational readiness, and will to fight, each one is prone to errors of miscalculation. And domestic political conditions in each country overlay these structural tensions, contributing to an increasingly confrontational relationship.

America's most pressing worry is the possibility of a war with China over Taiwan, as the head of US Indo-Pacific Command warns that Beijing might try to seize control of Taipei by 2027.[88] The United States also continues to fear the possibility of a clash with China in the South China Sea. Ben Buchanan and Fiona Cunningham warn that in any conflict between Washington and Beijing, "the difficulty of distinguishing between hacking for espionage and operational preparation of the environment, an essential precursor to most high-end cyber attacks," could introduce the risk of an "inadvertent escalation."[89]

Also of concern is the prospect of a trilateral arms race—a phenomenon, note Nicholas Miller and Vipin Narang, for which there is no precedent.[90] While the United States and Russia have agreed to extend New START, which is the one remaining pillar of the nuclear nonproliferation regime, both of them are modernizing their nuclear programs, along with China. China may be reluctant to enter into arms control discussions with the United States and Russia until it has roughly as many strategic deployed warheads as they do. Containing nuclear dangers in an age of rapid technological advances will be increasingly fraught. Eugene Rumer and Richard Sokolsky warn that "[t]he existing US–Russian strategic arms-control framework does nothing to limit the arms race in areas that are threatening and destabilizing to the balance of terror between the United States and Russia."[91] And James Acton explains how, in either a US–China or a US–Russia conflict, entanglement between nuclear and non-nuclear assets could "precipitate the use of nuclear weapons directly" and "frustrate efforts to manage nonnuclear escalation."[92]

Informal dialogues on such dangers are occurring, and they must continue. In December 2020, Fu Ying and John Allen reflected on a series of Track II dialogues they had led over the prior fifteen months on artificial intelligence-enabled military systems.[93] Since 2010, meanwhile, under the aegis of the Harvard Kennedy School, the Elbe Group has convened former military and intelligence officials from the United States and Russia to discuss difficult security issues that affect bilateral relations. As strategic tensions with Beijing and Moscow rise, though, it will be essential for Washington to sustain formal, high-level bilateral exchanges with them both: the imperative of diplomacy scales with the intensity of frictions. Members of Congress should avoid the temptation to score political points by appearing "tougher" than one another when it comes to China and Russia; "getting tough" is a slogan, not a prescription. One engages in difficult diplomacy not as an act of altruism or as an admission of weakness, but as an acknowledgment of reality: Beijing and Moscow are major powers with which Washington must coexist. Fiona Hill, senior director for European and Russian affairs on the National Security Council from 2017–19, makes the point succinctly: "Negotiating with your adversaries is what diplomacy is supposed to be about—as long as you have aides and note-takers present. Not talking makes no sense."[94] Sustained silence that calcifies antagonism is more liable to undercut America's vital national interests than piecemeal dialogue that encounters roadblocks.

The United States, China, and Russia should also consider establishing an official trilateral dialogue aimed at ensuring that strategic tensions are, in the words of Andrew Ehrhardt, "tamed by a modern framework of understanding—one in which the principal great powers aim . . . at deliberation and negotiation as opposed to efforts based solely on deterrence." Ehrhardt suggests as a model the ten days in October 1925 when leaders from Britain, France, and Germany convened in Locarno, Switzerland to address a range of issues that had strained their relations since the end of World War I.[95]

Theoretically, war is not necessary, of course, to transform dissatisfaction with an existing order into the foundation for a new one. The mere need to make such a statement is a damning indictment of humanity. Alas, war has often played that role. The Thirty Years' War (1618–48) concluded with the Peace of Westphalia, which gave rise to a phenomenon that is historically quite new: the nation-state. The French Revolutionary and Napoleonic Wars (1792–1815) concluded with the Congress of Vienna, which made the balance of power a more explicit organizing principle of European affairs. World War I (1914–18) yielded a noble—if, in retrospect, naïve—effort to avert a repetition of that cataclysm, the League of Nations. And World War II (1939–45), of course, birthed the framework, albeit tenuous, that persists to the present: the postwar order. The last of those conflicts has been the deadliest in human history. In an age of nuclear weapons, one can only hope that the next ordering moment does not emerge from the ashes of a great-power war; the horror of such an event tests the bounds of human comprehension. Unfortunately, though, inconceivability is not the same as impossibility—a conclusion that Washington, Beijing, and Moscow would all do well to heed.

While avoidance of war is the basic precondition for a durable order, it is hardly a satisfactory aspiration. Some observers had hoped, and may yet believe, that the pandemic could compel the establishment of a more resilient and capable system without the need for a kinetic catalyst. While there is no ready way to compare the systemic effects of a war with those of a health-cum-economic emergency, COVID-19 has illuminated about as vividly as possible the interlocking vulnerabilities that have arisen from—or at least have been exacerbated by—global interdependence, the glaring inadequacy of international institutions to the tasks with which they have been entrusted, and the near impossibility of mobilizing collective action amid deteriorating great-power tensions.

One of the gravest risks to humanity is that the United States, China, and Russia will come to regard investments in strategic stability—and in cooperative undertakings more broadly—as displays of strategic weakness. One might call it the risk of great-power nihilism, whereby the great powers end up focusing more on how to damage one another than on how to gird the postwar order for the challenges it now faces and will eventually confront. That Washington, Beijing, and Moscow would eventually have to reckon with the consequences of such posturing is not in doubt. Nor is it in doubt that transnational challenges will exact an ever greater human and economic toll. One question, however, does loom large: will the great powers have the foresight to cooperate more decisively now, or will they wait until they realize that they no longer have a choice?

PRINCIPLE 8   Rebalance in earnest toward the Asia-Pacific,
               with an economic focus

The first seven principles are built around the relationship between internal renewal and external competitiveness, the importance of viewing allies and partners outside the prism of strategic tensions with China and Russia, and the need for great-power cooperation in order to prevent war and manage transnational challenges. The eighth and final principle emphasizes the imperative of prioritization.

The United States has national interests around the world. At any given time, though, it has a finite pool of strategic assets it can invest. If every region of the world were roughly comparable in, say, population size, economic growth, and military expenditures, a foreign policy that accorded equal focus to each would be sensible enough. In truth, though, only one region presently is, and increasingly will be, central, no matter which metric one considers: the Asia-Pacific. It is telling that major powers outside the region, including the United Kingdom and the European Union, are formulating strategies designed to increase their influence there.

While China's resurgence furnishes one more justification for rebalancing toward the Asia-Pacific, such a reorientation would be merited even if one were to exclude that country from one's analysis. Indeed,

Nina Silove demonstrates that the United States had seriously begun contemplating that shift at least as early as the first term of the George W. Bush administration.[96] The region is home to three of America's most important allies—Australia, Japan, and South Korea—all vibrant democracies with large economies and powerful militaries. It is also home to the world's largest democracy and second-most populous country, India, which, despite its concerning illiberal turn in recent years, will be an increasingly vital partner.

Rebalancing does not involve an exclusive focus on the Asia-Pacific. The United States should intensify the process of economic integration with its two neighbors, harnessing the competitive potential of a more cohesive North American continent. It should reinvigorate the transatlantic project, which has long been the bedrock of the postwar order. And it should reimagine its relationship with an African continent that is home to some of the world's fastest-growing economies and that moves forward with growing confidence and promise, for all of the challenges that continue to beset it. But rebalancing entails, by definition, a reallocation of existing strategic assets: if one believes that Washington should accord top billing to the Asia-Pacific, holding all else equal, one cannot credibly urge it to maintain its traditional degree of focus on the Middle East.

The extent to which the United States has prioritized the region since the end of World War II means that it would be substantially invested—militarily, economically, and diplomatically—even if it were to scale back its commitments significantly over time. The volatility that has long plagued the region should disabuse China and Russia of any pretensions to regional dominance that they may harbor. In addition, there are possibilities for Washington to partner with them in the Middle East, especially Beijing, which depends heavily upon oil from the region and seeks greater stability there to facilitate the expansion of the Belt and Road Initiative.[97]

Following the drawdown of US forces from Afghanistan, some observers began warning once more that the United States would undermine its credibility if it were to "abandon" the Middle East. Accepting this proposition for argument's sake—and leaving aside the difficulty of determining when selective disengagement crosses over into abandonment—one should consider a corollary judgment: Washington undermines its credibility at least as much, if not more, when it continues to pursue unsuccessful policies, be it by volition or through inertia. The number, scope, and duration of the setbacks it has experienced in the Middle East, moreover, suggest that the problem has not been Washington's level of exertion as much as the thrust of its engagement. Philip Gordon, now deputy national security advisor to Vice President Kamala Harris, laments that "the US policy debate about the Middle East suffers from the fallacy that there is an external American solution to every problem, even when decades of painful experience suggest that this is not the case."[98]

The Biden administration has taken a number of early steps to demonstrate its commitment to the Asia-Pacific. The largest directorate of its NSC is focused on the region.[99] Its interim national security strategic guidance refers to the Asia-Pacific as the most strategically consequential theater.[100] The administration has made the reinvigoration of the Quad a central component of its foreign policy, and the first foreign leader to visit President Biden in person was then Prime Minister Suga.

The administration is also trying to scale back the American presence in the Middle East. In April 2021, when President Biden announced that the United States was going to withdraw all its troops from Afghanistan, thereby ending its longest war, he expressed exasperation with the view that such an undertaking would be precipitous: "[W]hen will it be the right moment to leave? One more year, two more years, ten more years? Ten, twenty, thirty billion dollars more above the trillion we've already spent?"[101]

The Taliban's resumption of power has raised fears that the Biden administration may prove unable to rebalance to the Asia-Pacific.[102] Daniel Byman contends nevertheless that Afghanistan is unlikely to reemerge as a safe haven for terrorism, in part because the United States' intelligence-gathering capabilities and capacity to conduct remote military operations have improved significantly over the past two decades.[103] In addition, Michael Mazarr doubts that the Taliban would have indefinitely tolerated a small US footprint; had it assessed that US forces intended to remain in Afghanistan for the long haul, it would have escalated its attacks on them. Eventually Washington would have had to make a choice: dispatch a significant number of additional troops in order to repel a new Taliban offensive—and thereby limit its ability to focus on the Asia-Pacific—or make an overdue exit.[104]

Now that its intervention in Afghanistan is finally over, the United States should commit to pursuing a narrower set of objectives in the Middle East—placing an emphasis on mitigating sectarian conflicts and promoting energy stability—and to relying upon reinvigorated diplomatic initiatives and enhanced intelligence cooperation with regional partners more than upon military instruments. And, as it aims to rebalance toward the Asia-Pacific, Washington should remember that, vital as its contributions are to the region's security order, the ultimate litmus test of its staying power will be its economic contributions. Lindsey Ford, now deputy assistant secretary of defense for South and Southeast Asia, and Zack Cooper conclude that "regional assessments of American decline are based largely on perceptions of waning US economic influence and its inward turn on trade."[105] The United States belongs to neither the RCEP nor the Comprehensive and Progressive Agreement for Trans-Pacific Partnership, and continued tariffs on China have had the unintended effect of reducing Washington's economic role in Southeast Asia.[106]

America's Great-Power Opportunity

No US foreign policy will return the world's strategic balance to its post-Cold War configuration. Discussions that consider how the United States can regain primacy in certain domains, whether regional or functional, can only lead it astray. Washington should not assume itself to be so indispensable to the evolution of geopolitics that the rest of the world will await its instructions before attempting to fashion a more resilient post-pandemic order. The United States will also have to exhibit greater humility; its allies and partners question its competence and reliability much more than they did even a decade earlier.

The American domestic landscape is also more embittered. Identifying four forces that have historically tested US democracy— "political polarization, conflict over who belongs in the political community, high and growing economic inequality, and excessive executive power"—Suzanne Mettler and Robert Lieberman contend the United States is confronting all of them simultaneously for the first time in its history.[107] And a growing number of observers discern the emergence of a "political sectarianism" whereby Republicans and Democrats "not only clash over policy and ideology, but see the other side as alien and immoral."[108] According to a poll taken a week after the January 6, 2021 insurrection at Capitol Hill, 54 percent of Americans think that the "biggest threat to the American way of life" comes from "[o]ther people in America, and domestic enemies."[109]

But fatalism, which periodically becomes fashionable, is no more justified than the hubris that attended the Soviet Union's collapse. The United States has defied many declinist forecasts, and there is no reason yet to conclude that its regenerative capacity is spent. Shortly after the insurrection, which officials in China and Russia gleefully cast as an indictment of US democracy, Maria Repnikova penned a counterintuitively hopeful analysis, arguing that the aftermath was not "a gift for authoritarian leaders bent on denouncing America's shortcomings so much as an opportunity for America to rebuild itself and its image worldwide."[110]

There is evidence to support her optimism. While the United States' response to COVID-19 during 2020 was appropriately criticized, a longer-term perspective paints a more favorable picture. The United States has administered more shots domestically than all other countries except China and India. And while it was a laggard on matters of global vaccine diplomacy, it is set to play an increasing role in vaccination efforts—not only because it has hundreds of millions of surplus doses but also because there are growing doubts about the efficacy of China's and Russia's vaccines. Ahead of the 2021 G7 summit, President Biden pledged that the United States would donate 500 million Pfizer-BioNTech doses to some 100 low- and middle-income countries over the coming year; at the conclusion of the gathering, moreover, he stated that Washington might be positioned to distribute an additional one billion doses "over 2022 going into 2023."[111] Meanwhile, a $1.9 trillion relief package, a massive infrastructure bill, and legislation to spur US investments in frontier technologies will all help enhance the country's competitiveness in the global economy.

An earlier chapter suggested that China is its own chief challenger. The same is true of the United States, whose long-term strategic prospects will turn far more on what it chooses to do and not to do. If it proves incapable of charting its path without invoking its competitors, China and Russia will have ample capacity, individually and in partnership, to lure it into peripheral contests and strategic detours that give it the illusion of purpose. If the United States instead embeds its management of great-power tensions within a forward-looking course of renewal, they will have considerably less capacity to distract it. Here, then, is its great-power opportunity: to reposition itself abroad and to rebuild itself at home in the service of affirmative undertakings, neither requiring external competitors to determine its direction nor awaiting their decisions before it makes its own.

Afterword

The first draft of this afterword was completed in January 2022. Russia's invasion of Ukraine the following month—a decision that stunned even many of the world's most distinguished scholars of the Kremlin—necessitated a revision. Imperiling perhaps the most sacrosanct of the postwar order's norms, that against territorial conquest, Moscow's destructive course surfaces a number of sobering realities, among them the fragility of Europe's peace, the endurance of interstate war, and the limits to US agency. As the United States is focused on containing the instability that emanates from the crisis over Ukraine, strategists are mulling over whether China may feel emboldened to make a move on Taiwan.

Most analysts contend that Beijing and Moscow are increasingly willing to countenance destabilizing actions because their self-confidence is expanding: their military capabilities are becoming more formidable, the argument runs, and they believe that the global strategic balance is shifting in their favor. But a growing number of analysts are anxious about the intentions of these two countries for the opposite reason: they argue that both are systemically declining and that President Xi and President Putin discern narrowing windows of opportunity for advancing core national interests.

While the United States' focus on China and Russia seems poised to sharpen apace, the discourse around great-power competition is increasingly likely to reflect this cleavage. Do Beijing and Moscow perceive geopolitical trends to be largely auspicious or unfavorable? Does Washington have more to fear from their continued relative ascent or from their prospective relative descent? Will the possibility of armed confrontation with them grow steadily or climax rapidly?

Debate over these questions will continue; there are no self-evident answers, and one hears esteemed voices on both sides. Chapter 3 noted that great-power competition has been cited to justify opposing policy choices. If, going forward, it is also invoked on the basis of opposing analytical judgments, its value as an orienting framework stands to diminish yet further.

In the meantime, an escalating crisis in Eastern Europe and the fear that war could break out over Taiwan have elicited a new wave of commentary on America's alleged weakness—commentary redolent of observations that followed Russia's annexation of Crimea in 2014. At least five rejoinders come to mind.

First, beyond overstating the United States' agency and understating the agency of its competitors, the charge of impotence discounts the number of serious strategic setbacks that the United States was unable to forestall even when its relative power was far greater. It behooves Washington to reckon with its constraints more fully, apply its power more selectively, and enlist its allies and partners more intensively: an international order cannot be sustained by—and should not be predicated upon—the actions of one country, no matter the immensity of its power. Russia's invasion of Ukraine is prompting not only Western Europe to exhibit renewed urgency in preserving stability on the continent, but also countries such as Hungary and the Czech Republic, which had been strongly aligned with the Kremlin before the fateful decision to invade. It is also stimulating China's neighbors to take further measures in support of their own defenses. As its relative preeminence is declining, the United States should encourage these trends.

Second, from the "loss" of China in 1949 through the US withdrawal from Afghanistan in 2021, observers have penned many a premature obituary for the credibility of the United States in world affairs. If one evaluates the United States' postwar foreign policy on the basis of specific outcomes, one may well conclude that the record has been dismal, successes only occasionally punctuating an arc of failure. But if one assesses that policy's contributions to, or at least association with, longer-term trends, one is likely to render a more favorable verdict: however embattled the postwar order and democratic governance may be today, they are far more entrenched than they were eight decades earlier.

Third, in dealing with China and Russia, the United States will rarely achieve dramatic breakthroughs or have the luxury of considering a range of satisfying policy courses. It will more often have to settle for quiet victories and weigh a set of unpalatable policy options. Other countries may not be able to do much to dissuade Beijing and Moscow from taking reckless actions, a realization that Russia's invasion of Ukraine places in stark relief. But this observation is no grounds for fatalism. Through nimble, patient, and sustained diplomacy, the United States and its allies and partners can reduce the likelihood of worst-case scenarios. If and when those scenarios do materialize, moreover, they can also impose significant military, economic, and diplomatic costs.

Fourth, the narrative according to which China and Russia are outwitting the United States downplays the extent to which the two are undercutting their respective national interests—China through heavy-handed diplomacy and Russia through continued irredentism. Consider the raft of consequences that Russia has brought upon itself. NATO is bolstering its military presence in Eastern Europe. Russia's access to the global financial system has been severely curtailed, as has its ability to import inputs that will be essential to its technological development. Germany has paused the certification of the Nord Stream 2 pipeline and, in a dramatic reversal of longstanding policy, sent lethal weapons to Ukraine. And, facing transatlantic opprobrium, Russia is now even more beholden to China. As for China itself, were it to attack Taiwan, it would immediately risk massive military retaliation from the United States, punishing economic sanctions from advanced industrial democracies, and an indefinite period of disruption to the supply of Taiwanese chips upon which its technological development still depends heavily; and in the long term it would risk the effects of a permanent rupture in its relations with the United States, a convergence between core US allies and partners that would come closer to approximating containment, and a substantial exodus of multinational corporations.

Fifth, mulling over the consequences that Russia is already experiencing as well as over the ones that China could experience underscores that the two countries, while estimable competitors, are manageable; their actions should influence US foreign policy without dictating its objectives. The point of making this comment is not to encourage insouciance but to discourage alarmism: the need for strategic equanimity is proportionate to the severity of competitive pressures.

China's growing economic heft and technological capacity are formidable competitive assets, as is the narrative momentum they generate. China is still on track to attain the world's largest economy well before the middle of the century, foreign direct investment in the mainland reached a record high in 2021, and China's integrated circuit output grew roughly twice as fast in 2021 as in the preceding year.[1] Even so, commercial pull can only go so far in overcoming strategic distrust. While advanced industrial democracies will not exhibit uniform intensity in contesting China's resurgence, the proliferation of bilateral, plurilateral, and multilateral agreements among them will form a steadily thicker patchwork of resistance; recent examples include the announcement of the AUKUS security partnership, the establishment of a transatlantic trade and technology council, and the signing of a reciprocal access agreement between Japan and Australia, Tokyo's first such pact.

Russia has demonstrated that it is an enduring power, one that cannot and will not be ignored amid a US desire to prioritize China. Since 2014 it has taken steps to render its financial system less vulnerable to new sanctions. And, having shattered the hope that post-Cold War Europe would not witness a large-scale land war, it has reactivated concerns over the possibility of great-power conflict. But conjectures that it could incrementally reconstitute its former empire are overwrought. If anything, its aggression against Ukraine has rendered that prospect even more distant.

As for the entente between China and Russia, the December 15, 2021 video summit between President Xi and President Putin and the two countries' joint statement on February 4, 2022 affirm its continued progress. But the partnership's difficulties are also coming into clearer view. Even as it seeks to strengthen its ties with China, Russia aims to avoid a future in which it exercises influence primarily as an adjunct to China's competitive efforts vis-à-vis the United States. At an in-person meeting with Narendra Modi, India's prime minister, that occurred shortly before the summit with President Xi, President Putin called

India "a great power" and "a time-tested friend."[2] While China would like to reduce India's role in shaping Central Asia's security architecture in the aftermath of America's withdrawal from Afghanistan, Russia would like to cooperate more closely with India. In addition, Russia's invasion of Ukraine leaves China in an awkward position, for China had endorsed the Minsk peace process and expressed support for Kiev's sovereignty and territorial integrity. While joining Russia in opposing NATO's expansion and calling for a global financial system that is less dollar-centric, China recognizes that the relationship between the two countries could intensify democratic alignment against China, if China is perceived as having sanctioned Russia's invasion.

Deepening Sino-Russian ties are nonetheless of growing concern to US policymakers. While the present rupture in US–Russia relations and the concomitant intensification of US–China distrust will limit their ability to manage that phenomenon for now, the United States should not assume that the entente will indefinitely go from strength to strength. It should approach the relationship by recalling the lesson of Aesop's fable about the wind and the sun: if the United States tries too hard to wrest Russia from China or leans too heavily on China to discipline Russia, it may compel the two to embrace each other even more closely. Assuming that eventually the United States and Russia are able to restore a baseline of diplomatic interaction, the United States should encourage Russia in the belief that it can enhance its own economic competitiveness and rebuild its own international standing over time, without depending too heavily upon any single relationship; a sustained US–Russia dialogue on arms control and heightened Russian outreach to countries such as India, Vietnam, and South Korea could inform a gradual recalibration that reinforces this belief. Washington should also convey to Beijing that it would be prudent for China to weigh the diplomatic ramifications of an association with Russia's destabilizing conduct.

On balance, the United States should regard China, Russia, and Sino–Russian ties as enduring challenges, not overwhelming forces. If the three countries are to coexist, as they must, they will have to sustain talks around strategic stability and discuss challenges that will implicate their shared national interests—even if they have appropriately modest expectations from such diplomacy and even if the suggestion of that interaction seems preposterous in light of Russia's invasion of Ukraine.

The most urgent priority, of course, is to avoid a great-power war. It is essential for the United States and Russia to preserve their deconfliction channels and update their crisis management protocols. After all, perilous as the situation in Europe is now, it would be exponentially worse were the world's two largest nuclear-armed powers to sever communication with each other. The United States and China have even more work to do on this front, for their mechanisms of military communication are far less advanced than those that exist between Washington and Moscow.

But the agenda for the United States, China, and Russia cannot be confined to avoiding a catastrophic confrontation; it must also include mitigating the risks posed by nuclear proliferation and hypersonic weapons, equipping international institutions to respond more quickly to future pandemics, and making more aggressive decarbonization pledges to combat climate change. While the response to the global financial crisis seemed to suggest that transnational challenges could mitigate strategic frictions, the aftermath of COVID-19 has made plain that each phenomenon is increasingly exacerbating the other. The foremost task of great-power diplomacy—bilateral (US–China and US–Russia) and, wherever possible, trilateral—must be to break that cycle. As fanciful as it may seem to consider a cooperative program in the present circumstances, even a limited one, the United States cannot realistically contemplate a world in which China and Russia are decoupled from the core of geopolitics while the United States manages to advance its vital national interests by bypassing or containing them.

It is self-evident, then, that managing strategic competition with Beijing and Moscow will be among the most important tasks of US foreign policy. But Washington should not organize its interactions with allies and partners solely around waging that competition, lest the pursuit of divergent approaches define or even derail those relationships. While order-level shocks such as Russia's aggression can galvanize the United States and its friends to make common cause in the short term, it is uncertain that such events can sustain the United States' diplomatic network in perpetuity: that is, short-term coalescence engendered by the missteps of competitors will not yield the longer-term framework necessitated by the realities of coexistence. Washington's task is to articulate a vision that can transcend the competitive challenges it now confronts and facilitate the emergence of that framework. After World

War II, it enlisted allies and partners in the task of constructing a postwar order that could bolster security and increase prosperity. It must now work with them to construct an updated system that, beyond restoring the hope for peace, can better withstand the stresses of globalization and mobilize resources for collective action.

If the United States is to be trusted with spearheading such an ambitious undertaking abroad, it must demonstrate greater effectiveness in addressing its challenges at home. COVID-19 has proven to be a frustratingly protean nemesis, having claimed some 950,000 American lives as of this writing. The 2022 midterm elections are likely to compound political polarization, making it still harder for the United States to govern and further reducing the appeal of its democratic example. A Pew Research Center report published in June 2021 noted that a median of just 17 percent of respondents across 16 countries believe US democracy to be worthy of emulation.[3] Looking to 2024, many allies and partners of the United States express anxiety that the vagaries of its domestic politics will increasingly jeopardize the stability of its foreign policy.

That the United States has renewed its competitive advantages during many previous periods of internal trial and external upheaval does not guarantee that it will be able to do so once more. But history serves both as antidote to fatalism and as exhortation to action: the United States can and should develop a new playbook to meet its present confluence of challenges. To that end, it should strive to reduce the role of external competitors in determining its aspirations, whether for the democratic example it seeks to cultivate or the international order it aims to advance. Regularly invoking China and Russia to justify its purposes will both project American anxiety and heighten the risk that these two competitors engage in miscalculations borne of hubris.

A final note: while no book can be completely up to date when it is published—the core text of *America's Great-Power Opportunity* was completed in the fall of 2021, and time permitted me to discuss Russia's invasion of Ukraine only briefly, in this revised afterword—I would submit that this act of aggression has actually underscored the book's principal arguments by illuminating so dramatically the chimera of US omnipotence. In accepting that it cannot hope to respond to every initiative that China and Russia announce or preempt every provocation that they launch, the United States will recognize that it can—and must—apply itself more creatively and energetically to devising a foreign policy that endures no matter what actions the two countries take. In addition to asking how external competition might stimulate US renewal, policymakers and observers should ask, more importantly, how this renewal could steady the country's competitive position over the long haul. Washington's capacity for sustained rebuilding at home and geopolitical initiative abroad should neither depend upon nor proceed from decisions in Zhongnanhai and in the Kremlin. If the United States moves forward with quiet confidence, vigilant but assured, it can seize its great-power opportunity.

Washington, DC
March 1, 2022

Notes

Chapter 1 Searching for a Post-Cold War Ballast

1 Though "Indo-Pacific" has largely displaced "Asia-Pacific" in US foreign policy discourse, there are analytical—and, it follows, prescriptive—risks to adopting this more capacious construct. See Van Jackson, "America's Indo-Pacific Folly: Adding New Commitments in Asia Will Only Invite Disaster," *Foreign Affairs* (March 12, 2021).

2 Danielle Pletka et al., "What Went Wrong in Afghanistan?" *Wall Street Journal* (August 20, 2021).

3 Jessica T. Mathews, "American Power after Afghanistan: How to Rightsize the Country's Global Role," *Foreign Affairs* (September 17, 2021).

4 "Come Home, America?" *Foreign Affairs*, 99.2 (March–April 2020).

5 For a fresh, wide-ranging reconceptualization of the factors that have historically shaped US grand strategy, see Elizabeth Borgwardt, Christopher McKnight Nichols, and Andrew Preston (eds.), *Rethinking American Grand Strategy* (New York: Oxford University Press, 2021).

6 Daniel W. Drezner, Ronald R. Krebs, and Randall Schweller, "The End of Grand Strategy: America Must Think Small," *Foreign Affairs*, 99.3 (May–June 2020), p. 108.

7 Francis J. Gavin and James B. Steinberg, "The Vision Thing: Is Grand Strategy Dead?" *Foreign Affairs*, 99.4 (July–August 2020), pp. 187–91.

8 Rebecca Friedman Lissner, "What Is Grand Strategy? Sweeping a

Conceptual Minefield," *Texas National Security Review*, 2.1 (November 2018), p. 57.

9 Van Jackson, "Wagering on a Progressive versus Liberal Theory of National Security," *Texas National Security Review*, 2.1 (November 2018), p. 179.

10 Colin Dueck, "The Future of Conservative Foreign Policy," *Texas National Security Review*, 2.1 (November 2018), p. 171.

11 Alex Pascal, "Against Washington's 'Great Power' Obsession," *Atlantic* (September 23, 2019).

12 James Kitfield, "New Arms Race Taking Shape amid a Pandemic and Economic Crisis: What Could Go Wrong?" Yahoo! News. June 6, 2020.

13 President George H. W. Bush, "Address before a Joint Session of the Congress on the Persian Gulf Crisis and the Federal Budget Deficit," Washington, DC. September 11, 1990. Transcript. https://www.presi dency.ucsb.edu/documents/address-before-joint-session-the-congress -the-persian-gulf-crisis-and-the-federal-budget.

14 President George H. W. Bush, *National Security Strategy of the United States* (Washington, DC: White House, 1991), p. v.

15 President George H. W. Bush, State of the Union address, Washington, DC. January 28, 1992. Transcript. https://millercenter.org/the-presi dency/presidential-speeches/january-28-1992-state-union-address.

16 John E. Ullmann, "Who Won Cold War? Japanese and Germans," *New York Times* (July 3, 1990).

17 John J. Mearsheimer, "Why We Will Soon Miss the Cold War," *Atlantic*, 266.2 (August 1990), p. 36.

18 Douglas Jehl, "CIA Nominee Wary of Budget Cuts," *New York Times* (February 3, 1993).

19 Robert D. Kaplan, "The Coming Anarchy," *Atlantic*, 273.2 (February 1994), p. 46.

20 Charles William Maynes, "America without the Cold War," *Foreign Policy*, 78 (1990), p. 5.

21 George F. Kennan, "The Failure in Our Success," *New York Times* (March 14, 1994).

22 Robert B. Reich, "Is Japan Out to Get Us?" *New York Times* (February 9, 1992).

23 Samuel P. Huntington, "The Erosion of American National Interests," *Foreign Affairs*, 76.5 (September–October 1997), pp. 29–30.

24 Josef Joffe, "America the Inescapable," *New York Times* (June 8, 1997).

25 Richard N. Haass, "What to Do with American Primacy," *Foreign Affairs*, 78.5 (September–October 1999), p. 37.

26 President George W. Bush, State of the Union address, Washington, DC. January 29, 2002. Transcript. https://millercenter.org/the-presi dency/presidential-speeches/january-29-2002-state-union-address.

27 Vice President Dick Cheney, speech delivered at the Los Angeles World Affairs Council, Beverly Hills, CA. January 14, 2004. Transcript. https://georgewbush-whitehouse.archives.gov/news/releases/2004/01 /20040114-7.html.

28 Senator Barack Obama, *The Audacity of Hope: Thoughts on Reclaiming the American Dream* (New York: Crown Publishers, 2006), pp. 304–6.

29 Richard Haass, testimony before the US Senate Foreign Relations Committee at the hearing *United States–China Relations in the Era of Globalization*, Washington, DC. May 15, 2008. Transcript. https:// www.govinfo.gov/content/pkg/CHRG-110shrg48013/html/CHRG -110shrg48013.htm.

30 Robert Kagan, "The September 12 Paradigm: America, the World, and George W. Bush," *Foreign Affairs*, 87.5 (September–October 2008), pp. 32–3.

31 Michael Kofman, "The August War, Ten Years on: A Retrospect- ive on the Russo-Georgian War," War on the Rocks. August 17, 2018.

32 Daniel W. Drezner, *The System Worked: How the World Stopped Another Great Depression* (New York: Oxford University Press, 2014), p. 14.

33 Thomas Donilon, press briefing at the White House, Washington, DC. June 8, 2013. Transcript. https://obamawhitehouse.archives.gov /the-press-office/2013/06/08/press-briefing-national-security-advisor -tom-donilon.

34 Ronald O'Rourke, *Renewed Great-Power Competition: Implications for Defense: Issues for Congress* (Washington, DC: Congressional Research Service, 2021), p. 25.

35 Anders Fogh Rasmussen, "A Strong NATO in a Changed World," speech at the Brussels Forum, Brussels. March 21, 2014. Transcript. https://www.nato.int/cps/en/natohq/opinions_108215.htm.

36 Walter Russell Mead, "The Return of Geopolitics: The Revenge of the Revisionist Powers," *Foreign Affairs*, 93.3 (May–June 2014), pp. 73–4.

37 Chris Buckley, "China Takes Aim at Western Ideas," *New York Times* (August 20, 2013).

38 Jane Perlez, "China's 'New Type' of Ties Fails to Sway Obama," *New York Times* (November 10, 2014).

39 "China's Xi to Make First State Visit to US as Both Flag Problems," Reuters. February 11, 2015.

40 Robert D. Blackwill and Ashley J. Tellis, *Revising US Grand Strategy toward China* (New York: Council on Foreign Relations, 2015), pp. 4, 20, 35, and 39.

41 Seth G. Jones et al., *Rolling Back the Islamic State* (Santa Monica, CA: RAND Corporation, 2017), p. xi.

42 Deputy Secretary of Defense Robert Work, speech delivered at the Center for a New American Security's Inaugural National Security Forum, Washington, DC. December 14, 2015. Transcript. https://www.defense.gov/Newsroom/Speeches/Speech/Article/634214/cnas-defense-forum.

43 John M. Richardson, *A Design for Maintaining Maritime Superiority, Version 1.0* (Washington, DC: Navy, 2016), p. 3.

44 Ash Carter, speech delivered at the Economic Club of Washington, DC. February 2, 2016. Transcript. https://www.defense.gov/Newsroom/Transcripts/Transcript/Article/648901/remarks-by-secretary-carter-on-the-budget-at-the-economic-club-of-washington-dc.

45 Josh Rogin, "The Pentagon's Lonely War against Russia and China," Bloomberg. November 11, 2015.

46 David B. Larter, "White House Tells the Pentagon to Quit Talking about 'Competition' with China," *Navy Times* (September 26, 2016).

47 President Donald J. Trump, inaugural address, Washington, DC. January 20, 2017. Transcript. https://trumpwhitehouse.archives.gov/briefings-statements/the-inaugural-address.

48 H. R. McMaster and Gary Cohn, "America First Doesn't Mean America Alone," *Wall Street Journal* (May 30, 2017).

49 Donald J. Trump, speech delivered at the 72nd session of the UN General Assembly, New York. September 19, 2017. Transcript. https://trumpwhitehouse.archives.gov/briefings-statements/remarks-president-trump-72nd-session-united-nations-general-assembly.

50 Donald J. Trump, *National Security Strategy of the United States* (Washington, DC: White House, 2017), pp. 27 and 25.

51 Jim Mattis, "Summary of the 2018 National Defense Strategy of the United States of America," Department of Defense. 2018, p. 4. https://dod.defense.gov/Portals/1/Documents/pubs/2018-National-Defense-Strategy-Summary.pdf.

52 Sarah Repucci and Amy Slipowitz, *Freedom in the World 2021: Democracy under Siege* (Washington, DC: Freedom House, 2021), pp. 2 and 4.

53 Andrea Kendall-Taylor, Erica Frantz, and Joseph Wright, "The Digital Dictators: How Technology Strengthens Autocracy," *Foreign Affairs*, 99.2 (March–April 2020), p. 112.

54 Elisabeth Vallet, "Border Walls Are Ineffective, Costly, and Fatal— But We Keep Building Them," *Conversation* (July 3, 2017).

55 Jan-Werner Müller, "False Flags: The Myth of the Nationalist Resurgence," *Foreign Affairs*, 98.2 (March–April 2019), p. 35.

56 Condoleezza Rice, "Promoting the National Interest," *Foreign Affairs*, 79.1 (January–February 2000), p. 47.

57 Amy Zegart, "The Urgent Race for Bigger Foreign-Policy Ideas," *Atlantic* (January 13, 2020).

58 Matthew Kroenig, "Washington Needs a Better Plan for Competing with China," *Foreign Policy* (August 7, 2020).

59 Telegram from Chargé d'Affaires in Moscow George F. Kennan to Secretary of State James F. Byrnes. February 22, 1946, p. 17. Transcript. https://digitalarchive.wilsoncenter.org/document/116178.pdf.

60 Henry Farrell and Abraham Newman, "Will the Coronavirus End Globalization as We Know It? The Pandemic Is Exposing Market Vulnerabilities No One Knew Existed," *Foreign Affairs* (March 16, 2020).

61 Samuel P. Huntington, "The US: Decline or Renewal?" *Foreign Affairs*, 67.2 (1988–9), p. 90.

62 "America the Confused: An Interview with Michèle Flournoy," *Octavian Report*, 4.4 (2019).

63 Damien Cave and Isabella Kwai, "Lesser Powers Link Up to Fill a Global Void," *New York Times* (May 12, 2020).

64 "COVID-19 Dashboard," Johns Hopkins University. 2021. https://coronavirus.jhu.edu/map.html.

65 "COVID-19 Vaccinations in the United States," Centers for Disease

Control and Prevention. 2021. https://covid.cdc.gov/covid-data-track
er/#vaccinations_vacc-total-admin-rate-total.

66 "Coronavirus (COVID-19) Vaccinations," Our World in Data.
December 10, 2021. https://ourworldindata.org/covid-vaccinations;
Olivia Goldhill, "States Are Sitting on Millions of Surplus COVID-19
Vaccine Doses as Expiration Dates Approach," STAT. July 20, 2021.
https://www.statnews.com/2021/07/20/states-are-sitting-on-millions
-of-surplus-covid-19-vaccine-doses-as-expiration-dates-approach.

67 Sue Halpern, "The Peril of Not Vaccinating the World," *New Yorker*
(June 3, 2021).

Chapter 2 Drawing Historical Analogies

1 "The Trump Era," *Economist* (November 12, 2016).

2 Stephen Kotkin, "Realist World: The Players Change, But the Game
Remains," *Foreign Affairs*, 97.4 (July–August 2018), p. 10.

3 Thomas F. Lynch III, "Introduction," in Thomas F. Lynch III (ed.),
Strategic Assessment 2020: Into a New Era of Great-Power Competition
(Washington, DC: NDU Press, 2020), p. 1.

4 Sarah Repucci and Amy Slipowitz, *Freedom in the World, 2021:
Democracy under Siege* (Washington, DC: Freedom House, 2021), pp. 1
and 10–11.

5 R. S. Foa et al., *The Global Satisfaction with Democracy Report 2020*
(Cambridge: Center for the Future of Democracy, 2020), p. 2.

6 The figure of 11 comes from John Keane, *The Life and Death of
Democracy* (New York: W. W. Norton, 2009), p. 730. The figure of
115 comes from "Electoral Democracies in Freedom in the World
2020," (Washington, DC: Freedom House, 2020). https://freedom
house.org/sites/default/files/2020-02/2020_List_of_Electoral_Democ
racies_FIW_2020.xlsx.

7 Daniel Treisman, "Is Democracy Really In Danger? The Picture Is
Not as Dire as You Think," *Washington Post* (June 19, 2018).

8 Steven Levitsky and Lucan Way, "The Myth of Democratic Recession,"
Journal of Democracy, 26.1 (January 2015), p. 54.

9 Martin Wolf, "The Fading Light of Liberal Democracy," *Financial
Times* (December 22, 2020).

10 Jonathan Freedland, "The 1930s Were Humanity's Darkest, Bloodiest
Hour: Are You Paying Attention?" *Guardian* (March 11, 2017).

11 "Turning Their Backs on the World," *Economist* (February 21, 2019).

12 Harold James, "Deconstructing Deglobalization," Project Syndicate. September 12, 2017.

13 Gita Gopinath, "The Great Lockdown: Worst Economic Downturn Since the Great Depression," International Monetary Fund. April 14, 2020.

14 "Recovery Delayed as International Travel Remains Locked Down," International Air Transport Association. July 28, 2020.

15 "COVID-19 could see over 200 Million more Pushed into Extreme Poverty, New UN Development Report Finds," UN News. December 3, 2020.

16 Gita Gopinath, "A Hobbled Recovery Along Entrenched Fault Lines," International Monetary Fund. October 12, 2021.

17 Steven A. Altman and Phillip Bastian, *DHL Global Connectedness Index 2020: The State of Globalization in a Distancing World* (New York: NYU Stern School of Business, 2020), p. 8.

18 Brian Deese, "The Biden White House Plan for a New US Industrial Policy," speech delivered at the Atlantic Council, Washington, DC. June 23, 2021. Transcript. https://www.atlanticcouncil.org/commenta ry/transcript/brian-deese-on-bidens-vision-for-a-twenty-first-century -american-industrial-strategy.

19 Zachary Karabell, "Will the Coronavirus Bring the End of Globalization? Don't Count on It," *Wall Street Journal* (March 20, 2020).

20 Henry Kissinger, "The Coronavirus Pandemic Will Forever Alter the World Order," *Wall Street Journal* (April 3, 2020).

21 Stephen M. Walt, *The Global Order after COVID-19* (Vienna: Institut für Sicherheitspolitik, 2020), p. 2.

22 Joseph S. Nye, Jr., "Post-Pandemic Geopolitics," Project Syndicate. October 6, 2020.

23 Richard Fontaine, "We Need an Atlantic Charter for the Post-Coronavirus Era," *Atlantic* (April 16, 2020).

24 Alastair Iain Johnston, "China in a World of Orders: Rethinking Compliance and Challenge in Beijing's International Relations," *International Security*, 44.2 (2019), p. 12.

25 Michael J. Mazarr, Timothy R. Heath, and Astrid Stuth Cevallos, *China and the International Order* (Santa Monica, CA: RAND Corporation, 2018), pp. 119–20.

26 Andrew Radin and Clint Reach, *Russian Views of the International Order* (Santa Monica, CA: RAND Corporation, 2017), p. 35.

27 Stanley Hoffmann, *World Disorders: Troubled Peace in the Post-Cold War Era* (Lanham, MD: Rowman & Littlefield, 1998), p. 215.

28 See, for example, Michael McFaul, "Cold War Lessons and Fallacies for US–China Relations Today," *Washington Quarterly*, 43.4 (2021), pp. 7–39; and Odd Arne Westad, "The Sources of Chinese Conduct: Are Washington and Beijing Fighting a New Cold War?" *Foreign Affairs*, 98.5 (September–October 2019), pp. 86–95.

29 Michael Martina and David Brunnstrom, "US, China Positions Ossify at Entrenched Tianjin Talks," Reuters. July 26, 2021; Vincent Ni, "Cold War or Uneasy Peace: Does Defining US–China Competition Matter?" *Guardian* (June 11, 2021); and Joseph S. Nye, Jr., "Cold War with China Is Avoidable," *Wall Street Journal* (December 30, 2020).

30 Laicie Heeley, "'World War C': How Did National Security Miss the Coronavirus?" *Things that Go Boom* podcast episode (May 21, 2020).

31 Eugene V. Rostow, testimony before the Senate Foreign Relations Committee at his confirmation hearing to be director of the Arms Control and Disarmament Agency, Washington, DC. June 22, 1981. Transcript, p. 49. https://books.google.com/books/download/Nomin ation_of_Eugene_V_Rostow.pdf?id=rUDT3hDuMtcC&output=pdf.

32 Taylor Downing, *1983: Reagan, Andropov, and a World on the Brink* (New York: Da Capo Press, 2018).

33 Patrick Porter, "Twilight Struggle: The Cold War Was Not Stable or Simple," War on the Rocks. August 3, 2015.

34 Margaret MacMillan, "Rebuilding the World after the Second World War," *Guardian* (September 11, 2009).

35 Margaret MacMillan, "Which Past Is Prologue? Heeding the Right Warnings from History," *Foreign Affairs*, 99.5 (September–October 2020), p. 20.

36 G. John Ikenberry, *A World Safe for Democracy: Liberal Internationalism and the Crises of Global Order* (New Haven, CT: Yale University Press, 2020), p. 257.

37 Michael M. Phillips and James Marson, "Russian Aggression Spurs Neighbors to Rebuild Defenses," *Wall Street Journal* (January 5, 2021).

38 John Darwin, *After Tamerlane: The Rise and Fall of Global Empires, 1400–2000* (New York: Bloomsbury Press, 2008), pp. 473–4.

39 Alina Polyakova, "Russia Is Teaching the World to Spy," *New York Times* (December 9, 2019).

40 Thomas Pepinsky and Jessica Chen Weiss, "The Clash of Systems? Washington Should Avoid Ideological Competition with Beijing," *Foreign Affairs* (June 11, 2021).

41 Bilahari Kausikan, "ASEAN's Agency in the Midst of Great-Power Competition," Australian Institute of International Affairs. October 30, 2020.

42 Avery Goldstein, "US–China Rivalry in the Twenty-First Century: Déjà vu and Cold War II," *China International Strategy Review*, 2.1 (June 2020), p. 50.

43 "Trade in Goods with China," United States Census Bureau. 2021. https://www.census.gov/foreign-trade/balance/c5700.html.

44 Yen Nee Lee, "5 Charts Show How Much the US and Chinese Economies Depend on Each Other," CNBC. September 28, 2020.

45 Eric Martin and James Mayger, "US–China Trade Booms as if Virus, Tariffs Never Happened" [*sic*], Bloomberg. July 22, 2021.

46 Andrew F. Krepinevich, *Preserving the Balance: A US Eurasia Defense Strategy* (Washington, DC: Center for Strategic and Budgetary Assessments), p. 39.

47 Ana Swanson, "It's a Made-in-China Holiday Season for Cooped-up Americans," *New York Times* (December 15, 2020).

48 Annabelle Timsit, "European Companies Have No Intention of Decoupling from China," Quartz. June 10, 2021; Mitsuru Obe, "Decoupling Denied: Japan Inc. Lays Its Bets on China," *Nikkei Asia* (February 10, 2021).

49 Thomas Hale et al., "Wall Street's New Love Affair with China," *Financial Times* (May 28, 2021).

50 Andrew Nathan, "An Anxious 100th Birthday for China's Communist Party: Can the Party Survive a Modernized China?" *Wall Street Journal* (June 26, 2021).

51 Steven Levitsky and Daniel Ziblatt observe that, "[s]ince the end of the Cold War, most democratic breakdowns have been caused not by generals and soldiers but by elected governments themselves." See their book *How Democracies Die* (New York: Broadway Books, 2018), p. 5.

52 Anna Lührmann et al., *Autocratization Surges, Resistance Grows: Democracy Report 2020* (Gothenburg: V-Dem Institute, 2020), pp. 6 and 9.

53 Ian Ona Johnson, "How an International Order Died: Lessons from the Interwar Era," *War on the Rocks.* August 5, 2021.

54 Stithorn Thananithichot and Kwankaow Kongdecha, "Pandemic Backsliding? A Comparative Study of Democracy Under the Virus," working paper for the King Prajadhipok's Institute. May 20, 2021.

55 President Xi Jinping, "Strengthening Cooperation among Political Parties to Jointly Pursue the People's Wellbeing," speech delivered at the CPC and World Political Parties Summit, Beijing. July 6, 2021. Transcript. http://www.xinhuanet.com/english/2021-07/07/c_131004 8196.htm.

56 John F. Harris and Bryan Bender, "Bill Perry Is Terrified: Why Aren't You?" *POLITICO Magazine* (January 6, 2017).

57 Sewell Chan, "Stanislav Petrov, 77; Soviet Who Helped Avert a Nuclear War," *New York Times* (September 19, 2017); Fred Kaplan, "Apocalypse Averted," *Slate* (February 18, 2021).

Chapter 3 Probing Great-Power Competition

1 Alexander Boroff, "What Is Great-Power Competition, Anyway?" Modern War Institute. April 17, 2020.

2 Stavros Atlamazoglou, "The US Is Preparing for a Fight with China in the Pacific: Here's How Army Special Operators Will Stay Relevant," *Business Insider* (September 22, 2020).

3 Transcript of "The Chessboard: The View from Congress," *Asia Chessboard* podcast episode, Center for Strategic and International Studies. May 18, 2020.

4 John J. Mearsheimer, *The Tragedy of Great Power Politics*, rev. edn. (New York: W. W. Norton, 2003), p. 4.

5 Peter M. Haas and John A. Hird (eds.), *Controversies in Globalization: Contending Approaches to International Relations*, 2nd edn. (Washington, DC: CQ Press, 2013), p. 249.

6 Peter Roberts and Sidharth Kaushal, *Competitive Advantage and Rules in Persistent Competitions* (London: Royal United Services Institute, 2020), p. 1.

7 Stephen D. Biddle, *American Grand Strategy After 9/11: An Assessment* (Carlisle: US Army War College, 2005), pp. 9 and 16.

8 Jacek Durkalec, Paige Gasser, and Oleksandr Shykov, *Workshop*

Summary: 5th Annual LLNL Deterrence Workshop (Livermore, CA: Lawrence Livermore National Laboratory, 2018), p. 2.

9 Katie Bo Williams, "What's Great-Power Competition? No One Really Knows," Defense One. May 13, 2019.

10 Transcript of "Military Implications of Great-Power Competition," *Defense 2020* podcast episode, Center for Strategic and International Studies. January 15, 2020.

11 Ville Sinkkonen and Bart Gaens, "Introduction: The Many Faces of Great-Power Competition," in Bart Gaens and Ville Sinkkonen (eds.), *Great-Power Competition and the Rising US–China Rivalry: Towards a New Normal?* (Helsinki: Finnish Institute of International Affairs, 2020), pp. 13–14.

12 Jared Keller, "After 17 Years of Fighting Terror, the US Makes a Disastrous Pivot," *Pacific Standard* (June 25, 2018).

13 Thomas Joscelyn, "How to Understand Our 'Great-Power Competition' with China," *Vital Interests* (January 15, 2020).

14 "Brown and Bipartisan Group of Lawmakers Raise Concerns with the Potential Reduction of Forces in Africa," website of Representative Anthony Brown. January 14, 2020. https://anthonybrown.house.gov /news/documentsingle.aspx?DocumentID=749.

15 Todd Harrison and Nicholas Harrington, "Bad Idea: Conflating Great-Power Competition with High-Intensity Conflict," Center for Strategic and International Studies. December 15, 2020.

16 Eric Robinson, "The Missing, Irregular Half of Great-Power Competition," Modern War Institute. September 8, 2020.

17 See, for example, Tim Ball, *Still the One: Great-Power Competition and Special Operations Forces* (Philadelphia, PA: Foreign Policy Research Institute, 2020).

18 See, for example, Seth Cropsey and Gary Roughead, "A US Withdrawal Will Cause a Power Struggle in the Middle East," *Foreign Policy* (December 17, 2019).

19 A prominent Australian research center has expressed concern over "an outdated 'superpower mindset' that regards the United States as sufficiently endowed in economic and military strength to not have to make strategic trade-offs": Ashley Townshend, Brendan Thomas-Noone, and Matilda Steward, *Averting Crisis: American Strategy, Military Spending, and Collective Defense in the Indo-Pacific* (Sydney: United States Studies Center, 2019), p. 22.

20 Austin Long, Linda Robinson, and Seth G. Jones, "Managing Chaos in an Era of Great-Power Competition," War on the Rocks. September 5, 2017.

21 Raphael S. Cohen, "America's post-COVID-19 Foreign Policy," *Hill* (May 25, 2020).

22 Klaus Knorr, *On the Uses of Military Power in the Nuclear Age* (Princeton, NJ: Princeton University Press, 1966), p. 21.

23 Oona A. Hathaway and Scott J. Shapiro, *The Internationalists: How a Radical Plan to Outlaw War Remade the World* (New York: Simon & Schuster, 2017), pp. 313–14.

24 Richard Ned Lebow, *Why Nations Fight: Past and Future Motives for War* (New York: Cambridge University Press, 2010), pp. 152–3.

25 Peter Layton, "Rethinking US Grand Strategy," *Small Wars Journal* (June 3, 2019).

26 Nishawn S. Smagh, *Intelligence, Surveillance, and Reconnaissance Design for Great-Power Competition* (Washington, DC: Congressional Research Service, 2020), p. 1.

27 Benjamin Jensen and Brandon Valeriano, *What Do We Know About Cyber Escalation? Observations from Simulations and Surveys* (Washington, DC: Atlantic Council, 2019), p. 1.

28 Eric Schmitt and Thomas Gibbons-Neff, "Russia Projects Increasing Influence in Africa, Worrying the West," *New York Times* (January 29, 2020).

29 Michael P. Fischerkeller and Richard J. Harknett, "What Is Agreed Competition in Cyberspace?" Lawfare. February 19, 2019.

30 Michael Miklaucic, "An Interview with General Joseph Votel, USA (Ret.)," *PRISM*, 9.1 (2020), p. 145.

31 Lawrence Freedman, "Who Wants to Be a Great Power?" *PRISM*, 8.4 (2020), pp. 5–6.

32 Donald Stoker and Craig Whiteside, "Blurred Lines: Gray-Zone Conflict and Hybrid War: Two Failures of American Strategic Thinking," *Naval War College Review*, 73.1 (2020), pp. 1–37.

33 Clyde Haberman, "'This Is Not a Drill': The Growing Threat of Nuclear Cataclysm," *New York Times* (May 14, 2018).

34 Odd Arne Westad, "The Cold War and America's Delusion of Victory," *New York Times* (August 28, 2017).

35 Simon Reich and Peter Dombrowski, "The Consequence of COVID-19: How the United States Moved from Security Provider

to Security Consumer," *International Affairs*, 96.5 (September 2020), p. 1260.

36 Cornell Overfield and Joshua Tallis, *Great-Power Relations: What Makes Powers Great and Why Do They Compete?* (Arlington, VA: CNA, 2020), p. 24.

37 Patrick M. Shanahan, *Indo-Pacific Strategy Report: Preparedness, Partnerships, and Promoting a Networked Region* (Washington, DC: Department of Defense, 2018), p. 1. The author was acting secretary of defense at the time.

38 Elbridge A. Colby and A. Wess Mitchell, "The Age of Great-Power Competition: How the Trump Administration Refashioned American Strategy," *Foreign Affairs*, 99.1 (January–February 2020), pp. 121 and 129.

39 Eric Edelman, "The US Role in the Middle East in an Era of Renewed Great-Power Competition," Hoover Institution. April 2, 2019.

40 Sam Mullins, "Great-Power Competition Versus Counterterrorism: A False Dichotomy," Just Security. October 23, 2020.

41 Paul McLeary, "China, Russia Press for Mideast Gains While US Talks of Withdrawal," *Breaking Defense* (January 14, 2020).

42 Nadia Schadlow, "The Conservative Realism of the Trump Administration's Foreign Policy," *Texas National Security Review* (November 30, 2018).

43 Mark D. Miles and Charles R. Miller, "Global Risks and Opportunities: The Great-Power Competition Paradigm," *Joint Force Quarterly*, 94 (July 2019), pp. 81 and 85.

44 Oriana Skylar Mastro, "China's End Run Around the World Order," *CATO Unbound* (March 14, 2018). Concerningly, great-power competition may not even be confined to the terrestrial realm; see William J. Broad, "US Counters Space Threat from China," *New York Times* (January 25, 2021).

45 Charles Kupchan, for example, concludes that "[t]he expansionist threats that both Russia and China pose to their neighbors mean that the same objective that guided US entry into World War II and the Cold War—to prevent the domination of Eurasia by a hostile power— still applies today and for the foreseeable future": *Isolationism: A History of America's Efforts to Shield Itself from the World* (New York: Oxford University Press, 2020), p. 368.

46 "Great-Power Competition," Wilson Center. 2021. https://www.wilso
ncenter.org/issue/great-power-competition.

47 The four quotations here come respectively from: Jim Garamone,
"Selva Describes Reality of Great-Power Competition," Department
of Defense. January 30, 2018; "Great-Power Competition," MITRE
Corporation. April 14, 2020; James A. Lewis, *Technological Competition
and China* (Washington, DC: Center for Strategic and International
Studies, 2018), p. 1; and Patrick Quirk and David Shullman, "Want to
Prevail against China? Prioritize Democracy Assistance," *Hill* (October
1, 2019).

48 Christopher Ashley Ford, "Relearning a Competitive Mindset in
Great-Power Competition," speech delivered at the Conference on
Strategic Weapons in the 21st Century, Washington, DC. March 14,
2019. Transcript. https://www.state.gov/re-learning-a-competitive-mi
ndset-in-great-power-competition.

49 Austin Doehler, "Great-Power Competition Is Too Narrow a Frame,"
Defense One. December 6, 2020.

50 Sinkkonen and Gaens, "Introduction," p. 16.

51 Daniel J. O'Donohue, *Joint Doctrine Note 1-19: Competition
Continuum* (Washington, DC: Joint Chiefs of Staff, 2019), pp. v, 7,
and 9.

52 Susanna V. Blume, "Fireside Chat with the 24th Secretary of
the Army and the 40th Chief of Staff of the Army," Center for a
New American Security. February 19, 2020, p. 16. https://s3.
amazonaws.com/files.cnas.org/documents/Fireside-Chat-with-
24th-Secretary-of-the-Army-and-the-40th-Chief-of-Staff-of-the-
Army.pdf?mtime=20200302122829.

53 Timothy Ray, speech delivered at the 20th Nuclear Triad Symposium,
Bossier City, LA. December 10, 2020. Video. https://www.youtube.com
/watch?v=TP4rSCRV0G8.

54 Sascha-Dominik Dov Bachmann, Doowan Lee, and Andrew Dowse,
"COVID Information Warfare and the Future of Great-Power
Competition," *Fletcher Forum of World Affairs*, 44.2 (2020), p. 12.

55 Nathan Freier, "Faster, Transient, Endless: How America Must
Adapt to Today's Great-Power Competition," Defense One. July 22,
2018.

56 Ali Wyne, "A Preliminary Critique of the 'Do Something Now'
Doctrine," War on the Rocks. April 2, 2014.

57 Stanley Hoffmann, "The Conduct of American Foreign Policy: The Perils of Incoherence," *Foreign Affairs*, 57.3 (1978), p. 468.

58 Arthur Schlesinger, Jr., "Russians and Cubans in Africa," *Wall Street Journal* (May 2, 1978).

59 Stanley Hoffmann, "Policy for the 70s," *LIFE Magazine* (March 21, 1969), p. 73.

60 Frank Hoffman, "Strategy as Appetite Suppressant," War on the Rocks. March 3, 2020.

61 Kerry Boyd Anderson, "The Challenge of Managing Great-Power Rivalry in the Middle East," *Arab News* (February 8, 2021).

62 Mordechai Chaziza, "Geopolitical and Geoeconomic Challenges to China's Silk Road Strategy in the Middle East," Middle East Institute. June 9, 2020.

63 Mona Yacoubian, *Understanding Russia's Endgame in Syria: A View from the United States* (Geneva: Geneva Center for Security Policy, 2021), p. 21.

64 Neta C. Crawford, *United States Budgetary Costs and Obligations of Post-9/11 Wars Through FY2020: $6.4 Trillion* (Providence, RI: Watson Institute for International and Public Affairs, 2019).

65 Peter Martin and Roxana Tiron, "Yesterday's Wars Didn't Prepare the Pentagon for Tomorrow's China," Bloomberg. August 2, 2021.

66 James A. Winnefeld, Michael J. Morell, and Graham Allison, "Why American Strategy Fails: Ending the Chronic Imbalance Between Ends and Means," *Foreign Affairs* (October 28, 2020).

67 Odd Arne Westad, *The Global Cold War: Third World Interventions and the Making of Our Times* (New York: Cambridge University Press, 2005), p. 38.

68 Christopher Hemmer, *American Pendulum: Recurring Debates in US Grand Strategy* (Ithaca, NY: Cornell University Press, 2015), p. 55.

69 "Bin Laden: Goal Is to Bankrupt US," CNN. November 1, 2004.

70 *The 9/11 Commission Report: Final Report of the National Commission on Terrorist Attacks upon the United States* (New York: W. W. Norton, 2004), p. 169.

71 Daniel Byman, "Eighteen Years on: The War on Terror Comes of Age," *CTC Sentinel*, 12.8 (September 2019), p. 4.

72 Jennifer Lind and Daryl G. Press, "Reality Check: American Power in an Age of Constraints," *Foreign Affairs*, 99.2 (March–April 2020), p. 47.

Chapter 4 Managing a Resurgent China

1 Josh Hawley, "It's Time to Rethink America's Foreign Policy Consensus," speech delivered at the Center for a New American Security, Washington, DC. November 12, 2019. Transcript. https://www.hawley.senate.gov/senator-hawleys-speech-rethinking-americas-foreign-policy-consensus.

2 David Brooks, "How China Brings Us Together," *New York Times* (February 15, 2019).

3 Janan Ganesh, "A Common Enemy Could Heal the US Partisan Divide," *Financial Times* (January 23, 2019).

4 World Bank, "GDP (current US$): China, United States." World Bank. 2021. https://data.worldbank.org/indicator/NY.GDP.MKTP.CD?locations=CN-US.

5 Alyssa Leng and Roland Rajah, "Chart of the Week: Global Trade through a US–China Lens," *Interpreter* (December 18, 2019).

6 Stephen S. Roach, "When China Sneezes," Project Syndicate. February 24, 2020.

7 Sebastian Horn, Carmen M. Reinhart, and Christoph Trebesch, "How Much Money Does the World Owe China?" *Harvard Business Review* (February 26, 2020).

8 Robert S. Ross, *Chinese Security Policy: Structure, Power, and Politics* (New York: Routledge, 2009), p. 153.

9 "Defending Taiwan is Growing Costlier and Deadlier," *Economist* (October 10, 2020).

10 Gregory B. Poling, "The Conventional Wisdom on China's Island Bases Is Dangerously Wrong," War on the Rocks. January 10, 2020.

11 Department of Defense, *Military and Security Developments Involving the People's Republic of China 2020* (Washington, DC: Department of Defense, 2020), pp. i–ii.

12 "China's Approach to Global Governance," Council on Foreign Relations. 2021. https://www.cfr.org/china-global-governance.

13 Bonnie Bley, "The New Geography of Global Diplomacy: China Advances as the United States Retreats," *Foreign Affairs* (November 27, 2019).

14 Anonymous, *The Longer Telegram: Toward a New American China Strategy* (Washington, DC: Atlantic Council, 2021), p. 21.

15 Kenneth Lieberthal and Wang Jisi, *Addressing US–China Strategic*

Distrust (Washington, DC: Brookings Institution, 2012), p. 22.

16 "Document 9: A ChinaFile Translation," *ChinaFile* (November 8, 2013).

17 Ellen Nakashima, "Indictment of PLA Hackers Is Part of Broad US Strategy to Curb Chinese Cyberspying," *Washington Post* (May 22, 2014).

18 Thomas Donilon, "The United States and the Asia-Pacific in 2013," speech delivered at Asia Society New York, New York. March 11, 2013. Transcript. https://asiasociety.org/new-york/complete-transcript-thomas-donilon-asia-society-new-york.

19 Department of Defense, *Military and Security Developments Involving the People's Republic of China 2020*, p. 13.

20 Mark Mazzetti et al., "Killing CIA Informants, China Stifled US Spying," *New York Times* (May 21, 2017).

21 Donald J. Trump, *National Security Strategy of the United States* (Washington, DC: White House, 2017), p. 25.

22 Chad P. Bown, "US–China Trade War Tariffs: An Up-to-Date Chart," Peterson Institute for International Economics. March 16, 2021.

23 Simon Denyer, "Move over, America. China Now Presents Itself as the Model 'Blazing a New Trail' for the World," *Washington Post* (October 19, 2017).

24 Michael R. Pompeo, "Communist China and the Free World's Future," speech delivered at the Richard Nixon Presidential Library, Yorba Linda, CA. July 23, 2020. Transcript. https://2017-2021.state.gov/communist-china-and-the-free-worlds-future-2/index.html.

25 Scott Kennedy, "Thunder out of Congress on China," Center for Strategic and International Studies. September 11, 2020.

26 "The US Innovation and Competition Act: Senate Passes Sweeping $250 Billion Bill to Bolster Scientific Innovation and Compete with China," Sidley Austin LLP. June 16, 2021; Catie Edmondson, "Countering China, Senate Unites on a Bill to Pour Aid into Tech," *New York Times* (June 9, 2021).

27 Bob Davis and Lingling Wei, "The Soured Romance between China and Corporate America," *Wall Street Journal* (June 5, 2020).

28 Laura Silver, Kat Devlin, and Christine Huang, "Most Americans Support Tough Stance toward China on Human Rights, Economic Issues," Pew Research Center. March 4, 2021.

29 Robin Wright, "Why Trump Will Never Win His New Cold War with China," *New Yorker* (July 29, 2020).

30 Janan Ganesh, "America's Eerie Lack of Debate on China," *Financial Times* (July 15, 2020).

31 Ganesh Sitaraman, "Mapping the China Debate," Lawfare. May 26, 2020.

32 Samuel P. Huntington, "The US: Decline or Renewal?" *Foreign Affairs*, 67.2 (1988/9), pp. 76–96.

33 Joseph R. Biden, Jr., *Interim National Security Strategic Guidance* (Washington, DC: White House, 2021), p. 21.

34 Michael Martina, Yew Lun Tian, and David Brunnstrom, "US to Stress Need for 'Guardrails' in Sherman's Talks in China," Reuters. July 24, 2021.

35 Biden, *Interim National Security Strategic Guidance*, p. 8.

36 Catherine Wong, "US–China Relations: Beijing Takes Pointers from Mao in Protracted Power Struggle with US," *South China Morning Post* (August 2, 2021).

37 Wang Yi, speech delivered at the Council on Foreign Relations, New York. September 28, 2018. Transcript. https://www.cfr.org/event/conversation-wang-yi.

38 Fu Ying, "China and US Can Have Cooperative Competition," *New York Times* (November 25, 2020).

39 Xi Jinping, "Secure a Decisive Victory in Building a Moderately Prosperous Society in All Respects and Strive for the Great Success of Socialism with Chinese Characteristics for a New Era," speech delivered at the 19th National Congress of the Communist Party of China, Beijing. October 18, 2017. Transcript. http://www.chinadaily.com.cn/china/19thcpcnationalcongress/2017-11/04/content_34115212.htm.

40 Evelyn Cheng, "Xi at Communist Party Anniversary: China Won't Accept 'Sanctimonious Preaching' from Others," CNBC. July 1, 2021.

41 Peter Berkowitz, *The Elements of the China Challenge* (Washington, DC: Department of State, 2020), p. 7.

42 Andrew Scobell et al., *China's Grand Strategy: Trends, Trajectories, and Long-Term Competition* (Santa Monica, CA: RAND Corporation, 2020), p. 21.

43 Oriana Skylar Mastro, "The Stealth Superpower: How China Hid

Its Global Ambitions," *Foreign Affairs*, 98.1 (January–February 2019), p. 31.

44 An example is Michael D. Swaine, "A Counterproductive Cold War with China: Washington's 'Free and Open Indo-Pacific' Strategy Will Make Asia Less Open and Less Free," *Foreign Affairs* (March 2, 2018).

45 Aaron L. Friedberg, "An Answer to Aggression: How to Push Back Against Beijing," *Foreign Affairs*, 99.5 (September–October 2020), p. 150.

46 Nadège Rolland, *China's Vision for a New World Order* (Seattle, WA: National Bureau of Asian Research, 2020), p. 51.

47 Daniel Tobin, testimony before the US–China Economic and Security Review Commission at the hearing *A "China Model?" Beijing's Promotion of Alternative Global Norms and Standards*, Washington, DC. March 13, 2020, p. 9. Transcript. https://www.uscc.gov/sites/default/files/testimoni es/SFR%20for%20USCC%20TobinD%2020200313.pdf.

48 Joel Wuthnow, "Deciphering China's Intentions: What Can Open Sources Tell Us?" *Asan Forum* (July 29, 2019).

49 Jessica Chen Weiss, "Nationalism and the Domestic Politics of Chinese Foreign Policy: Lessons for the United States," Working Paper for the Penn Project on the Future of US–China Relations. 2021, p. 15. https://cpb-us-w2.wpmucdn.com/web.sas.upenn.edu /dist/b/732/files/2021/04/Jessica-Chen-Weiss_Nationalism-and-the -Domestic-Politics-of-Chinese-Foreign-Policy_Updated.pdf.

50 Sui-Lee Wee, "Drop in Births Risks Stunting China's Growth," *New York Times* (May 12, 2021).

51 *World Population Prospects 2019*, vol. 2: *Demographic Profiles* (New York: United Nations Department of Economic and Social Affairs, 2019), p. 388.

52 Orange Wang, "China GDP Growth Last Year Was 6.1 Percent, Slowest Rate for 29 Years," *South China Morning Post* (January 17, 2020).

53 Amanda Lee, "China Debt: Has It Changed in 2021 and How Big Is It Now?" *South China Morning Post* (June 5, 2021).

54 Ding Yi, "China 'Unlikely' to Reach Goal of 70% Self-Sufficiency in Chip Production, Report Says," Caixin Global. May 25, 2020.

55 Debby Wu, Sohee Kim, and Ian King, "Why the World Is Short of Computer Chips, and Why It Matters," Bloomberg. April 26, 2021.

56 Keith Zhai, Julie Zhu, and Cheng Leng, "How Billionaire Jack Ma Fell to Earth and Took Ant's Mega IPO with Him," Reuters. November 5, 2020.

57 Yanzhong Huang, "America's Political Immune System Is Overreacting to China," *Foreign Policy* (September 8, 2020).

58 Thomas Hale and Leslie Hook, "China Expands Coal Plant Capacity to Boost Post-Virus Economy," *Financial Times* (June 24, 2020).

59 Steven Lee Myers, Keith Bradsher, and Chris Buckley, "Extreme Weather Challenges City Life in China," *New York Times* (July 27, 2021).

60 Chun Han Wong, "'Their Goal Is to Make You Feel Helpless': In Xi's China, Little Room for Dissent," *Wall Street Journal* (November 27, 2020).

61 Richard McGregor, "Xi Jinping's Strength Is China's Weakness," *New York Times* (November 9, 2020).

62 Anna Fifield, "Taiwan's 'Born Independent' Millennials Are Becoming Xi Jinping's Lost Generation," *Washington Post* (December 26, 2019).

63 John Sudworth, "China Needs to Show Taiwan Respect, Says President," BBC. January 14, 2020.

64 Demetri Sevastopulo, "Japan Vows to Support US in Opposing 'Coercion' from China," *Financial Times* (April 17, 2021).

65 Keith Bradsher, Austin Ramzy, and Tiffany May, "In Hong Kong, a Banner Day for Democracy," *New York Times* (November 25, 2019).

66 Joel Wuthnow, *System Overload: Can China's Military Be Distracted in a War over Taiwan?* (Washington, DC: National Defense University, 2020), p. 19.

67 Steven Erlanger, "In This Crisis, US Sheds Its Role as Global Leader," *New York Times* (March 22, 2020).

68 Arvind Subramanian, "China Has Blown Its Historic Opportunity," Project Syndicate. July 20, 2020.

69 Ken Moriyasu and Wajahat Khan, "Malaysia Says China's Maritime Claims Have No Legal Basis," *Nikkei Asia* (July 31, 2020).

70 Sebastian Strangio, "At ASEAN Meetings, US, China Spar over Maritime Disputes," *Diplomat* (September 10, 2020).

71 Ed Davies, "Indonesia Hails 'New Era' for US Ties, Hosts Biggest Joint Military Drills," Reuters. August 5, 2021.

72 "NATO Recognizes China 'Challenges' for the First Time," *Deutsche Welle* (December 3, 2019).

73 "Stoltenberg Urges NATO Unity amid Challenges from China, Russia," Radio Free Europe/Radio Liberty. June 8, 2020.

74 Louise Guillot, "Europe Has Been 'Naive' about China, EU Official Says," POLITICO. May 3, 2020.

75 "EU's Top Diplomat Urges 'More Robust Strategy' toward China," Associated Press. May 25, 2020.

76 Patrick Wintour, "Dawn of Asian Century Puts Pressure on EU to Choose Sides, Says Top Diplomat," *Guardian* (May 25, 2020).

77 Mikko Huotari, Anja Manuel, and Boris Ruge (eds.), *Mind the Gap: Priorities for Transatlantic China Policy: Report of the Distinguished Reflection Group on Transatlantic China Policy* (Washington, DC: Aspen Strategy Group, 2021).

78 Catherine Wong, "Too Soon, Too Loud: Chinese Foreign Policy Advisors Tell 'Wolf Warrior' Diplomats to Tone It Down," *South China Morning Post* (May 14, 2020).

79 Peter Hirschberg, "Internal Chinese Report Warns Beijing Faces Tiananmen-like Global Backlash over Virus," Reuters. May 4, 2020.

80 Zheng Bijian, "China's 'Peaceful Rise' to Great-Power Status," *Foreign Affairs*, 84.5 (September–October 2005), pp. 22 and 24.

81 Yan Xuetong, "How China Can Defeat America," *New York Times* (November 21, 2011).

82 Michael Schuman, "How Xi Jinping Blew It," *Atlantic* (November 19, 2020).

83 Drew Hinshaw, Sha Hua, and Laurence Norman, "Pushback on Xi's Vision for China Spreads beyond US," *Wall Street Journal* (December 28, 2020).

84 Some observers of China argue in fact that the world has more to fear from its potential decline than from its continued ascent. See, for example, Michael Beckley, "The United States Should Fear a Faltering China: Beijing's Assertiveness Betrays Its Desperation," *Foreign Affairs* (October 28, 2019).

85 Gerald Segal, "Does China Matter?" *Foreign Affairs*, 78.5 (September–October 1999), p. 24.

86 Justin Sherman, "Is the US Winning Its Campaign against Huawei?" Lawfare. August 12, 2020.

87 Dan Strumpf, "Huawei's Revenue Hits Record $122 Billion in 2019 Despite US Campaign," *Wall Street Journal* (December 30, 2019).

88 Drew Hinshaw, "Allies Wary of US Stance on Huawei and 5G," *Wall Street Journal* (April 9, 2020).

89 James Kynge, "Developing Countries Sign Huawei Deals despite US Espionage Warnings," *Financial Times* (May 15, 2021).

90 Chris Miller, "America Is Going to Decapitate Huawei," *New York Times* (September 15, 2020).

91 Dan Wang, "China's Sputnik Moment? How Washington Boosted Beijing's Quest for Tech Dominance," *Foreign Affairs* (July 29, 2021).

92 Bob Davis and Lingling Wei, *Superpower Showdown: How the Battle between Trump and Xi Threatens a New Cold War* (New York: HarperCollins, 2020), p. 409.

93 Adam Segal, "The Coming Tech Cold War with China: Beijing Is Already Countering Washington's Policy," *Foreign Affairs* (September 9, 2020).

94 Department of Defense, *Military and Security Developments Involving the People's Republic of China 2020*, p. vi.

95 Tweet by Thomas Shugart. September 16, 2020. https://twitter.com /tshugart3/status/1306311607568404481.

96 Mark T. Esper, speech delivered at the RAND Corporation, Santa Monica, CA. September 16, 2020. Transcript. https://www.defen se.gov/Newsroom/Transcripts/Transcript/Article/2351152/secretary -of-defense-engagement-at-rand-corporation-complete-transcript.

97 Denny Roy, "China Won't Achieve Regional Hegemony," *Washington Quarterly*, 43.1 (2020), p. 111.

98 Timothy R. Heath, Derek Grossman, and Asha Clark, *China's Quest for Global Primacy: An Analysis of Chinese International and Defense Strategies to Outcompete the United States* (Santa Monica, CA: RAND Corporation, 2021), p. 176.

99 Chun Han Wong, "China's Xi Jinping Tightens Grip on Domestic Security Forces in First Broad Purge," *Wall Street Journal* (August 18, 2020).

100 Tanner Greer, "China's Plans to Win Control of the Global Order," *Tablet* (May 17, 2020).

101 David O. Shullman, "How China Is Exploiting the Pandemic to Export Authoritarianism," War on the Rocks. March 31, 2020.

102 Sheena Chestnut Greitens, "Surveillance, Security, and Liberal Democracy in the Post-COVID World," *International Organization*, 74.S1 (December 2020), pp. E169–E190.

103 Jessica Chen Weiss, "A World Safe for Autocracy? China's Rise and the Future of Global Politics," *Foreign Affairs*, 98.4 (July–August 2019), p. 100.

104 Elbridge Colby and Robert D. Kaplan, "The Ideology Delusion: America's Competition with China Is Not About Doctrine," *Foreign Affairs* (September 4, 2020).

105 While America's capacity to shape China's internal evolution is limited, Washington should not assume that President Xi's tenure marks its culmination. See John Culver, "Xi Jinping's China May Not Last Forever," Lowy Institute. September 24, 2020. https://interactives.lowyinstitute.org/features/china-rules-based-order/responses/jinping-china.

106 Emily Feng, "As US Views of China Grow More Negative, Chinese Support for Their Government Rises," NPR. September 23, 2020.

107 Jessica Chen Weiss and I argue that "Washington must push back against Beijing in ways that Beijing can absorb without being discredited with its domestic audience." See "The US Shouldn't Try to Out-China China," *New York Times* (September 3, 2020).

108 Evan S. Medeiros and Ashley J. Tellis, "Regime Change Is Not an Option in China: Focus on Beijing's Behavior, Not Its Leadership," *Foreign Affairs* (July 8, 2021).

109 Jonathan Cheng, "China Exports Boom to Record Year, While COVID-19 Ravages Global Economy," *Wall Street Journal* (January 14, 2021).

110 Henry Farrell and Abraham Newman, "The Folly of Decoupling from China: It Isn't Just Perilous, It's Impossible," *Foreign Affairs* (June 3, 2020).

111 David Shepardson, "Some 3,500 US Companies Sue over Trump-Imposed Chinese Tariffs," Reuters. September 25, 2020.

112 Bob Davis, "Business Groups Call on Biden to Restart Trade Talks with China," *Wall Street Journal* (August 5, 2021).

113 Nicholas R. Lardy, "Foreign Investments into China Are Accelerating despite Global Economic Tensions and Restrictions," Peterson Institute for International Economics. July 22, 2021.

114 Liza Lin, "China's Trillion-Dollar Campaign Fuels a Tech Race with the US," *Wall Street Journal* (June 11, 2020).

115 Frank Tang, "China Unveils 'Strategic Emerging Industries' Plan

in Fresh Push to Get Away from US Technologies," *South China Morning Post* (September 24, 2020).

116 Ryan Hass and Zach Balin, "US–China Relations in the Age of Artificial Intelligence," Brookings Institution. January 10, 2019.

117 Tom Hancock, "China Is Exporting More Sophisticated Products Despite Trade War," Bloomberg. August 3, 2021.

118 Anna Gross and Madhumita Murgia, "China Shows Its Dominance in Surveillance Technology," *Financial Times* (December 26, 2019).

119 Valentina Pop, Sha Hua, and Daniel Michaels, "From Lightbulbs to 5G, China Battles West for Control of Vital Technology Standards," *Wall Street Journal* (February 8, 2021).

120 Jeffrey Wilson, "RCEP Will Redraw the Economic and Strategic Map of the Indo-Pacific," *Strategist* (September 21, 2020).

121 Scott Malcomson, "How China Became the World's Leader in Green Energy: And What Decoupling Could Cost the Environment," *Foreign Affairs* (February 28, 2020).

122 Kristine Lee, "The United States Can't Quit on the UN: When America Withdraws, China Wins," *Foreign Affairs* (September 24, 2020).

123 Bethany Allen-Ebrahimian, "The US Gives Far More Money to the WHO Than China Does," Axios. April 15, 2020.

124 Vijay Gokhale, "China Doesn't Want a New World Order: It Wants This One," *New York Times* (June 4, 2020).

125 Li Laifang, "Enlightened Chinese Democracy Puts the West in the Shade," Xinhua. October 17, 2017.

126 John Ruwitch, "In George Floyd Protests, China Sees a Powerful Propaganda Opportunity," NPR. June 3, 2020.

127 David Wertime, "Chinese Propagandists Seize on George Floyd Protests," POLITICO. June 2, 2020.

128 Josh Campbell, "Global Conflict Watchers Issue Warning of 'Unfamiliar Danger' ahead of US Election," CNN. November 1, 2020.

129 Gerry Shih, "China Is Awash with Schadenfreude over US Election Tumult," *Washington Post* (November 5, 2020).

130 James S. Lay, Jr., *United States Objectives and Programs for National Security* (Washington, DC: National Security Council, 1950), p. 9.

131 Robert Gilpin, *War and Change in World Politics* (Cambridge:

Cambridge University Press, 1981), p. 31.

132 Jude Blanchette, "China's Fifth Plenum: Reading the Initial Tea Leaves," Center for Strategic and International Studies. October 30, 2020.

133 "Upbeat Xi Says Time on China's Side as Turmoil Grips US," Bloomberg. January 12, 2021.

134 Gideon Rachman, "China Is Still a Long Way from Being a Superpower," *Financial Times* (July 19, 2021).

135 Jude Blanchette, "The United States Has Gotten Tough on China. When Will It Get Strategic?" Center for Strategic and International Studies. July 17, 2020.

136 Elizabeth C. Economy, *The Third Revolution: Xi Jinping and the New Chinese State* (New York: Oxford University Press, 2018), p. 250.

137 Audrye Wong, "How Not to Win Allies and Influence Geopolitics: China's Self-Defeating Economic Statecraft," *Foreign Affairs*, 100.3 (May–June 2021), pp. 44–53.

138 *World Population Prospects 2019*, vol. 2, p. 1163.

139 Martin Wolf, "China Is Wrong to Think the US Faces Inevitable Decline," *Financial Times* (April 27, 2021).

140 Kevin Rudd notes the Chinese leadership's concern that the Biden administration "might form an effective coalition of countries across the democratic capitalist world with the express aim of counter-balancing China collectively." See his "Short of War: How to Keep US–Chinese Confrontation from Ending in Calamity," *Foreign Affairs*, 100.2 (March–April 2021), p. 65.

141 Nicholas Kitchen and Michael Cox explain that the prevailing order at a given time "has a huge amount of inertia built into it," a reality that privileges that system's principal architects. See their "Power, Structural Power, and American Decline," *Cambridge Review of International Affairs*, 32.6 (2019), p. 747.

142 David Uren, "Southeast Asia Will Take a Major Economic Hit if Shipping Is Blocked in the South China Sea," *Strategist* (December 8, 2020).

143 Alan Beattie, "Global Governance and the Gap of 7," *Financial Times* (June 10, 2021).

144 William Schomberg and Elvira Pollina, "Italy's Draghi Says G7 Had to Be Frank about China," Reuters. June 13, 2021.

145 Roland Oliphant, "G7 Unveil West's Rival to China's Belt and Road

Scheme with $40 Trillion Green Investment," *Telegraph* (June 12, 2021).

146 Bernhard Bartsch et al., *Dealing with the Dragon: China as a Transatlantic Challenge* (New York: Asia Society, 2020), p. 33.

147 Laura Höflinger, "Interview with India's External Affairs Minister," *Der Spiegel* (November 17, 2019).

148 Geoff Dyer and George Parker, "US attacks UK's 'Constant Accommodation' with China," *Financial Times* (March 12, 2015).

149 Scott Morris, *Responding to AIIB: US Leadership at the Multilateral Development Banks in a New Era* (New York: Council on Foreign Relations, 2016), p. 15.

150 Rana Hasan, *Meeting Asia's Infrastructure Needs* (Manila: Asian Development Bank, 2017), p. vii.

151 Melanie Burton, "US Diplomat Says Confident Australia Can Ensure Telecom Security," Reuters. May 24, 2020.

152 Natalie Herbert, "China's Belt and Road Initiative Invests in African Infrastructure and African Military and Police Forces," *Washington Post* (April 30, 2021).

153 Yuen Yuen Ang, "Demystifying Belt and Road: The Struggle to Define China's 'Project of the Century,'" *Foreign Affairs* (May 22, 2019).

154 Jennifer Hillman and David Sacks, *China's Belt and Road: Implications for the United States* (New York: Council on Foreign Relations, 2021), p. 5.

155 "Creating Alternatives to China's Belt and Road," *Financial Times* (April 24, 2021).

156 Bob Davis and Drew FitzGerald, "US Pushing Effort to Develop 5G Alternative to Huawei," *Wall Street Journal* (February 4, 2020).

157 Stu Woo, "The US Is Back in the 5G Game," *Wall Street Journal* (May 26, 2021).

158 David E. Sanger, "Strategic Narcissism," *New York Times* (December 20, 2020).

159 Melvyn P. Leffler, "China Isn't the Soviet Union: Confusing the Two Is Dangerous," *Atlantic* (December 2, 2019).

160 "Joe Biden Is Determined that China Should Not Displace America," *Economist* (July 17, 2021).

161 John Van Reenen, *Innovation Policies to Boost Productivity* (Washington, DC: Brookings Institution, 2020), p. 7.

162 Jared Council, "White House Announces $1 Billion Plan to Create AI, Quantum Institutes," *Wall Street Journal* (August 26, 2020).

163 Tom McKay, "Here's What's in the Senate's Massive Bill Funding the Tech War with China," Gizmodo. August 6, 2021.

164 *Losing Talent: An Economic and Foreign Policy Risk America Can't Ignore* (Washington, DC: NAFSA, 2019), pp. 5, 2, and 6.

165 Ishan Banerjee and Matt Sheehan, "America's Got AI Talent: US' Big Lead in AI Research Is Built on Importing Researchers," MacroPolo. June 9, 2020.

166 David Wertime, "China Just Won the First US Presidential Debate," POLITICO. October 1, 2020.

167 Rory Truex, "What the Fear of China Is Doing to American Science," *Atlantic* (February 16, 2021).

168 Elizabeth Redden, "Reconsidering the 'China Initiative,'" *Inside Higher Ed* (March 2, 2021).

169 James Goldgeier and Bruce W. Jentleson, "The United States Is Not Entitled to Lead the World: Washington Should Take a Seat at the Table, but Not Always at Its Head," *Foreign Affairs* (September 25, 2020).

170 Samantha Power, "The Can-Do Power: America's Advantage and Biden's Chance," *Foreign Affairs*, 100.1 (January–February 2021), p. 12.

171 "Transcript: NPR's Full Interview with Secretary of State Tony Blinken," NPR. February 16, 2021.

172 Martin Arnold and Valentina Romei, "Europeans Reassess the Double-Edged Sword of Trade with China," *Financial Times* (April 27, 2021).

173 Kurt M. Campbell and Jake Sullivan, "Competition Without Catastrophe: How America Can both Challenge and Coexist with China," *Foreign Affairs*, 98.5 (September–October 2019), pp. 96–110.

174 Kurt Campbell and I discuss five of them in "The Growing Risk of Inadvertent Escalation between Washington and Beijing," Lawfare. August 16, 2020.

175 Jeff M. Smith, "Strategic Autonomy and US–Indian Relations," War on the Rocks. November 6, 2020.

176 Hervé Lemahieu and Alyssa Leng, *Lowy Institute Asia Power Index: Key Findings 2020* (Sydney: Lowy Institute, 2020), p. 12.

177 Evan A. Feigenbaum, "Asia's Future beyond US–China Competition,"

Carnegie Endowment for International Peace. September 9, 2020.

178 Samuel Brannen, "Four Scenarios for Geopolitical Order in 2025–2030: What Will Great-Power Competition Look Like?" Center for Strategic and International Studies. September 16, 2020.

179 Lee Hsien Loong, "The Endangered Century: America, China, and the Perils of Confrontation," *Foreign Affairs*, 99.4 (July–August 2020), p. 59.

180 Heiko Maas, *Policy Guidelines for the Indo-Pacific* (Berlin: Federal Foreign Office, 2020), p. 9.

181 Scott Morrison, speech delivered at Policy Exchange, London. November 23, 2020. Transcript. https://www.pm.gov.au/media/uk-policy-exchange-virtual-address.

182 Yanzhong Huang, "When the US and China Fight, It Is the Environment that Suffers," *New York Times* (October 12, 2020); Kiran Stacey, "Wuhan Lab Row Threatens US–China Cooperation in Science," *Financial Times* (June 10, 2021).

Chapter 5 Assessing Russia's Conduct and the Sino-Russian Entente

1 Michael McFaul, "How to Contain Putin's Russia: A Strategy for Countering a Rising Revisionist Power," *Foreign Affairs* (January 19, 2021).

2 Willian Courtney and Howard J. Shatz, "Why Russia Struggles to Feed Its Great-Power Addiction," *National Interest* (May 9, 2020).

3 Andrew Anthony, "Mark Galeotti: 'We Should Laugh at Russia More,'" *Guardian* (February 9, 2019).

4 Zack Cooper, "Bad Idea: 'Great-Power Competition' Terminology," Center for Strategic and International Studies. December 1, 2020.

5 Joseph S. Nye, Jr., "How to Deal with a Declining Russia," Project Syndicate. November 5, 2019.

6 Tweet by Anton Barbashin. January 5, 2021. https://twitter.com/abarbashin/status/1346606126201241607.

7 Kathryn E. Stoner, "The US Should Stop Underestimating Russian Power," *Wall Street Journal* (December 23, 2020).

8 Simon Saradzhyan and Nabi Abdullaev, *Measuring National Power: Is Vladimir Putin's Russia in Decline?* (Cambridge, MA: Belfer Center for Science and International Affairs, 2018), p. 11. An intermediate answer posits that it is "neither a rising nor a declining power, but . . . a nation

in stagnation." See Jeffrey Edmonds et al., *Artificial Intelligence and Autonomy in Russia* (Arlington, VA: CNA, 2021), p. 2.

9 Michael Kofman, "Bad Idea: Dismissing Russia as a Declining Power in US Strategy," Center for Strategic and International Studies. December 18, 2020.

10 Dmitri Trenin and Thomas Graham, "How to Safely Manage US–Russian Great-Power Competition," Carnegie Moscow Center. December 11, 2020.

11 "Should US Foreign Policy Focus on Great-Power Competition? *Foreign Affairs* Asks the Experts," *Foreign Affairs* (October 13, 2020).

12 Mark Montgomery and Eric Sayers, "Make China the Explicit Priority in the Next NDS," Center for a New American Security. July 27, 2020.

13 Vladimir Putin, annual address to the Federal Assembly of the Russian Federation, Moscow. April 25, 2005. Transcript. http://en.kremlin.ru/events/president/transcripts/22931.

14 Vladimir Putin, speech at the Munich Security Conference, Munich. February 10, 2007. Transcript. http://en.kremlin.ru/events/president/transcripts/24034.

15 Luciano Fontana, "Vladimir Putin: Interview to the Italian Newspaper *Corriere della Sera*," *Corriere della Sera* (June 7, 2015).

16 Seva Gunitsky, "One Word to Improve US Russia Policy," *New Republic* (April 27, 2018).

17 Nikolas Gvosdev, "'Because It Is': Russia, the Existential Great Power." 2007. Unpublished article.

18 Anne-Sylvaine Chassany, "The West Should Pay Attention to Russia and China's Vaccine Diplomacy," *Financial Times* (February 10, 2021).

19 Vladimir Putin, "A New Integration Project for Eurasia: The Future in the Making," *Izvestia* (October 3, 2011).

20 A recent report finds that "Russia faces multiple challenges in implementing its lofty ambitions, given its shaky economic foundations and the opposition to its plans even in its immediate neighborhood in post-Soviet Eurasia, let alone at a global level": Samuel Charap et al., *Russian Grand Strategy: Rhetoric and Reality* (Santa Monica, CA: RAND Corporation, 2021), p. 171.

21 Robert Person, "Four Myths about Russian Grand Strategy," Center for Strategic and International Studies. September 22, 2020.

22 Henry Foy and Max Seddon, "Rising Poverty and Falling Incomes

Fuel Russia's Navalny Protests," *Financial Times* (February 6, 2021).

23 Clara Ferreira Marques, "Economic Reality Is Dragging Russia Toward Climate Acceptance," Bloomberg. August 13, 2021.

24 Jeremy Bowen, "Syria War: Assad under Pressure as Economic Crisis Spirals," BBC. June 15, 2020.

25 Sarah A. Topol, "The View from Moscow," *New York Times* (June 30, 2019).

26 Joshua Yaffa, "Believe It or Not," *New Yorker* (September 14, 2020), p. 30.

27 Jon Allsop, "How Should We Think about Russian Disinformation?" *Columbia Journalism Review* (September 15, 2020).

28 Franklin Foer, "The 2016 Election Was Just a Dry Run," *Atlantic*, 325.5 (June 2020), p. 48.

29 Richard Stengel, "Domestic Disinformation Is a Greater Menace than Foreign Disinformation," *Time* (June 26, 2020).

30 Emily Bazelon, "Freedom of Speech Will Preserve OUR Democracy," *New York Times* (October 18, 2020).

31 Adam Entous, "A Devil's Bargain," *New Yorker* (June 29, 2020), pp. 35 and 43.

32 David Ignatius, "The Russians Manipulated Our Elections: We Helped," *Washington Post* (April 24, 2020).

33 Charles E. Ziegler, "A Crisis of Diverging Perspectives: US–Russian Relations and the Security Dilemma," *Texas National Security Review*, 4.1 (2020/1), p. 31.

34 One analysis concludes that "the core mission of the US–Russia relationship moving into the 2020s is to disincentivize further Russia–China convergence": Nikolas K. Gvosdev, "Russia's Impact on US National Interests: Maintaining a Balance of Power in Europe and Asia," *Russia Matters* (August 5, 2020).

35 Rose Gottemoeller et al., "Why We Still Need to Rethink Russia Policy: A Rebuttal," *POLITICO Magazine* (September 25, 2020).

36 Serge Schmemann, "The Promise of the Biden–Putin Summit," *New York Times* (June 15, 2021).

37 Fyodor Lukyanov, "Trump's Defense Strategy Is Perfect for Russia," *Washington Post* (January 23, 2018).

38 Haley Britzky, "The Army Thinks China Will Surpass Russia by 2028. Here Is How the Service Is Planning to Take Them On." Task and Purpose. September 20, 2019.

39 For an example that focuses on the two countries' disinformation efforts, see Jean-Baptiste Jeangène Vilmer and Paul Charon, "Russia as a Hurricane, China as Climate Change: Different Ways of Information Warfare," War on the Rocks. January 21, 2020.

40 Eric Tucker, "FBI Official: Russia Wants to See US 'Tear Ourselves Apart,'" Associated Press. February 24, 2020.

41 Avril Haines, *Foreign Threats to the 2020 US Federal Elections* (Washington, DC: Office of the Director of National Intelligence, 2021), pp. 5 and 7.

42 Zbigniew Brzezinski, *The Grand Chessboard: American Primacy and Its Geostrategic Imperatives* (New York: Basic Books, 1997), p. 55.

43 Andrea Kendall-Taylor and David Shullman, *Navigating the Deepening Russia–China Partnership* (Washington, DC: Center for a New American Security, 2021), p. 1.

44 "Crude Oil Prices: 70-Year Historical Chart," Macrotrends. 2021. https://www.macrotrends.net/1369/crude-oil-price-history-chart.

45 Evan A. Feigenbaum, "The United States Is Driving Russia and China Together Again," *International Herald Tribune* (December 28, 2000).

46 Daniel R. Coats, *Statement for the Record: Worldwide Threat Assessment of the US Intelligence Community* (Washington, DC: Office of the Director of National Intelligence, 2019), p. 4.

47 Angela Stent, "Russia and China: Axis of Revisionists?" paper for the Brookings Institution's Global China Initiative (February 2020), p. 1. https://www.brookings.edu/wp-content/uploads/2020/02/FP_2020 02_russia_china_stent.pdf.

48 Nahal Toosi, "Biden Fears What 'Best Friends' Xi and Putin Could Do Together," POLITICO. June 14, 2021.

49 Vasily Kashin observes that "Russia believes US domestic politics is too chaotic and extremist to make any dealmaking or subtle maneuvers very likely": quoted in Kathrin Hille et al., "US Urged to Exploit Cracks in Russia–China Relationship," *Financial Times* (July 26, 2020).

50 Stephen J. Hadley and Paula J. Dobriansky, "Navigating the Growing Russia–China Strategic Alignment," strategic insights memo for the Atlantic Council (June 29, 2020), p. 2. https://www.atlanticcouncil. org/wp-content/uploads/2020/07/SIM-Russia-China-Relationship-FINAL-PDF-1.pdf.

51 Eugene Rumer, Richard Sokolsky, and Aleksandar Vladicic, *Russia in*

the Asia-Pacific: Less than Meets the Eye (Washington, DC: Carnegie Endowment for International Peace, 2020), p. 36.

52 Jeremy Friedman, *Shadow Cold War: The Sino-Soviet Competition for the Third World* (Chapel Hill, NC: University of North Carolina Press, 2015), p. 2.

53 Melinda Liu, "Xi Jinping Has Embraced Vladimir Putin—for Now," *Foreign Policy* (October 3, 2019).

54 Bethany Allen-Ebrahimian, "China Takes a Page from Russia's Disinformation Playbook," Axios. March 25, 2020.

55 Andrea Kendall-Taylor and David Shullman, "A Russian–Chinese Partnership Is a Threat to US Interests: Can Washington Act Before It's Too Late?" *Foreign Affairs* (May 14, 2019).

56 Bobo Lo, "The Sino-Russian Partnership and Global Order," *China International Strategy Review*, 2.2 (December 2020), p. 319.

57 John Pomfret, "45 Years Ago, Kissinger Envisioned a 'Pivot' to Russia: Will Trump Make It Happen?" *Washington Post* (December 14, 2016).

58 World Bank, "GDP (Current US$): China, Russian Federation." 2021. https://data.worldbank.org/indicator/NY.GDP.MKTP.CD?locations=CN-RU.

59 Andrew Higgins, "China's Not Far, but for Russian Town the Worry Is for Business, Not Germs," *New York Times* (February 25, 2020).

60 Yaroslav Trofimov and Thomas Grove, "Weary Russia Tries to Avoid Entanglement in US–China Spat," *Wall Street Journal* (June 22, 2020).

61 Scott Neuman, "As Relations with US Sour, Xi Describes Putin as 'Best Friend' at Moscow Meeting," NPR. June 6, 2019.

62 Artyom Lukin, "The Russia–China Entente and Its Future," *International Politics*, 58.3 (June 2021), p. 377.

63 See tweet by Ali Wyne. August 15, 2020. https://twitter.com/Ali_Wyne/status/1294720269886554113.

64 Sergey Radchenko, "The Sino-Russian Relationship in the Mirror of the Cold War," *China International Strategy Review*, 1.2 (December 2019), p. 281.

65 Dmitri Trenin, "Russia Analyst: China and Russia Are Partners, but Not quite Allies," *Defense News* (December 2, 2019).

66 Tom O'Connor, "China Calls Russia's Talk of Possible Military Alliance 'Positive,' with 'No Limit' to Their Ties," *Newsweek* (October 23, 2020).

67 Nadège Rolland, "A China–Russia Condominium over Eurasia," *Survival*, 61.1 (February–March 2019), p. 8.

68 Charles A. Kupchan, "The Right Way to Split China and Russia: Washington Should Help Moscow Leave a Bad Marriage," *Foreign Affairs* (August 4, 2021).

69 Maria Repnikova and Alexander Gabuev, "Why Forecasts of a Chinese Takeover of the Russian Far East Are just Dramatic Myth," *South China Morning Post* (July 14, 2017); Michael Khodarkovsky, "So Much Land, so Few Russians," *New York Times* (September 17, 2016).

70 Michael R. Gordon, "Russia–China Theme: Contain the West," *New York Times* (April 24, 1997).

Chapter 6   Seizing America's Great-Power Opportunity

1 See, for example, Daniel H. Nexon, "Against Great-Power Competition: The US Should Not Confuse Means for Ends," *Foreign Affairs* (February 15, 2021); Emma Ashford, "Great-Power Competition Is a Recipe for Disaster," *Foreign Policy* (April 1, 2021); and Joseph S. Nye, Jr., "America's New Great-Power Strategy," Project Syndicate. August 3, 2021.

2 David E. Sanger, "Defying US, China and Russia Set the Tone for a Cold, New Era," *New York Times* (March 21, 2021).

3 William J. Burns, *The Back Channel: A Memoir of American Diplomacy and the Case for Its Renewal* (New York: Random House, 2020), p. 9.

4 Kori Schake, *Safe Passage: The Transition from British to American Hegemony* (Cambridge, MA: Harvard University Press, 2017), p. 19.

5 Bud Greenspan, *The Olympians' Guide to Winning the Game of Life* (Santa Monica, CA: General Publishing Group, 1997), p. 40.

6 John Thornhill, "To Maintain Tech Supremacy the US Must Avoid 'Military–Civil Fusion,'" *Financial Times* (March 11, 2021).

7 James T. Areddy, "What the US Can Learn from China's Infatuation with Infrastructure," *Wall Street Journal* (April 3, 2021).

8 Jonnelle Marte, "Fed's Powell: China's Approach to Digital Currency Would Not Work in US," Reuters. April 28, 2021.

9 Stein Emil Vollset et al., "Fertility, Mortality, Migration, and Population Scenarios for 195 Countries and Territories from 2017 to 2100: A Forecasting Analysis for the Global Burden of Disease Study," *Lancet*, 396.10258 (October 2020), pp. 1300–1 and 1303.

10 Kalpana Sunder, "Indian Migrants Flock to Canada as Trump-Era Rules Make US Less Attractive," *South China Morning Post* (March 31, 2021).

11 Evan Burke, *Trump-Era Policies toward Chinese STEM Talent: A Need for Better Balance* (Washington, DC: Carnegie Endowment for International Peace, 2021).

12 Alison Snyder, "China's STEM PhD Push," Axios. August 5, 2021.

13 Henry Farrell and Abraham L. Newman, "Weaponized Interdependence: How Global Economic Networks Shape State Coercion," *International Security*, 44.1 (2019), pp. 42–79.

14 Catie Edmondson, "Stimulus Puts Deficit Hawks in Lonely Spot," *New York Times* (January 3, 2021).

15 Shawn Tully, "The US Now Has a Debt Level That Rivals Italy's," *Fortune* (January 14, 2021).

16 Byrne Hobart, "Why the US Dollar Could Outlast the American Empire," *Palladium Magazine* (December 5, 2020).

17 See, for example, Patrick Porter, *A World Imagined: Nostalgia and Liberal Order* (Washington, DC: CATO Institute, 2018).

18 Amrita Narlikar and Nora Müller have written an illuminating primer on revitalizing multilateralism against the backdrop of an eroding postwar order: *Making It Matter: Thought Experiments for Meaningful Multilateralism* (Berlin: Körber Multilateralism Lab, 2021).

19 Fu Ying, "The US World Order Is a Suit That No Longer Fits," *Financial Times* (January 6, 2016).

20 G. John Ikenberry, "The Next Liberal Order: The Age of Contagion Demands More Internationalism, Not Less," *Foreign Affairs*, 99.4 (July–August 2020), p. 142.

21 Evan Osnos, "Blaming Beijing," *New Yorker* (May 18, 2020), p. 13.

22 Fintan O'Toole, "Donald Trump Has Destroyed the Country He Promised to Make Great Again," *Irish Times* (April 25, 2020).

23 Tom McTague, "The Decline of the American World," *Atlantic* (June 24, 2020).

24 Michel Crozier, Samuel P. Huntington, and Joji Watanuki, *The Crisis of Democracy: Report on the Governability of Democracies to the Trilateral Commission* (New York: New York University Press, 1975), p. 106.

25 Aaron Blake, "The New American 'Malaise,'" *Washington Post* (December 12, 2014).

26 President Harry S. Truman, "Remarks upon Presenting the Wendell Willkie Awards for Journalism," speech delivered at the National Press Club, Washington, DC. February 28, 1947. Transcript. https://www.presidency.ucsb.edu/documents/remarks-upon-presenting-the-wendell-willkie-awards-for-journalism.

27 Michael J. Klarman, *From Jim Crow to Civil Rights: The Supreme Court and the Struggle for Racial Equality* (New York: Oxford University Press, 2004), p. 182.

28 "How It Happened: Transcript of the US–China Opening Remarks in Alaska," *Nikkei Asia* (March 19, 2021).

29 David Pilling, "'Everybody Has Their Eyes on America': Black Lives Matter Goes Global," *Financial Times* (June 20, 2020).

30 Dominic Tierney, "Does America Need an Enemy?" *National Interest*, 146 (November–December 2016), p. 60.

31 Evan Osnos, "Fight Fight, Talk Talk," *New Yorker* (January 13, 2020), p. 34.

32 Noah Smith, "Techno-Optimism for the 2020s," author's blog. December 3, 2020.

33 Janan Ganesh, "America's Best Hope of Hanging Together Is China," *Financial Times* (February 16, 2021).

34 Rachel Myrick, "Do External Threats Unite or Divide? Security Crises, Rivalries, and Polarization in American Foreign Policy," *International Organization* (April 20, 2021), pp. 1–38.

35 Flora Lewis, "Time to Be Steady," *New York Times* (May 5, 1990).

36 Bethany Allen-Ebrahimian and Shawna Chen, "How US–China Tensions Can Fuel Anti-Asian Racism," Axios. March 23, 2021; Julia Hollingsworth, Yong Xiong, and David Culver, "Trump-Era Policy That Shut Out Top Chinese Students Could Be Hurting America More Than Beijing," CNN. August 9, 2021.

37 Greg Jaffe, "Lessons in Disaster: A Top Clinton Advisor Searches for Meaning in a Shocking Loss," *Washington Post* (July 14, 2017).

38 Timothy Garton Ash, "Hearts Don't Beat Faster for 'the Rules-Based International Order,'" *Financial Times* (September 10, 2020).

39 Richard Fontaine, "Great-Power Competition Is Washington's Top Priority—but Not the Public's: China and Russia Don't Keep Most Americans Awake at Night," *Foreign Affairs* (September 9, 2019).

40 Thomas G. Mahnken, *Forging the Tools of 21st-Century Great-Power*

Competition (Washington, DC: Center for Strategic and Budgetary Assessments), p. 36.

41 Jonathan Monten et al., "Americans Want to Engage the World: The Beltway and the Public Are Closer than You Think," *Foreign Affairs* (November 3, 2020).

42 Mark Hannah and Caroline Gray, *Diplomacy and Restraint: The Worldview of American Voters* (New York: Eurasia Group Foundation, 2020), p. 10.

43 Bruce Stokes, "US Electorate Shows Distrust of the Realities of Foreign Policy," Chatham House. September 4, 2020.

44 Salman Ahmed and Rozlyn Engel (eds.), *Making US Foreign Policy Work Better for the Middle Class* (Washington, DC: Carnegie Endowment for International Peace, 2020), p. 3.

45 One does not need to accept that the United States is in relative decline to question whether Americans will support a steadily more consuming competition with China and Russia. Indeed, counter-intuitively, Michael Beckley arrives at this conclusion on the basis of the opposite analytical assessment: because America's aggregate power is set to increase in relation to that of other great powers, Washington will become more self-reliant and less interested in devoting resources to undertakings that seem tangential to its vital national interests. See "Rogue Superpower: Why This Could Be an Illiberal American Century," *Foreign Affairs*, 99.6 (November–December 2020), pp. 73–86.

46 Jeremy Shapiro, "Ask Not What Your Country Can Do for Foreign Policy," War on the Rocks. July 7, 2020.

47 Carter C. Price and Kathryn A. Edwards, *Trends in Income from 1975 to 2018* (Santa Monica, CA: RAND Corporation, 2020), p. 1.

48 Chad Stone et al., "A Guide to Statistics on Historical Trends in Income Inequality," Center on Budget and Policy Priorities. January 13, 2020.

49 Chuck Collins, "Updates: Billionaire Wealth, US Job Losses, and Pandemic Profiteers," Inequality.org. October 18, 2021.

50 David Leonhardt and Yaryna Serkez, "The US Is Lagging behind Many Rich Countries: These Charts Show Why," *New York Times* (July 2, 2020).

51 Mike Stobbe, "US Life Expectancy in 2020 Saw Biggest Drop since WWII," Associated Press. July 21, 2021.

52 "America's Wars," Department of Veterans Affairs. November 2020. https://www.va.gov/opa/publications/factsheets/fs_americas_wars.pdf.

53 David Crow, "The Next Virus Pandemic Is Not Far Away," *Financial Times* (August 6, 2020).

54 Christopher Flavelle, Brad Plumer, and Hiroko Tabuchi, "Storms Exposing a Nation Primed for Catastrophe," *New York Times* (February 21, 2021).

55 Christopher Flavelle, "Climate Change Could Slash Global Wealth, an Insurance Giant Warns," *New York Times* (April 23, 2021).

56 Michael J. Mazarr, "Time for a New Approach to Defense Strategy," War on the Rocks. July 29, 2021.

57 Bruce W. Jentleson, "Refocusing US Grand Strategy on Pandemic and Environmental Mass Destruction," *Washington Quarterly*, 43.3 (2020), pp. 7–29.

58 Robert M. Gates, "Reflections on the Status and Future of the Transatlantic Alliance," speech delivered at the Security and Defense Agenda, Brussels. June 10, 2011. Transcript. https://www.atlanticcouncil.org/blogs/natosource/text-of-speech-by-robert-gates-on-the-future-of-nato.

59 Edward White, "South Korea Aims for Military Independence as Asia Threats Rise," *Financial Times* (January 6, 2021).

60 Sudip Kar-Gupta, "Macron: Europe Needs Its Own Sovereignty in Defense, even with New US Government," Reuters. November 15, 2020.

61 Ben Westcott, "Australia Announces $186 billion in Defense Spending amid Rising Tensions in the Indo-Pacific," CNN. July 1, 2020.

62 Hana Kusumoto, "Japan's Cabinet Approves Largest-ever Defense Budget for Coming Fiscal Year," *Stars and Stripes* (December 21, 2020).

63 Kishi Nobuo, *Defense of Japan 2021* (Tokyo: Ministry of Defense, 2021), pp. 2 and 19.

64 White, "South Korea Aims for Military Independence."

65 Richard Bush, Bonnie Glaser, and Ryan Hass, "Don't Help China by Hyping Risk of War over Taiwan," NPR. April 8, 2021.

66 Samuel Brannen, "World Order after Covid-19," Center for Strategic and International Studies. May 28, 2020.

67 Rorry Daniels, *Creating a Favorable Balance of Power in the Indo-Pacific: Views from the US and Its Allies and Partners* (New York: National Committee on American Foreign Policy, 2021), p. 6.

68 Ivan Krastev and Mark Leonard, *The Crisis of American Power: How Europeans See Biden's America* (London: European Council on Foreign Relations, 2021), p. 23.

69 Walter Russell Mead, "Eurocrats Are from Pluto," *Wall Street Journal* (February 1, 2021).

70 Michael Crowley and Steven Erlanger, "Biden Is Finding a Shifting Transatlantic Alliance on China and Russia," *New York Times* (February 19, 2021).

71 Daniel Michaels, "European Business Leaders Want a Stronger Hand with China, Not Decoupling," *Wall Street Journal* (July 4, 2021).

72 Kori Schake, "The US Doesn't Know How to Treat Its Allies," *Atlantic* (March 28, 2021).

73 Frances Z. Brown and Thomas Carothers, "Washington's Democracy Dilemma: Crafting a Democracy Strategy in an Age of Great-Power Politics," *Foreign Affairs* (July 23, 2021).

74 Josep Borrell, *A New EU–US Agenda for Global Change* (Brussels: European Commission, 2020), pp. 1–3.

75 Susan Thornton, "The Quad (finally) Delivers: Can It Be Sustained?" *Interpreter* (April 12, 2021).

76 Anne-Marie Slaughter, "There Is a Way to Keep America Globally Engaged," *Financial Times* (November 18, 2020).

77 William Burr, "US Intelligence and the Detection of the First Soviet Nuclear Test, September 1949," National Security Archive. September 22, 2009.

78 D. W. Brogan, "The Illusion of American Omnipotence," *Harper's Magazine*, 205 (December 1952), pp. 23–4.

79 Erica D. Borghard, "A Grand Strategy Based on Resilience," War on the Rocks. January 4, 2021.

80 Rana Mitter, "The World China Wants: How Power Will—and Won't—Reshape Chinese Ambitions," *Foreign Affairs*, 100.1 (January–February 2021), p. 169.

81 Paul Kennedy, "The Great Powers, Then and Now," *International Herald Tribune* (August 14, 2013).

82 Deborah Jordan Brooks et al., "The Demographic Transition Theory

of War: Why Young Societies Are Conflict Prone and Old Societies Are the Most Peaceful," *International Security*, 43.3 (Winter 2018/19), pp. 53–95.

83 Paul Musgrave, "The Beautiful, Dumb Dream of McDonald's Peace Theory," *Foreign Policy* (November 26, 2020).

84 Christopher Layne, "Coming Storms: The Return of Great-Power War," *Foreign Affairs*, 99.6 (November–December 2020), p. 42.

85 Bear F. Braumoeller, *Only the Dead: The Persistence of War in the Modern Age* (New York: Oxford University Press, 2019), p. 16.

86 Aaron Clauset, "Trends and Fluctuations in the Severity of Interstate Wars," *Science Advances*, 4.2 (February 21, 2018), p. 2.

87 Tanisha M. Fazal and Paul Poast, "War Is Not Over: What the Optimists Get Wrong About Conflict," *Foreign Affairs*, 98.6 (November–December 2019), pp. 75–7 and pp. 79–81.

88 Lara Seligman, "US Warns of China's Growing Threat to Taiwan," POLITICO. March 16, 2021.

89 Ben Buchanan and Fiona S. Cunningham, "Preparing the Cyber Battlefield: Assessing a Novel Escalation Risk in a Sino-American Crisis," *Texas National Security Review*, 3.4 (2020), p. 55.

90 Nicholas L. Miller and Vipin Narang, "Is a New Nuclear Age upon Us? Why We May Look Back on 2019 as the Point of No Return," *Foreign Affairs* (December 30, 2019).

91 Eugene Rumer and Richard Sokolsky, "Why the New START Extension Could Be the End of Arms Control as We Know It," *POLITICO Magazine* (February 7, 2021).

92 James M. Acton, "Escalation through Entanglement: How the Vulnerability of Command-and-Control Systems Raises the Risks of an Inadvertent Nuclear War," *International Security*, 43.1 (2018), p. 60.

93 Fu Ying and John Allen, "Together, the US and China Can Reduce the Risks From AI," *Noema* (December 17, 2020).

94 Fiona Hill, quoted in Edward Luce, "America Is Back—and Wants Everyone to Focus on China," *Financial Times* (June 18, 2021).

95 Andrew Ehrhardt, "The Return of Great-Power Diplomacy," Engelsberg Ideas. January 27, 2021.

96 Nina Silove, "The Pivot Before the Pivot: US Strategy to Preserve the Power Balance in Asia," *International Security*, 40.4 (2016), pp. 45–88.

97 Ashley Rhoades and Dalia Dassa Kaye, "China Does Not Have to Be America's Enemy in the Middle East," *War on the Rocks*. April 19, 2021.

98 Philip H. Gordon, *Losing the Long Game: The False Promise of Regime Change in the Middle East* (New York: St. Martin's Press, 2020), p. 22.

99 Ken Moriyasu, "Biden's Indo-Pacific Team Largest in National Security Council," *Nikkei Asia* (February 11, 2021).

100 Joseph R. Biden, Jr., *Interim National Security Strategic Guidance* (Washington, DC: White House, 2021), p. 10.

101 Joseph R. Biden, Jr., "Remarks by President Biden on the Way Forward in Afghanistan," White House, Washington, DC. April 14, 2021. Transcript. https://www.whitehouse.gov/briefing-room/speec hes-remarks/2021/04/14/remarks-by-president-biden-on-the-way -forward-in-afghanistan.

102 Michael Martina, David Brunnstrom, and Idrees Ali, "Contrary to Intent, Biden's Afghan Pullout Could Undermine Asia Shift," Reuters. August 19, 2021.

103 Daniel Byman, "Will Afghanistan Become a Terrorist Safe Haven Again? Just Because the Taliban Won Doesn't Mean Jihadis Will," *Foreign Affairs* (August 18, 2021).

104 Tweet by Michael Mazarr. August 16, 2021. https://twitter.com/MM azarr/status/1427459275631349764.

105 Lindsey Ford and Zack Cooper, "America's Alliances after Trump: Lessons from the Summer of '69," *Texas National Security Review*, 4.2 (2021), p. 115.

106 David Dollar and Jonathan Stromseth, "US Must Urgently Rethink Its Economic Policies in Asia," *Nikkei Asia* (February 17, 2021).

107 Suzanne Mettler and Robert C. Lieberman, *Four Threats: The Recurring Crises of American Democracy* (New York: St. Martin's Press, 2020), pp. 5–6.

108 Nate Cohn, "Growing Threat to American Democracy: Us vs. Them," *New York Times* (April 22, 2021).

109 Linley Sanders, "Americans Now See Other Americans as the Biggest Threat to Their Way of Life," YouGov America. January 20, 2021.

110 Maria Repnikova, "No, the Chaos in America Is Not a Gift to Autocrats," *New York Times* (January 18, 2021).

111 Joseph R. Biden, Jr., "Remarks by President Biden in Press Conference," Cornwall. June 13, 2021. Transcript. https://www.wh itehouse.gov/briefing-room/speeches-remarks/2021/06/13/remarks -by-president-biden-in-press-conference-2.

Notes to Afterword

1 Paul Hannon, "Foreign Investment Bounced Back Last Year but Did Little to Ease Supply Strains," *Wall Street Journal* (January 19, 2022); Che Pan, "US-China Tech War: Chinese Semiconductor Output Surged 33 Percent Last Year, Double the Growth Rate in 2020," *South China Morning Post* (January 17, 2022).
2 Shubhajit Roy and Krishn Kaushik, "Putin Meets PM Modi: 'India Great Power, Friendly Nation, Time-Tested Friend,'" *Indian Express* (December 6, 2021).
3 Richard Wike et al., "America's Image Abroad Rebounds with Transition from Trump to Biden," Pew Research Center. June 10, 2021.

Index